Praise for the Bo

"The Cook-Off Mystery series by Devon Delaney is a very tasty treat of a series. Readers will be glued to their seats wrestling with continuing reading the story or getting up to get a tasty treat to eat . . . I highly recommend getting something to eat before you sit down to indulge yourself in the story . . ."

—*Cozy Mystery book Reviews*

"This is a very fun and rollicking mystery that stays light-hearted even as the case gets more complicated, building toward a get-all-of-the-suspects-together-in-a-room conclusion. Cooking, holiday celebrations, and moving family drama all make for the perfect end-of-the-year escape."

—*Kings River Life*

"I've read several in the series and enjoyed them all. It was interesting to see Sherry acting as a judge rather than a competitor. The book kept my interest from the beginning but any book that combines cookies and murder has to be interesting. The characters are varied and seem like a lot of fun. I look forward to more in this series."

—Alicia F.

Books by Devon Delaney

Cook-Off Mysteries

Expiration Date
Final Roasting Place
Guilty as Charred
Eat, Drink and Be Wary
Double Chocolate Cookie Murder
A Half-Baked Alibi

A Half-Baked Alibi

A Cook-Off Mystery

Devon Delaney

A Half-Baked Alibi
Devon Delaney
Copyright © 2022 by Devon Delaney
Cover design and illustration by Dar Albert, Wicked Smart Designs

Beyond the Page Books
are published by
Beyond the Page Publishing
www.beyondthepagepub.com

ISBN: 978-1-954717-80-0

All rights reserved under International and Pan-American Copyright Conventions. By payment of required fees, you have been granted the non-exclusive, non-transferable right to access and read the text of this book. No part of this text may be reproduced, transmitted, downloaded, decompiled, reverse engineered, or stored in or introduced into any information storage and retrieval system, in any form or by any means, whether electronic or mechanical, now known or hereinafter invented without the express written permission of both the copyright holder and the publisher.

This is a work of fiction. Names, characters, places, and incidents either are the product of the author's imagination or are used fictitiously, and any resemblance to actual persons, living or dead, business establishments, events or locales is entirely coincidental. The publisher does not have any control over and does not assume any responsibility for author or third-party websites or their content.

The scanning, uploading, and distribution of this book via the Internet or via any other means without the permission of the publisher is illegal and punishable by law. Your support of the author's rights is appreciated.

Chapter 1

Sherry flung her arm to the side with such force she knocked her water bottle off the bedside table. The resulting clatter woke Chutney. Abandoning the comfort of his human's side, the dog sought refuge on the floor. Sherry cradled her bandaged hand tight to her chest. She searched for her pillow and found the puffy rectangle lying askew beside her head, reminding her of the trouble she had repositioning it in the night with only one fully functional hand. She peered over the edge of her bed at her Jack Russell terrier, who glared back with concerned brown eyes.

"Sorry, boy. That was quite a dream. Can't recall most of the details but the image of the dead body is burned in my brain." Sherry's apologetic tone did little to calm Chutney's agitation. His small paws tapped out a steady beat as he paced back and forth across the wooden bedroom floor until Sherry rose from beneath her quilt. The action was a struggle. Her hand was markedly less sore than it was the previous day, but still not ready to aid in hoisting her out of bed.

She managed to retrieve her robe from the foot of the bed and wriggle her arms into the sleeves. As she fumbled with the tie to secure the robe, her phone rang. She gave up the notion of closing the robe, grabbed the phone off the bedside table and sat on the corner of her bed.

"Good morning, Sherry. Hope I'm not calling too early. Just checking on the patient."

Sherry glanced down at the splotched gauze secured with tape around her right hand. "Good morning, Amber. Thanks for checking in. The patient's hand is definitely still a bit sore. Leaking a little ooze, too."

"Ugh, sounds gruesome." Sherry's friend and workmate made a sympathetic moan.

"How many times can I say I regret trying to hold a raw sweet potato with one hand and dice it with the other? How could I be so careless and cavalier?"

"That's the pain meds talking. You know you can do most anything in the kitchen, even with one hand tied behind your back."

"Thanks, I think." Sherry sighed. "Actually, I'm officially off the medication. Just taking over-the-counter stuff, as needed. The healing is underway, so the stitches are beginning to alternate between aching, itching, pinching and tingling."

"I suggest taking it easy again today," Amber said. The words were delivered with hesitation.

Sherry imagined Amber was chomping at the bit to get together in the kitchen to practice her contest recipe. Amber's prescription for more rest was coming from her trained medical side, not the enthusiastic ever-improving cooking contest side.

"I would take it easy, except that I committed to taking a ride on Don's new boat to pick up some passengers in Long Island." She caught her reflection in the mirror on the opposite wall. She had a hard time believing she could make herself presentable out of the disarray she saw. She retracted that thought. One of the reasons she fell for Don was his ability to love her despite her paucity of makeup and the fashion trappings many other women committed to. She did think she could benefit from some mascara and blush if she was leaving the house.

"That sounds like a fun time with Don. Be careful, though. No manual labor. The age-old maritime saying all hands on deck does not apply to you."

"Message received," Sherry said.

On the other end of the phone all hesitation was abandoned. "I'm so sorry you had to withdraw from the cook-off due to your injury. I know how sad you are to miss the event. I can't express enough my gratitude for your potential help in prepping me for my second plunge into the cooking competition world."

"I don't know if I'll be of any help. I mean, you got all the way to the finals of this week's national cook-off on your own. Who says you need any additional guidance?"

"Believe me," Amber implored. "I do need you. You're one of the country's premier cooking competition veterans."

"If I ever need a public relations agent, I'm coming straight to you. You make my silly hobby sound very important. You understand I'm doing what I love to do and sometimes win cash and valuable prizes as a bonus."

"You can be as humble as you like about your cooking prowess but you're a national treasure and I should take advantage of your availability. If for nothing else, I'd like to tap into your calming influence and experienced thinking patterns. Before I retired from my marriage and family therapy practice, I was in my element helping even the most difficult of clients. We had our share, that's for sure. I could be calm under stress because I was well versed in the crazy that people can bring to a situation. In the kitchen, and especially the contest kitchen, I'm a whole other person, wading through uncharted waters minute by minute, employing all my wiles to stay afloat."

Sherry laughed. "You make cook-offs sound very dramatic."

"My way of reeling you in." Amber returned the chuckle.

"I'm here for you, my friend. I recommend we work on your recipe presentation, technique and overall contest time management. If I've learned anything over all the years I've been competing in cooking contests, it's that those are the three most important elements to rein in and get a grip on," Sherry said as she mentally scanned some of the troubles she'd had in past cook-offs. "I've had every type of circumstance from outdoor cook-offs in the pouring rain, blistering heat and freezing cold, to indoor cook-offs with malfunctioning ovens and incorrect ingredients provided. The crazy can be brought to a cook-off too, you know. Thinking on my feet isn't always my greatest asset, except in the kitchen, for some reason."

"I need as many pep talks as you can muster up," Amber said. "My Asparagus Lasagna Blooms are waiting for any last-minute tweaking you suggest."

"Come by the house after your shift at the Ruggery and we'll get started. In the meantime, wish Don and me luck on his inaugural trip. He's very excited to get his new business venture underway. Goodbye financial world, hello watery world of commuter boat transport."

"Perfect. Good luck and be careful."

"Speaking of career changes, how is Pep doing at the Ruggery?" Sherry asked.

"Your brother has been doing a bang-up job subbing for you at the store while your hand mends."

Sherry envisioned Pep, bundling skeins of yarn for hooked-rug-hungry customers with the same love and care their father, Erno, employed over his many decades of store management.

"Except Pep has this habit of juggling yarn balls in front of our customers when he doesn't know they're watching," Amber said with a mischievous laugh.

The idyllic image of her younger brother hard at work under the tutelage of their father evaporated. "That sounds like the Pep I know and love. I'd wager he does know the customers are watching and that's the reason he puts on a show. I know Dad's loving having his only son, Pep's wife, and his first grandchild living back in Augustin. Giving him a hand at the Ruggery while my hand is on the mend is frosting on the cake."

"Erno is over the moon that another member of the Oliveri clan is getting to know the ins and outs of the family business."

"I hope he's prepared for the fact Pep may not stay on at the store long-term. Charlotte's lucky enough to be able to perform her marine biology research locally for the next two years, but that doesn't mean Pep has decided the hooked rug store is his first choice of employment. I don't want to end Dad's dream for his son to take over the business one day, should he ever decide to slow down and retire." Sherry heard a rattle of what she assumed were dishes coming through the phone's speaker. "Are you in the middle of breakfast?"

"Just getting my presentation platter in order to bring to your house for our practice session."

"Speaking of the cook-off, I had the most horrific dream before I woke in a panic this morning." Sherry inhaled a halting breath when a sudden chill seized her core. "I dreamt I was admiring the appliance prize package that was on display at the cook-off."

"The gorgeous stainless-steel appliances advertised for the grand prize winner?" Amber released a sigh. "The cook-off pamphlet had a full-page photo of the prize. I could really use those beauties."

"Yes, they're beauties. That was the good part of the dream. The bad part came when I closed in to get a look at the inside of the to-die-for stove and to my horror there was a body stuffed inside."

Amber squealed. "How awful! Putting my therapist hat on for a moment, I'd have to say you might have deep-seated emotions concerning your cooking competitions that you might want to work through. Maybe you've been involved in one too many cook-off murders."

"Not at all," Sherry said with a hint of defense. "I think the remnants of the pain medication Urgent Care pumped into me a few days ago expanded my imagination."

Amber let out a note of skepticism. Sherry visualized Amber's habit of tucking her strawberry-blonde hair back behind her ears when she was in the midst of making an educated point. Chances were she had performed a hair tuck while analyzing Sherry's dream.

"First of all, the murders I've had any involvement with one way or another haven't been specifically cook-off murders." Emphasis on the word *cook-off*. "They just happen to have occurred either before, during, or after a cook-off."

Amber offered no rebuttal.

"Your silence speaks volumes. You're not convinced. I don't want my hobby given the stigma that it's in any way a haven for homicidal lunatics. If you thought there was any danger in a cook-off you wouldn't have let me convince you to enter the Kitchen Royalty Use Your Noodle Recipe Cook-off. Right?"

"Absolutely right. I dragged my feet entering the contest, not because of any potential mishap, but rather I was petrified to go up against the likes of one of the country's best amateur cooks—namely, you. I'm sorry you had that nightmare. Let me reassure you, I don't even think anything larger than a Thanksgiving turkey and a few side dishes would fit in an oven, but I'd rather not entertain the thought much longer. So, no worries there. Was that all you dreamt?"

"All I can remember." Sherry paused. On her bedside table was a notepad she kept in case a midnight flash of recipe creation brilliance crossed her mind and she needed to jot down the idea. On the small paper was a doodle of bells. Bells? Oh, yes, wedding bells. "I almost forgot. I had a dream Don asked me to marry him."

"Whoa, whoa, whoa. You almost forgot that dream? Now that's a dream I should analyze."

Sherry distanced the phone from her ear when Amber's voice amplified.

"You can put on your retired therapist hat if you'd like. I prefer your Ruggery managerial hat," Sherry said. "My dreams are nothing but random thoughts running amok in my brain."

"You two have no big announcement to make?" Amber asked.

"Don and I have become quite close, yes. It's early days. You must know by now, I don't rush into anything without studying the situation from all angles. No big announcement on this side of the phone." Sherry glanced down to the floor, where Chutney had curled up on top of a pair of yesterday's socks. The effort required at bedtime to remove the socks and the rest of her clothing before putting on her pajamas with one good hand frustrated Sherry to the point she left the discarded clothes where they fell. "When we were at Urgent Care the other night, Don may have made a passing reference to our future together. But, you know, people say things in the chaos of an emergency. Maybe he thought my life was on the line and panicked." Sherry let loose a cautious giggle.

"Or he wants to marry you," Amber said.

Sherry hoisted herself off the corner of the bed. Phone to her ear, she passed by the mirror. A severe case of bedhead stared back at her. Framing her pretty face was a snaggle of highlighted dark blonde hair tumbling almost to her shoulders. "If he saw me right now, he'd reconsider any thought of spending his life with me. I'm definitely on the worse side of for better or worse."

"I'm not believing you," Amber said.

"How in the world am I going to wash my hair with one hand? The situation is nearly beyond repair. If I'd known I couldn't get my hand wet for this many days I would have washed my hair the morning before my accident."

"Sherry, that's impossible. When you're able to predict the future, call me. I'd have plenty of uses for that talent."

"Ha," Sherry laughed.

"I'm sure you look as wonderful as ever. Maybe your hair is a bit more like a rat's nest after a restless night of sleep. That's to be expected. I'll bring you a can of dry shampoo. It's the greatest invention since the bagel slicer."

"Please don't mention slicing anything," Sherry said. "At least for a day or two longer. And yes, I'll accept your offer of the dry shampoo. In the meantime, I have a fashionable baseball cap from last year's Fall Fest Cookoff to tuck my hair under."

"When are you going out?"

As she considered Amber's question, Sherry navigated the stairs, phone in one hand and bandaged hand sliding along the railing. "Very soon. I'm meeting Don at the marina. After I withdrew from the cook-off and volunteered my restricted services in whatever way I could be useful, I was put in contact with a woman, Rickie O'Dell, who will soon be on her way from Long Island. She's apparently made the commute between Long Island, Augustin and Boston by car a number of times over the last couple weeks and is tired of the gridlock traffic. She heads the cook-off organization committee and I offered Don's services to ferry her and a few cook-off participants from Long Island back to Augustin. Then I'll taxi them to the Sound Shore Lodge, where most are staying during the cook-off."

"That sounds like the best way to travel," Amber said.

"We'll see. Fingers crossed for a smooth journey. I want Don to be encouraged he's done the right thing by following his entrepreneurial aspirations. I should be back home in a couple of hours and then Team

Amber-Sherry will work on your Spring Thyme Asparagus Lasagna Blooms."

"Team Am-Sher all the way. Text me when you return. Have fun. Oh, I have to make a stop at the Sound Shore Lodge sometime this morning to check in with the contest committee and pick up my contestant welcome packet and credentials. Maybe I'll see you over there."

"Hey, would you like to make the crossing with us?" Sherry asked. "Last-minute invite, but why not?"

"I thought you'd never ask. I'd love to. I better get a move on if I'm going to go."

"Great. I'll text you the exact time when Don settles on one."

After Sherry dressed for the day, she gave Chutney a short walk. Back inside, Sherry scooped out some dry nuggets and placed Chutney's shiny metal bowl down on his doggie place mat. Every task she performed took twice the amount of time with only one hand. While Chutney munched, she found her typed cook-off recipe on the green marble counter. She found a pen and made a note on her to-do list to ask the contest officials whether she could enter the same recipe next year since the Shortcut African Groundnut Flat Noodle Stew would never get a chance to compete in this year's event. Cubing the sweet potato for the recipe was the action that injured her hand. From mishandling the tuber she learned a hard lesson to keep her cooking techniques by the book or suffer the consequences.

Sherry searched the kitchen counter for a second sheet of paper. She found Amber's recipe for Spring Thyme Asparagus Lasagna Blooms in a pile of papers. She scanned the ingredient list. Sherry's first inclination was to check whether Amber had creatively showcased both a Kitchen Royalty–brand condiment and any form of a noodle in her cook-off recipe, as contest rules required. In that case, she would have a leg up on the competition. As she was reading the recipe a twinge of envy ran through her core. Kitchen Royalty, the largest sponsor of the cook-off, produced some of Sherry's favorite recipe accompaniments and was in large part the reason for Sherry's desire to compete. A blast of discomfort bolted through her hand as she manipulated the page.

After she centered Amber's recipe sheet on the counter, Sherry slid the reusable grocery bag containing the jar of mango chutney she had purchased for her own practice sessions to the side. As the glass jar rattled inside the bag, Sherry was reminded how she used Kitchen Royalty mango chutney in a number of variations, including salad dressings, sandwich spreads, and in the case of her chosen recipe, as a tangy sweet flavor enhancer for her African stew entrée.

"I have to stop torturing myself. I'll have plenty of other opportunities to compete in the future."

She checked the wall clock for the time. "I need to get dressed and get down to the marina." She glanced at her dog, who returned a look of satisfaction for a breakfast well-served. "Almost time to test my one-handed driving skills. Can't be more dangerous than my knife-wielding skills."

Chapter 2

Sherry checked the time on her phone as she neared the water's edge. She had some extra time to marvel at the renovations to the new and improved Augustin Marina before she was to meet Don. If her memory served her correctly, the last time she visited the dockmaster's shed, while in the midst of hunting for a murderer, the tiny building was the only structure between the parking lot and the docks. Added to the landscape since that time was a snack shack, a nautically themed outhouse and a stylish wandering stone pathway.

"Gorgeous scenery."

A voice from behind startled Sherry and she caught her toe on the first stone on the walkway. She regained her balance and turned to see a man in a windbreaker, sweatpants and sunglasses.

"I visited this town years ago and this marina was a neglected mess," he continued. "Glad the town has come to their senses and cleaned this place up. It was a diamond in the rough."

"Lovely. I'm not much of a boater but I do appreciate the natural beauty of the shore," Sherry replied.

"I heard there's going to be a boat shuttle service between here and Long Island. I can't wait to take the voyage. I'd much rather be out on the water than sitting in traffic," the man said as he nodded his head. "Have a great day." He headed in the direction of the adjacent wetland's boardwalk.

"Thank you," Sherry called after him. "You, too." Sherry's mind jumped to an unusual place. That stranger and Amber would make a nice-looking couple. Amber's sleek build and headful of wavy reddish-blonde hair and his athletic frame and rugged, welcoming face were perfect complements to one another.

The thought passed as quickly as it had arrived. Sherry continued her inspection of the marina's improvements. "I'm so happy for Don. He's come on board at the right time. Augustin is re-embracing its maritime history and bringing it into the present."

One item that remained from her last visit to the waterfront months ago was the huge anchor braced against the remnants of a stone wall. She shuddered as her memory returned to the image of a body tied to the rusting metal. The scene of the murder she helped solve was transformed into a memorial to Augustinians lost at sea. A plaque was affixed to the wall the anchor leaned against that read *Lost at sea, always found in our hearts.*

Upon closer inspection, she read only one name on the list, *Sylvester, faithful canine companion.*

"Glad to know Augustin may not have suffered any human casualties at sea. Sorry, Sylvester, I'm sure you were a wonderful companion of the furry variety."

"One thing I've learned about you is I shouldn't worry that you talk to yourself often." Footsteps crunching on the pebbled path from the restrooms grew nearer.

Sherry turned to see a tall man with day-old stubble on his face and a sun hat with earflaps on his head. His plaid flannel shirtsleeves were rolled up, revealing the hefty biceps he was developing since his work on the boat began. The skin on his face, once pale from years of indoor office work, was bronzed, despite his efforts at sun protection. Don's green eyes boasted well-earned laugh lines at their corners.

A hug and kiss later, the couple began a walk down the dock. Sherry watched the man who owned a growing portion of her heart smile broadly as he regarded the vessel docked in front of them with the same level of admiration she regarded her winning cook-off entries. Passion for her hobby kept her happy and engaged and she was glad Don found what drove his. As she observed his quiet reverence for his new toy, she whispered a small thank-you for that day that brought them together.

Deep down Sherry admitted part of the attraction was the circumstance under which the two met. The thought of the wine store where he helped her choose a variety that would be the foundation for a winning balsamic-merlot reduction, despite the fact he was a competitor in the same contest, made his selection her drink of choice since that afternoon.

"Excited for our journey?" Don asked.

Sherry heard Don's question but chose to bask in deep reflection in the warmth of her memory.

"Hey, Sherry. You in there?" Don turned and faced Sherry as he came to a halt a few feet away from the front of his blue, gold, and white boat.

She admired the mercifully long canopy over the outdoor seats that promised to keep out the late spring sun's burning rays. The indoor cabin was available to those unwilling to face the elements. Four rows of cushioned seats sat twelve passengers. Toward the bow of the boat was Don's captain's chair and his command console with all the bells and whistles Sherry couldn't name or give the function of if she tried.

Don lifted her sunglasses "You're so quiet."

"Sorry. I was reminiscing about how we met." Sherry surprised herself with her sentimentality.

"Don't get all gushy on me. I have to captain you safely across the Long Island Sound without distraction. I can't be all lovey-dovey. This is serious business." Don's voice took on a deep intonation that brought a grin to Sherry's lips.

"Yes, sir. Or should I say, Aye, aye, Captain." Sherry saluted Don with her bandaged hand. She followed him to the edge of the dock. "This is an amazing boat."

"I struggled with the size. In the end, I had to choose the model for any type of weather contingency. Indoor space and outdoor space for enough passengers to earn a profit. If commuters are paying a premium for my service they'll want comfort and choice."

"I'm very excited Amber will also be joining us. She's an avid supporter of your new venture and wanted to be a part of your first crossing."

"That's great news," Don said.

"I didn't give her much advance notice but she should be here any minute. She stopped at the lodge to pick up some cook-off welcome goodies." Sherry glanced at the time on her phone.

"Since you can't give much manual help . . ." Don began as he glanced at Sherry's wound.

"Hey, I have one good hand," Sherry said with a whimper.

"As I was about to say, I have a special task for you that doesn't require hands. You can help me read the radar."

"That sounds like an important job, one I have zero experience in. How about if I take on the job of supplying pleasant conversation?"

Don stepped onto the bow of his boat from the short gangplank and reached back for Sherry's good hand. He guided her to the captain's bridge. Sherry watched closely as he double-checked the instruments.

"Gorgeous. And I'm really not a boat person. Let's see, would people rather sit in gridlock traffic or enjoy the ocean breeze while sipping a latte and reading the paper?"

"I'm going to hire you to write my advertising copy," Don said.

"You can't afford me. How many people are we picking up?"

"I believe four or five, not including our second mate, Amber. A woman named Rickie O'Dell provided me with a list, one of which is herself. She said possibly more to come."

"She's the cook-off organizer-in-chief. I'm so glad this all worked out."

"Her note also said the group we're picking up needs to be in Augustin within the next two hours, so whoever shows up on time to catch the inaugural Captain Don's Commuter Cruiser passage is who we ferry across the Sound. All I was told is they're associated with Wednesday's cook-off and I've been paid for one group round trip."

"Can we wait a minute longer for Amber?" As Sherry finished her question her phone rang. "Amber, are you almost here?"

"I'm so sorry. I told everyone I was making the crossing and at the last second Erno asked if I could work earlier today. He has a dentist appointment he forgot he had. I had one foot out the door to come down to the marina."

"No problem. We'll miss you. We even had a special title ready for you. Second mate," Sherry said.

"A promotion. Save the position for me for next time," Amber said. "Have a successful trip."

Sherry turned to Don. "You heard? She can't make it."

"I heard. Too bad."

As the boat rumbled away from the dock Sherry studied the man at the helm of the boat. The brilliant sunlight highlighted the few gray flecks in his facial stubble. He was relaxed for the moment, while taking in all the details of his surroundings. Sherry shifted her sights to the horizon, anticipating the coast of Long Island coming into focus as the boat neared its destination. She would never tell Don, but she would prefer to be driving the round trip by car, as she had yet to embrace too much time on the salt water. She hugged her insulated windbreaker tight around her as the boat's speed increased. Her baseball cap threatened to come lose until she pulled it down tighter.

The temperature began to drop and she was relieved she followed her instinct to overdress. Despite her efforts to keep her coat from fluttering, the material billowed out as the wind slipped underneath. Sherry bent toward Don's ear in hopes he could hear her over the engine's rumbling. "You're still happy with your decision to leave the financial world behind and follow your dreams of starting a water commuter company?"

"So far, so good," Don answered, increasing the volume of his voice over the boat's engine roar. The vague reply left Sherry yearning for more insight, but she left it at that.

When they reached Port Diamante, Long Island, Don parked his boat in the visitor slip. He asked Sherry to remain on board while he checked in with the dockmaster. The portable gangplank was attached and the boat was ready to receive passengers.

"Don't untie anything. I don't want to go floating off without the captain on board," she said and laughed.

Moments later, when Don returned, he wore a sour expression. He jumped aboard and fiddled with some ropes.

"They're not all here yet." Don tipped his head in the direction of a couple making their way down the dock toward the boat. "I'll give the stragglers ten minutes but it's not fair to those who are on time. That's the way I'm going to run this line. On time or out of luck."

"You might want to reconsider running such a tight ship when dealing with Augustin passengers. Plenty of folks in Augustin live by the philosophy that timetables are merely suggestions." She glanced in Don's direction. His tight jaw loosened.

"Duly noted." Don said. He turned his attention to the approaching passengers. "Good morning. Welcome to the *Current-Sea*. Let me help you aboard." As Don reached for the hand of the woman nearing, he added, "This is my first mate, Sherry. She can't shake hands due to a cooking mishap."

Sherry's face warmed as all heads pivoted in her direction. "Good morning," she said with a meek grin. She offered her left hand to the woman dressed in a floral-print raincoat and gleaming white sneakers. A silky earth-tone scarf encircled her head. "What a beautiful scarf. You'll have to show me how you wrapped your hair so artistically with it."

"Thank you. My mother taught me and her mother taught her. I'm Livvy Washington. So nice to meet you. I'm so sorry my husband, Gray, is running late. If we can wait for him, I would appreciate it, but I understand if we can't." Her light brown face twisted into a scowl. "I always remind him to be more considerate, but you can't teach an old dog new tricks."

"Not a problem. Please, take a seat inside or outside. Whichever you prefer. While the weather is cooperating I suggest outside," Sherry said. "We are able to expand or contract the inside shelter as needed, which is a wonderful design feature of this boat." She side-eyed Don, whose mouth curled into a smile.

Livvy smoothed her raincoat under her backside. She took a seat in the row of cushioned low-backed seats behind the captain's chair, where she immediately pulled her phone from her coat pocket. Sherry glanced at

Don, who pinched his lips tight again. He held his hand out a second time and offered assistance to a couple waiting to board.

"We are Jean and Curt McDonald. So nice to meet you two." The man clutching his wife's hand and a suitcase made his way off the dock and onto the boat without assistance.

"I'm Don, and this is Sherry."

"We drove up from Virginia to compete in the cook-off," Jean said as she found a seat. She tucked her small suitcase close to her legs.

"Jean's competing," Curt corrected. "I'm here to cheer her on and take advantage of the perks, such as this boat ride and tomorrow's pre-competition festivities." Curt generated a chuckle that tussled the wiry sideburns protruding from his floppy sun hat.

"We got as far as Long Island and decided we'd had enough traffic. Thanks to the cook-off organizers for offering this alternative to road rage," Jean added. She kept her hand on the handle of her rolling suitcase.

"Can we store that for you to give you more legroom?" Sherry asked, pointing to the small suitcase.

"No, thank you," Jean said. She wedged the suitcase between her seat and Curt's. "My prized Swiss cutlery collection is inside, and if that gets misplaced, I won't be able to function. The set cost an arm and a leg. I should insure it, it was so expensive. Top of the line. I wonder if you know which brand I'm talking about."

"Let me guess," Sherry said with a sly grin. "Could it be the Hunziker?"

"You do know your equipment. Took me years to work up the confidence to spend the money on knives that can cut through bone as if it's butter. I've practiced my Tidewater Smothered and Stuffed Chicka-Noodle Casserole recipe using my six-inch carving knife, so I'd be lost without it."

Beside her, Curt was patting his extended belly. "She's made the dish so many times I'm the one who's smothered and stuffed."

"I completely understand," Sherry said. "About the coveted knife set, that is."

"Have you been in a cook-off before?" Curt asked.

Sherry caught a glimpse of Don's wry smile. "Yes, a few. As a matter of fact, my recipe was chosen to compete in the finals of this year's Kitchen Royalty Use Your Noodle Recipe Cook-off." She held up her bandaged hand. "Then this happened. One practice session too many. Now I'm on the sidelines rooting for my friend who's participating."

"Burn?" Jean asked.

"Knife slip," Sherry said.

"Wait a minute. Are you Sherry Oliveri?" Jean blurted out. She sat up at attention and uncrossed her legs. "I heard she was in the cook-off and had to withdraw due to a mishap. I mean you, not she."

Sherry lifted her eyebrows and smiled. In her peripheral vision she saw Don nodding. "It was only a matter of time," he whispered.

"You are Sherry Oliveri. No wonder you're so familiar with knife sets that get the job done. I was hoping to meet you while we were in Augustin and learn how you've done so well over the years. There has to be a formula to your winning. I have to admit I'm sorry about your accident but relieved I'm not competing against you." Jean dropped the handle of her suitcase. "Can you give me a few pointers now that you're not competing?"

"Dear, take it easy. You're scaring the woman," Curt said with a hint of a Southern drawl.

Sherry opened her mouth to respond, but before she could a voice rang out.

"Hello, everyone. My name is Rickie O'Dell." A woman dressed in khakis and a quilted coat boasting the famous British high-end plaid lining exposed at the wrists and collar sashayed across the dock to the boat's hull. Before Don could extend a hand, the woman crossed the watery gap between the dock and the *Current-Sea* as if she were more than a bit familiar with boarding a boat. "You must be Don Johnstone." She put down her luggage and shook Don's hand. "I'm with the cook-off organizing committee."

"Hi, I'm Sherry. You're the chairwoman of the cook-off, isn't that right?"

"That's me. Unless you have a complaint, then that's someone else." She bellowed a laugh. "Judging by your hand, you must be Sherry Oliveri." Rickie acknowledged the others seated in the boat. "The McDonalds from Virginia and Mrs. Washington from Boston. Are we expecting your husband, Gray? My list indicated he hoped to take this ride."

"Yes. We're hoping so, too." Livvy lifted her eyes for a split second before returning her attention to her phone.

Rickie sat down and focused her attention on Don. "I've made this trip back and forth by car at least four times over the last two months attending to details. Southern New Jersey might as well be on Mars when you have to drive through the jam-packed boroughs of New York City. So many cars.

I'm so glad to get off the road and out on the water. This is the way to travel. Sherry was so kind to offer your services." Rickie turned her attention to Livvy, who remained seated. "And I can't thank the Washingtons enough. Real lifesavers."

"What do you mean?" Sherry asked.

"You didn't hear?" Rickie asked. "The cook-off had a last-minute snafu. The supplier of the appliance package, which is a large part of the grand prize, ran into trouble when the company was handed a nationwide recall of their products for a safety issue with the power source."

"I heard murmurings," Sherry said.

"Losing a sponsor after all the write-ups are out to the press and public is a bad look for the cook-off, but quickly remedied when I was given the name of the Washington Appliance Center. The cook-off was saved in the eleventh hour." Rickie turned her attention to Livvy. "Where is your husband? I have yet to meet the man who agreed to step in at the last moment with the appliance prize package."

"We were on vacation in the Hamptons when the store called us and said they had been approached to offer a prize package to your prestigious cook-off. We didn't even have time to head home to Boston to pick up the appropriate work attire. We'll be sporting Hamptons chic for the next few days whether it's appropriate attire for the cook-off events or not. Maybe we can return to the beach for a few days since we have to pick up our car in Long Island anyway before we return to Boston." Livvy laughed. "I'm afraid Gray was running a bit late getting himself out of vacation mode and missed our car service to the boat. He shouldn't be too far behind, although he's not answering my texts. I've been reaching out to him for the last hour. When he wasn't at the hotel at departure time, I left without him. I didn't want to miss the boat." Livvy's tone seemed pleasant but, at the same time, carried an edge.

"We'll wait a few more minutes, then he may have to find an alternate mode of transport," Don said as he checked the radar.

A few minutes passed with the passengers sitting in near silence on the boat. Rickie and Livvy were attending to their phones and the McDonalds were poring over what Sherry recognized as a printout of the cook-off event schedule. Sherry kept checking in on Don's mood and was satisfied he was taking the delay in stride. It wasn't too long before he began glancing at the time with increasing frequency. Relief from the mounting uneasiness came when a breathless voice called down from the head of the dock.

"Excuse me, is this the commuter boat to Augustin, Connecticut? Livvy, is that you?"

"That's got to be Livvy's husband," Sherry said as she watched Don spring from his seat.

"Better late than never," Livvy said.

"Sorry, everyone. Thanks for waiting. I'm Gray Washington." The broad, dark-complected man accepted Don's help getting aboard the boat.

"I'm Don, this is Sherry, Rickie, Jean and Curt. When you find a seat, we'll set off. Everyone's decided to sit outside. The choice is up to you," Don said. "Secure your bag under your seat if it fits."

Sherry nodded a greeting to Gray while taking note that Livvy did no more than lift her eyes from her phone screen for a split second. Instead of taking a seat close to his wife, Gray parked himself next to Rickie. With such close space between seats there was not much chance of a private conversation until the motor powered up. That didn't seem to stop Gray from addressing Rickie in a tone charged with indignation.

"Thank you for the opportunity to sponsor the cook-off. My good fortune does seem to come at a cost. I have the previous appliance sponsor, Walter Hemphill, calling my shop day and night using profanity-laced rants. My manager is beside himself," Gray said.

Rickie's response diffused Gray's animosity expertly with a polite overtone. "I can't thank you enough for stepping in at the last moment. I regret the previous sponsor was blindsided with the recalls of his product, but he has to understand the cook-off's predicament. We cannot offer a tainted prize package. I had to choose another sponsor."

Sherry whispered in Don's ear. Don cleared his throat, stood and faced his passengers. "A quick safety note. Life vests are stored in the storage chest at the rear of the boat. If you feel you'd like to wear one now you may, or if, heaven forbid, we encounter an emergency, the lid flips up and the vests inside easily zip on. In a minute I'll begin backing out at slow speed before heading out into open water. Hold on to your hats and enjoy your trip."

Rickie led a soft round of applause and Don's face bloomed with pride. After Don took his captain's seat, Sherry kept her sights alternating between the boat's high-definition rear camera and the passengers behind her as the vessel backed from the dock. She made every attempt to appear as if she weren't overhearing the conversation between Gray and the other passengers, but her pinched facial expression may have betrayed her.

"It's bringing a certain amount of trouble to my business. When I was hoping for good publicity all I'm getting is an outcry for taking away Hemphill's products," Gray said over the engine's escalating hum.

"I couldn't help but overhear what you said. The Hemphill appliances aren't part of the prize package anymore? I was gung-ho to win a new stainless steel smart refrigerator, oven and matching dishwasher from their uber-luxury line," Jean said.

"Ours is luxurious, too," Gray said. He huffed a prolonged groan. "My belief in my products is so strong I cut my vacation short and hightailed it over to Augustin, a town I never even heard of, while coordinating long-distance with my Boston store. Priority shipping at the highest cost to my business to get everything to the cook-off on time and keep my wife happy. Do you know how complicated the logistics of all that is? This boat ride is the only form of relaxation I've had in days. Worth leaving the car behind for."

Livvy raised her voice. "Gray, this is a good chance for us to showcase our wares. The extra effort required is all worth it."

"In the end, you'll be happy with your decision to join the cook-off. You and your wife's business came highly recommended." Rickie turned her attention to Jean. "Yes, we changed suppliers at the last minute for an even better line of product. Cook your best and you will be in contention for a delightful surprise."

"That's my intention," Jean said with a nod. She patted her equipment case.

"The contestants are getting a tour of the cook-off venue layout at the Augustin Convention Center tomorrow morning. If the shipment arrives on time the appliances will be on view for motivation and inspiration to the cooks. I'll be asking Sherry for her help in showing the contestants around since we are fortunate enough to have a seasoned veteran of cooking contests at our disposal," Rickie said. "Isn't that right, Sherry?"

Sherry opened her mouth to reply. Her words were drowned out by Don's proclamation.

"We are on our way, folks. I'm powering up, so square yourselves to your seat," Don said as he slid the throttle forward.

Sherry was surprised how much she enjoyed the ride. As the Augustin Harbor came into view she worked at identifying as many coastal landmarks as she could from the boat's vantage point. Her challenge was interrupted when a voice cried out.

"Don!"

Sherry jerked her head around to see who was frantically calling Don. Jean was waving her arms overhead. Sherry's sights shifted in the direction Jean began pointing. She gasped. Sherry poked her elbow in Don's ribs and he shot her an aggressive look that sent a chill down her spine.

"What are you doing?" he shouted. "I could have crashed."

Sherry couldn't get any words past her lips. She silently begged him to understand what she was thinking. She gestured wildly as the jet ski closed in diagonally. Don's face blanched and he yanked back the throttle.

"Hold on!" Don called out.

Unattended luggage and unoccupied seat cushions catapulted forward as the boat responded to Don's sudden command to come to a stop. When Sherry lifted her head after lurching forward, she scanned the surroundings for the jet ski and the hooded driver. Sherry watched the machine skipping over the waves and out of sight.

"That was a close one," Jean said with a mighty exhale.

Sherry surveyed the passengers. "Everyone okay?" Her gaze stalled on Gray. "Are you feeling ill? Your face is rather . . ." She reconsidered using *gray* as her description of his suddenly pallid complexion, ". . . pale."

"I'm fine. Shouldn't have had a meal so close to departure." Gray rubbed his stomach. "Not digesting very well. Something's coming back up."

"We don't need any more details," Livvy said. She addressed Sherry. "He'll be fine. He's had trouble with seasickness before."

"Everyone else okay?" Sherry asked. She was addressing the passengers, but her attention was on Don.

"Someone's suitcase got crunched. Make that two suitcases got crunched," Gray said as he left his seat to right the life preserver chest, which had traveled across the glistening wooden deck and taken some suitcases for a ride.

Jean sprang from her seat. "My case," she shrieked. "I lost my grip."

"Mine, too," Rickie said. "Bad choice to use my old suitcase. I thought I'd give it one more trip before I bought a new one and that was a mistake." She stood to collect items the broken closure let escape from her bag.

"I'll get them," Curt said. He joined Gray and together they returned the life vest chest to the stern of the boat and suitcases to their rightful owners. Livvy's suitcase suffered a bent wheel, while Don's travel coffee mug lost its lid and liquid contents.

"Now I know everything needs to be better secured," Don whispered to

Sherry. "That's what these trial runs are all about. The learning curve is steep out on the water and I want to keep everyone safe no matter what the odd occurrence."

Chapter 3

With the commute complete and the *Current-Sea* safely docked at the Augustin Marina, everyone disembarked. Sherry joined in the thank-yous to Don for an exciting and mostly successful commute from Long Island. She reserved a kiss and a private word of encouragement for him after the other passengers made their way to the parking lot.

"Job well done, Captain. We were all very safe in your capable hands."

"Thanks," Don said. "I could have used a lot less drama." He took Sherry's hand. "I'm sad I won't see you tonight. I hope the dinner is as good at my sister's house as it is at yours, but I doubt that's a possibility. She said you must come next time."

"I will. I promised Amber I'd do a recipe run-through with her and I don't want to put a time limit on the project. She's really keen on taking home a prize. That's an attitude I can work with."

"I can see by the twinkle in your eye you're going to give it all you've got. Have a good night." Don headed back to the boat after blowing an additional kiss in Sherry's direction.

Sherry rejoined the group in the marina parking lot. Rickie was speaking to everyone while referring to a piece of paper in her hand.

"Sherry, the McDonalds will be catching a car service to the Sound Shore Lodge." She gestured in the direction of an idling sedan. "Does your offer to drive myself and the Washington's to the lodge still stand?" Rickie asked.

"Absolutely. Right this way." Sherry and her charges crossed the parking lot, luggage in tow.

"Gray, I got a text saying your store has delayed the delivery of the refrigerator, oven and dishwasher set until the late afternoon," Rickie said as everyone settled into their seats in Sherry's car. "Would you please put the urgency rush in process? I'm getting worried."

"I'm doing my best. I got a text from my trucker saying he had a devil of a time getting his truck to start," Gray said.

"But the truck's on its way, right? So, all is well," Rickie said with a superficial lightness. "The cook-off will be a complete success." Rickie leaned forward from the backseat and closed in on Sherry's ear. "Nearly all the cooks are staying at the lodge. Tomorrow they'll be shuttled to the convention center for orientation. That's when I was hoping you could lend a hand. I have plenty of assistants and volunteers but no one with your valuable expertise."

"I'm planning on it," Sherry said. "What do you need me to concentrate on?"

"During the orientation, I'd use you on the cook-off floor to circulate between cook stations, making sure your assigned group of cooks is familiar with how their stove works and they know their recipe ingredient locations."

"I'm looking forward to helping," Sherry said. "The convention center is within walking distance of the Sound Shore Lodge. I would bet, unless it rains, people would enjoy the walk."

Rickie dismissed Sherry's suggestion by changing the subject. "Have you ever had any problems as a competitor during any of your cook-offs? I'm asking because I'd like a feeling for what could go wrong."

"Good question. One thing organizers grapple with at every cook-off, the unknown. Just when I think I've witnessed every possible scenario of mishaps a new one rears its ugly head," Sherry said with a laugh. "Best suggestion is to give a thorough orientation and hope the cooks are good listeners."

"That is half the battle," Rickie said. "If they're nervous or distracted they'll miss valuable information."

"Just do the best you can doling out information and hope for the best. Without an orientation cooks can waste valuable time trying to turn on a brand of oven they're unfamiliar with. Imagine trying to figure out where your recipe ingredients are being stored or where the medium-sized saucepan you specified might be hiding without prior knowledge of the cook-off's layout."

"We don't want anyone put in that situation." Rickie's confidence was both reassuring to Sherry and somewhat naïve if this was her first venture into the cooking competition world. Problems were sure to occur.

"Here we are," Sherry announced as she steered her car toward the parking lot of the Sound Shore Lodge. The main building in front of them overlooked Half Moon Harbor. Sherry remembered when the lodge's property consisted of a dilapidated house, neglected for years yet sitting on one of the most scenic plots of land along Augustin's coast. Despite the fact her hometown boasted many historic buildings that leant their charm to careful preservation by historic-minded citizens, the house could not be saved. Sherry considered what replaced the neglected house as a better use of the property everyone could enjoy. Yards below the property was the beach. Reached by venturing down a bluff, and rocky rather than sandy, sunbathers and swimmers were dissuaded from making the trek. Walks and hikes were what the beach was primarily used for.

"What a lovely setting," Livvy said. "Wouldn't want to sleepwalk down that hill. I bet kids love to run up and down the path to the beach."

Sherry slowed the car to give her passengers time to take in the scenery. She found herself caught in a flashback to her youth when she and her siblings, Pep and Marla, snuck onto the property and climbed down the overgrown path to the water. Sherry made the mistake of taking off her flip-flops to enjoy the water, only to have the sharp clam and oyster shell bits cut her feet. From her vantage point behind the wheel, the lodge owners had left the beach as wild as it was. Those who preferred a more barefoot-friendly beach could head to the public beach, which was within easy walking distance.

"The cook-off will provide a shuttle bus between the lodge and the Nutmeg Motor Inn, also to the cook-off venue at the convention hall and downtown Augustin, which is so convenient. Honestly, everything is within walking distance depending on your energy level. If you brought comfortable shoes, that's the mode of transport I suggest," Sherry said.

She parked her car after she let off her passengers near the walkway to the lodge's main entrance. Sherry took her time surveying the scene as the warming midday sun lit up the sky. When she arrived at the check-in desk, Livvy and Gray were having words.

"I told you I wanted a separate room," Livvy insisted.

"That money comes out of our business. Do you know how much this place costs?" Gray hissed. He turned to face the customer service agent behind the desk. "The contest will only pay for one room. Fine. We will stay with the original reservation she made without my knowledge for two rooms, three nights." He tossed his credit card onto the counter.

"Excuse me. Is this the line for the check-in?" asked a man carrying a leather briefcase.

Sherry glanced toward the man and noted the intensity of his glare. He looked as if he were taking in every detail of Sherry's face.

"Yes. I'm not in line. I'll step aside," Sherry said.

"I'm not in it either, I'm looking for a couple who should be checking in about now." He scanned the room before his sights settled on the service counter. "There they are, right in front of me."

"Are you with the cook-off?" Sherry asked. "My name is Sherry. I'm assisting the contestants over the next few days if you need anything."

"Nice to meet you. My name is Bart Foster." He glanced at the Washingtons, who were winding up their business at the check-in desk. The couple made a move closer to Sherry.

"That's okay, Sherry. I can take over from here," Livvy said as she stepped between Sherry and Bart. "Welcome to Augustin, Bart. Hope your train ride was pleasant."

Bart shook hands with Gray. "Very pleasant, thanks. Good to be here. I've checked in over at the Nutmeg Motor Inn. I've been waiting for you since before breakfast."

"I told you we'd be here by midmorning," Livvy said.

Sherry stepped back from the group's huddle. She caught sight of Rickie and the McDonalds entering the lodge, followed by a boisterous group of women dressed in cook-off aprons. Over the animated conversation, Sherry heard someone call her name.

Rickie was waving in her direction. "Sherry, I'd like to give you a lanyard with your cook-off credentials and an official cook-off management apron to wear whenever you're on duty, which if I have my way, will be often."

Sherry came to the fast realization her offer to lend Rickie a hand, if needed, had evolved into a full-blown job. At least the timing worked out well, as she wasn't planning on returning to work at the Ruggery for a few more days. Her brother, Pep, would have to take up the slack at the store while she concentrated on the cook-off and related activities. He was already on call since Sherry's accident, what's a few more hours on duty going to hurt?

"Tonight, there's an early buffet dinner for the contestants here at the lodge. Some may choose to go off on their own and explore the town, while others will take advantage of the contest footing the dinner bill, which is what I recommend. Why not? Free is free." Rickie threw her hands open.

"The dinners are one of the best parts of cook-offs. Seeing the other cooks out at play sheds new light on who they are out of the kitchen," Sherry said. "Untie those aprons and let your hair down until the real competition begins."

A moment later Rickie excused herself when her name was called out from across the room.

"I arrived early this morning, and while I was waiting for the

Washingtons I talked to a contestant who knew you," Bart said as he closed in.

"Knew me? Who?" Sherry said.

"Amber Sherwin. She and I were milling around the lobby and I struck up a conversation with her. She said she was local and proceeded to share that the famous Sherry Oliveri had influenced her to enter the contest. She's very proud to call you her friend."

"Thank you. That's very nice of her," Sherry said.

"Said it's only her second cook-off. Nice she knows some of the others associated with the cook-off," Bart said.

"I didn't realize she did," Sherry said.

"She seemed to have a few friends," Bart said. "As the lobby filled up, she excused herself to go greet someone across the lobby."

"Wonder who she knows?" Sherry said.

"I didn't get any names, sorry. Just wanted to share her compliment with you. See you later." Bart left Sherry's side. The void was immediately filled by Rickie.

"Well, that was nice. Now, the last job I have left for you today is walking the Washingtons over to the convention center to meet the appliance package delivery. Would you be willing?" Rickie handed Sherry a piece of paper. "Refer to this drawing to get your bearings when you're inside the building. It's a massive space and very easy to get turned around. The signage isn't up yet."

Sherry studied the rendering of the convention center layout and found the marked outline for the prize package location.

"I appreciate it. I want to give the Washingtons reassurance. The good news is the delivery should be here any minute. Amazing what a little old-fashioned urging can accomplish."

"Good. Yes, I did sense some tension. Glad the delivery is moving at warp speed suddenly," Sherry said.

"While you're showing them the location, I need to put a Band-Aid on a contestant airport pickup miscue. I'm available by text if there's a problem you can't solve. Oh, and one warning. Be prepared for pushback on the location from the delivery service people," Rickie said. "It's the devil to get large items through the narrow doorways and down the hall, but it's the only way in. The first floor was originally designed for lectures, speaking engagements and such, not for trade shows and certainly not cook-offs with tons of large equipment."

"Nothing comes easily," Sherry said.

"I was told the building was renamed Augustin Convention Center after years of being called the Colonial Lecture Hall. The original name was terribly limiting, wouldn't you say?"

"I edit the town's weekly newsletter and I've been privy to much of the inside secrets of name changes of long-standing institutions in town. Change of any sort doesn't happen without years and years of debate, studies, polls and votes. That's what makes Augustin a stronghold of tradition, often much to the chagrin of the younger generation, who prefer instant action," Sherry explained.

"The charm of small-town New England. My team managed to set up all the cooking stations with the necessary ovens and a number of small refrigerators, et cetera, so I know it can be done. Nothing comes easy, as you said. I had to field so many complaints from suppliers delivering equipment over the last few days I was forced to head to Long Island twice to recruit more members from our office over there."

"I'll bring my most persuasive temperament," Sherry said with a degree of trepidation. There seemed to be bad consequences looming if this delivery operation wasn't on point and she wasn't sure she wanted to shoulder that burden.

Questions popped into her head but were never voiced when Rickie called out, "Gray and Livvy? Can I see you over here, please?" Rickie waved the Washingtons in closer.

The couple approached with Bart Foster trailing behind.

"Rickie, this is our friend Bart Foster. He's here to watch the cook-off," Gray said. Bart shook Rickie's hand. Gray turned his attention to his phone. "I just got a text the delivery is five minutes away."

"Sherry will take you over to the convention center to meet the truck," Rickie said.

Gray's prevalent forehead lines broadcast his concern. "You're not coming?" he asked Rickie.

"I've got a fire to put out. Don't worry. Sherry's a veteran of cook-offs. She can handle any situation," Rickie said with such a calm delivery Sherry almost believed her.

"Mind if Bart joins us?" Livvy asked.

"Sure. Hold on a minute." Rickie put up her index finger. "I'll secure him a pass for the next couple days. Please don't spread the word around. I won't do it for anyone else who hasn't filed the event paperwork with me.

You two have been the cook-off's salvation so I owe you one. Now we're even." Rickie winked. "Take my lanyard for the time being and I'll get a replacement." She handed Bart a Cook-off Helping Hands credential to wear around his neck. Rickie reached in her pants pocket. "Sherry, I'm lending you a copy of the convention hall key. This copy works on the side door, which is where deliveries should be received. Fingers crossed everything fits where it's supposed to."

Sherry received the key and put it safely in her coat pocket. "Mind if we walk? It's not too far. Otherwise, I could get my car from the lot and pick you up," Sherry said.

"Walking is fine," Gray said with little enthusiasm.

"The view is lovely," Livvy said to Bart.

"The entire town is quaint and lovely," Bart said. "I could see living here."

Sherry bloomed with a sense of pride her little town was making such an instant impact on visitors.

By the time the foursome reached the expansive brick convention center the delivery truck was idling at the side entrance. The driver was pacing from the door of the building to the rear of the truck and back again, hands on hips, shaking his head. He was gesturing to a robust man in overalls, leaning on the truck's cab.

Before anyone could greet the man and his truck mate, he spoke. "No way. Can't do it. Isn't there a delivery entrance? Otherwise, we're going to have to shoehorn these things through the doorways. Is this the only way inside for deliveries? You can't squeeze a watermelon through a keyhole, you know."

Sherry waved the sheet of paper in her hand. "This is the service and delivery entrance." She nodded to emphasize her belief in the impossible. "Let me show you how this is going to work."

"What a headache," Gray said to Livvy.

"We need to convince them it's happening," Sherry said. After a few minutes of explaining the tight doorway and slim long hallway was the only way into the cavernous room, the deliverymen were dissuaded from returning their load to Boston. Sherry exhaled a sigh of relief. She unlocked the convention center's delivery door with the key Rickie lent her.

The deliverymen got to work unloading the shipment. After climbing into the body of the truck, one of the men addressed Gray.

"Before we left your warehouse, we got this forwarded email from your showroom." He held up his phone. "Says Washington Appliances will regret this. Weird, right? Gave me the heebie-jeebies. I don't need any trouble. I've got a wife and kids and I need this job."

Gray puffed out his cheeks. "Bart? Know anything about this?"

Bart and Livvy exchanged a long look of concern.

"Nothing to worry about. Everything's fine," Bart said.

A cool breeze chilled Sherry's neck. She pulled up her coat collar. "If you're ready to start unloading, I'll prop the door open," Sherry said.

Out of the corner of her eye she spotted Bart and Livvy in a muted conversation. As she looked on, Bart was writing in a palm-size notebook while Livvy seemed to be doing all the talking. Sherry quickly refocused on the job at hand when Gray bellowed a stop order.

"Wait a minute. Hold up. Easy, guys. This stuff's valuable. No one wants dented goods," Gray directed. A bang, a crash and a groan later, Sherry moved in to inspect the damage.

"The security camera's smashed," Sherry said. "The top of the refrigerator swiped it and knocked it down."

"How's the refrigerator?" Gray asked as he trotted over. He ran his hand along the top rim of the stainless steel giant. "No damage here, thank goodness. The camera's the only casualty." He picked up the cracked mirrored glass dome and the embedded camera and set them aside. "I'll advise Rickie. Couldn't be helped."

The remainder of the delivery went without mishap. Gray directed the deliverymen until the truck was empty and the men's shirts were stained with sweat. "Good job. You're the best."

"Thanks, boss. I sure hope whoever sent that email threat was only kidding around," the man said as he climbed into the cab of the truck. The engine rumbled to life. They blasted the horn, flipped a wave goodbye and drove out of sight.

"You didn't seem concerned about the email threat," Sherry said.

"My store forwarded me the email. I saw it this morning. I didn't want to add fuel to the fire, but I am beyond concerned," Gray said.

Sherry studied the man's face. His dark skin camouflaged under-eye circles from a distance. Up close Sherry could see evidence of sleepless nights on the man's face. Livvy and Bart stepped aside and began a conversation that didn't include Gray.

"Glad that's done. From here on out it's the contest's responsibility to move the goods to the winner's house," Gray said as he dusted his hands together. "Now we have no responsibilities until day after tomorrow, when we introduce the prize package at the awards ceremony."

Sherry smiled at the man whose mood swung from dismal to content over the last few hours. "I can recommend some activities in Augustin if you're interested. And some great restaurants."

"Livvy? Come and listen to this," Gray said. "Sherry has some recommendations for sights and eating spots in town."

Livvy and Bart made their way over to Sherry. Bart was tucking his notepad inside his coat.

"I was telling Bart about the jet ski incident this morning," Livvy said. "He doesn't think it was any random guy out for a joy ride. He thinks there was ill intent."

"If that's the case it could have been one of Hemphill's henchmen. The guy wants to see me fail because he went from the northeast's largest luxury appliance dealer to bottom of the barrel," Gray said. "I wouldn't put it past the man to try to embarrass me in front of your cook-off audience."

A ripple of goose bumps crept up Sherry's arms. She didn't want to be in the middle of a conflict, especially one involving her favorite hobby. "I'm sure that won't be the case. Come on. I'll walk you all back to the lodge."

Sherry again used the quarter-mile stroll back to the lodge to revisit her youth. Thick bramble bushes lined the edge of the path that veered off toward the beach below. The property had been preserved in its same wild state she recalled, and as a result, Sherry mentally returned to the day she and her siblings trespassed, urged on by the promise of the broken-down house being haunted. They weren't disappointed when they tested the porch floorboards and were rewarded with the planks groaning like an otherworldly chorus of specters. A moment later the floor gave way when Pep, the weightiest of the siblings, took one step too many. The result was a scraped leg and the fastest foot race back to the safety of the Oliveri house the siblings had ever run.

"This is a lovely walk," Livvy said. "I'm glad we didn't drive."

Sherry, startled out of her daydream by the comment, nodded in agreement. "There used to be a house over there where the lodge now sits. You can make out the edges of the foundation under the tall grasses. Takes me back to times when I tested my somewhat lacking adventurous side in my youth."

"That's not what I've heard," Bart said. "I've heard you are quite the amateur sleuth. That's pretty adventurous if you ask me."

"Something I fell into unintentionally for the most part," Sherry said. "And hopefully, never again."

Chapter 4

After escorting the Washingtons and Bart from the convention hall to the Sound Shore Lodge's lobby, Sherry texted Amber that she was free to meet for their recipe practice session. As she typed the final word, a pang of regret, or possibly frustration, rang through her. She wouldn't be in the kitchen making final preparations for another cook-off performance for herself. This being the first and only time she was ever sidelined from a cook-off after she qualified to compete should have provided enough solace for her to let the feeling pass quickly, but instead she wallowed in self-pity until she pulled her car into her driveway. Amber was there to greet her, cooking supplies bundled in her arms.

Sherry greeted her friend and coworker with a welcoming smile. The thought passed through Sherry's mind that their relationship had come full circle since they met at a cook-off years ago. Amber was a newbie at her first cook-off, which she entered on a whim after the breakup of her marriage. On hiatus from her family and marriage therapy practice, Amber took a chance on a new hobby. Sherry was the veteran competing in her umpteenth cooking contest. Seeing her warm smile, Sherry was reminded of the immediate connection she felt to Amber. Sherry saw Amber as a yin to her yang. Amber was confident, soft-spoken and easygoing. Sherry leaned toward cautious, inflexible, a creature of habit. Despite their differences, one thing led to another and on Sherry's recommendation Amber relocated to Augustin and began working as a manager in Erno Oliveri's hooked rug store. Sherry was reminded of the value of that decision nearly every day she saw her friend, this day being no exception. Seeing her friend anxious to perfect her cook-off recipe under her tutelage was a badge of honor, Sherry admitted to herself.

"Hi!" Sherry pulled out her key to unlock the paneled front door of her small colonial house.

"You look lost in thought," Amber said.

Sherry struggled to wriggle the house key into the ancient brass lock. She knew the dance she had to perform to get the key to turn the tumbler, requiring hand and wrist gyrations with one hand and a coaxing of the knob with another. A tall order under the circumstances. She was resigned to using shoulder pressure to loosen the tight fit. Once open, she found Chutney perched inside the door, wagging his tail.

"Just remembering how we met and how far we've come," Sherry said.

"I pat myself on the back every day for having the foresight to hound you into a friendship when we met at your first cook-off."

"Now you're stuck with me. Be careful what you wish for." Amber followed Sherry into the kitchen. "If I win the cash prize at the cook-off I'm going to buy you one of those newfangled door locks that only need your phone to unlock. And there's a camera to see who's knocking when you're inside. Anyone who lives alone should have one. Me included."

"Can't say no to that," Sherry said. "Time for me to modernize."

"Did I give you more incentive to perfect my recipe?" Amber asked and laughed.

"I don't need any. I'm so happy to get into the kitchen to help you," Sherry said with a wide grin. She bent down and ruffled Chutney's fur. "If I can't compete, I want you to do your best work."

"I can't wait to firm up a few aspects of my recipe that I know I can do better, with the help of your expertise."

"I've read through your recipe once and I think it's a winner."

Amber laid the printout on the counter behind the supplies.

"I have a copy right here," Sherry said as she held up a piece of paper.

"I've brought my copy. I've made a few notes." Amber slid the paper across the counter next to Sherry's printout.

Sherry scanned Amber's typed recipe for Spring Thyme Asparagus Lasagna Blooms containing circled words, highlighted sentences and lots of underlining. Exclamation points accented the margin. Sherry let her mind drift to how she herself approached cook-off prep day in a very different manner. No printout served as a backup to her memorizing the recipe. The reasoning behind her method was her knowledge of each recipe's origin. Her recipes almost always contained a nod to her upbringing and favorite childhood ingredients. She cooked what was familiar to her, yet always with a modern twist that would catch the judge's eye. Memorizing her recipes was an essential level of familiarity she strove for in order to be ready to compete.

"Do you prepare the entire recipe the day before a cook-off, to make sure you have every base covered?" Amber asked.

"I don't. I only work on sections, like the sauce or the filling. If the recipe doesn't flow for me a day or two before the actual event, I've chosen the wrong recipe to enter."

"I'm not that confident," Amber said.

"You are. I'm just nitpicky. You do you. I'd wager most cooks do the entire recipe. Even when I say it out loud it makes the most sense to practice the recipe from start to finish. I'm the oddball."

"Obviously your method works for you," Amber said and laughed. "If how you do things isn't broken, don't fix it."

"You unpack the ingredients and I'll get the pans out. Did you bring knives?" Sherry asked.

"I didn't," Amber said. She finished unpacking and tucked away her empty tote bags. "My knives are not the greatest. I'll run out and buy a new set when we're done. I know how important proper and consistent knife cuts are to the judges."

Sherry opened her knife drawer. "Now's not the time to be bringing untested cutlery to a cook-off. Especially a knife you've never held before." She raised her bandaged hand. "I did this after knowing my new knife set for only a month." Sherry pulled out three knives in various sizes. "The best knives on the market. We'll use them today and if you like them, you'll be using them at the cook-off."

"You're the best," Amber said. "I'll be very careful."

Below their knees, Chutney took up his clean-up-the-spill stance. "Watch your step," Sherry warned. "The cleanup crew is down below."

An hour and a half later, Amber and Sherry had rolled up the last of the al dente lasagna noodles with sausage, soft herb cheese and lightly steamed asparagus nestled inside. They were baked to a golden brown perfection. Amber's Kitchen Royalty condiment choice was prepared pesto, which she used to top the baked dish.

"A pop of color and a burst of savory goodness the judges will love," Sherry commented. "If this isn't a taste of spring, I don't know what is." Sherry stepped back to let Amber arrange her presentation platter. You've definitely punched me in the face with flavor. I smell and taste a winner here. Do you have room for all those new appliances when you win?" Sherry scanned her kitchen. "Throw any my way if you don't need them."

"You're putting the cart before the horse," Amber said with a smile. "Speaking of new . . ." She lightened her tone and wrinkled her forehead. "I love the knives." Amber glanced at Sherry's bandaged hand. "I'm guessing you're not using them for a few days. Trimming the asparagus will take on a more professional uniform appearance if I can use this knife." Amber held up the six-inch knife she'd trimmed the tough ends of the asparagus off with. "I never invested in a knife set while I was married. It's been on my wish list as a single gal learning her way around the kitchen.

Today has definitely proven a great knife is worth the expense."

Sherry's expression beamed brilliance. "Of course. A contestant we ferried over from Long Island earlier today had the same knife set she was guarding with her life. That reminded me to check with you as to whether you had a knife set that could compete with hers. She got my competitive juices flowing with the pride she had for her equipment." Sherry's lower lip protruded slightly.

"Let's clean the whole knife set and we'll put it in a special travel case for you. When the other cooks see you toting the knife set, don't be surprised if they just roll over and give up." Sherry snickered at her joke. She handed Amber a kitchen towel. "I'm sorry to say, you have to do the dirty work. And please be careful."

She handed Amber the knives one by one to wash. Sherry laid a towel down on the counter on which to rest the washed knives.

"How was the trip to Long Island on Don's fancy commuter boat?"

Sherry pondered the question for a moment. "Very nice, for the most part, but not without a close call."

"Oh, no. What happened?"

"A jet skier gave us a run for the money with a near miss. Maybe a young hotdogger out for a springtime jaunt."

"Did you learn any inside info on the cook-off from the organizer?" Amber smiled a sly smirk.

"One interesting tidbit. Apparently, there was a last-minute switcheroo from the cook-off appliance prize package supplier. The Hemphill luxury product line we saw advertised in the cook-off paperwork ran into a snag and they went with another supplier. Something about the first set of appliances being recalled nationwide. Rickie O'Dell, the woman in charge, played down the significance of the swap." Sherry studied Amber's placid expression. "You don't seem surprised at that news."

"I had heard," Amber said.

"Oh, okay. Meanwhile, a contestant named Jean McDonald and her husband, Curt, were banking on the original top-of-the-line stove, refrigerator and dishwasher. They enjoy excellence. She's the one with the same knife set as me." Sherry cocked her head toward the clean knives laying on the towel. "The prize package was a great draw for them entering the contest."

"I would give you any appliance I couldn't use, if I were lucky enough to win. Count on that."

Sherry peered over at her stove. "My trusty stove has served me well. I could never replace her until she wants to replace me." A shudder traveled from the bottom of Sherry's neck and down her spine. "I just got goose bumps. I remembered the dream I had last night." She walked over to her oven and cautiously opened the door. "The body in an oven you won."

"I remember the gory part, but you never mentioned I won the oven. You dreamt I won the cook-off? You forgot that minor detail. That's a great omen!"

"Did you hear me? There was a body in the oven you won."

"No problem. With a good cleaning it's good as new."

Sherry's mouth fell agape.

"I'm kidding," Amber said.

"The first part of the same dream was when Don asked me to marry him."

"That's pretty significant, wouldn't you say?"

Amber's eagerness for the reply gave Sherry pause. Did her friend really believe Sherry should be engaged to the man she had been dating less than a year? Not an unheard-of amount of time for an engagement, but on Sherry's life timetable a year was a very short amount of time to come to any sort of decision of that magnitude. She was engaged to her first husband for a year and a half after dating for five years. Rushing to the altar for a second time was something she had no intention of doing.

"I already told you. I dreamt Don asked me to marry him. That's it. Funny thing is, when I woke up, I wasn't completely sure it was a dream or whether he maybe did ask me."

"Let's revisit your dream. Have you two had this conversation? Don't answer if I'm sticking my nose somewhere it doesn't belong."

"The only time we may have come anywhere close to touching on the subject was the night he rushed me to the urgent care facility when I sliced my hand. I'm certain he couldn't think of any other way to comfort me, and at the same time was feeling terribly uncomfortable in the situation."

"What did he say?" Amber helped herself to a glass of water.

"I was about to be stitched up and he said he would like to spend the rest of his life with me even if it included mopping up messes like we left behind in the kitchen that night."

Amber tipped her head toward her shoulder. "Not exactly a proposal but very romantic indeed. Gotta take the bad with the good."

"My ex-husband, Charlie, chose not to take the bad with the good so it was nice to hear Don would stick by me. Remember I said it was a dream. Don hasn't proposed. Even though he has taken the next step and moved across the sound to live closer, that's as far as we've gone. And I'm fine with the way things are for now."

"A move that's aimed, for all intents and purposes, in the right direction," Amber said.

"Can we put this subject to rest and get finished with the cleanup? I'm working at half capacity and it's taking longer than it should." Sherry held up her bandaged hand. "You must have a million things on your agenda to get to before tomorrow's contestant orientation."

"I do. One less, now that you've offered up your wonderful knife set. I do have to tell your father I won't be in to work at the Ruggery at all tomorrow, or at least until the afternoon. I have the contestant lunch, orientation, and the field trip to the Augustin Playhouse. The latter is optional but I'd sure love to go. I'd like to opt in because I've never been to the playhouse and I've heard such wonderful things about it. It's an integral part of Augustin history."

"Yes, don't miss that. Rickie told me the contestants are in for a behind-the-scenes look at the current play production, titled *Scrambled*. Has a cooking theme, along with a murder mystery to solve. How fun is that?"

"Great connection to the cook-off and the host town. Rickie O'Dell is really doing a good job scheduling entertainment for the contestants and making them feel pampered," Amber said. "If I'd known cook-offs were so much fun I would have taken your advice sooner to enter a second."

Sherry smiled despite the fact she wished it were her joining the group of pampered cooks over the next few days. "Cook-offs are days-long celebrations of food, cooks and the host region. That's why they're so wonderful."

"Scary and wonderful," Amber added.

"Did I tell you Pep's new food truck will be at the cook-off orientation for about two hours at lunchtime. He won't be at the Ruggery, either. Dad's just going to have to man the store himself until we can make it back," Sherry said.

In the next room, Chutney began a tirade of barking.

"What could he be complaining about?" By the time Sherry reached the front door Pep was entering her house.

"Speak of the devil."

"You were speaking of me? I'm honored. Hello, to my two favorite people," Pep announced. "I stopped by to see what progress has been made on Amber's recipe. Sherry told me you two were up to no good today on Sherry's first day back to almost being fully functional."

"We accomplished all sorts of good," Amber said. She stood behind Sherry holding her platter of lasagna roll-ups. "Let's get back in the kitchen and I'll pack you and your family some leftovers."

"We'd love that," Pep said. "With Sherry not in the cook-off this year I didn't think I'd have any chance tasting any of the contestants' food. Since I moved back to Augustin, I'm always her willing taste tester and now I'll be yours." He patted his stomach. "Getting a dad bod since the baby was born."

"Hardly," Sherry said.

"What's your recipe?" Pep asked.

"I'll handle this," Sherry said. "Lasagna noodles, cooked al dente, are stuffed with sausage and asparagus, rolled up and nestled in a baking dish. Each is bathed with a layer of spreadable garlic-herb cheese, a touch of fig jam, a dash of champagne vinegar, smidge of Dijon mustard and sprinkled with chopped tomatoes, shallots and more cheese. Topped with a kiss of pesto and a dusting of ground hazelnut." Sherry's eyebrows danced as she finished her description of Amber's dish. "See how I put the love into your lasagna roll-ups? That's what the judges are looking for. Your passion, your creativity, your motivation."

"Phew. That was intense," Pep said. He swiped his hand across his forehead. "I'm buying what you're selling."

"Coming right up." Sherry searched in her upper cabinets for a storage container that would hold two servings for her brother and his wife.

"Charlotte will love this. She's no longer a full-time vegetarian. This is right up her alley."

"Sherry, a reminder, you were going to supply a travel protector for the knives I'm borrowing."

Sherry returned to the upper cabinet and pulled something down from deep within. "Could you hold that open for me?" She collected and packed three of her knives in a padded zippered carrying case. "Here you are, my dear."

"Thank you." Amber cradled the knife case to her chest. "I'll take very good care of them."

"Is there something else you need, Pep? You don't usually pop in unannounced without a good reason. Plus, I thought you'd be busy preparing to feed the contestants tomorrow," Sherry asked.

"You know me so well," Pep said. "Yes, there's something else." Pep shifted his sights to Amber. "I have a question for Amber to consider."

Amber closed the lid on the container she filled with her lasagna asparagus roll-ups. She turned and handed the food to Pep. "A question for me?"

"I'm looking for a sous chef for my yet-to-be-named food truck. I serve brunch and lunch items, so the day would end around three. Would you be interested? Not tomorrow, as I know you're going to be occupied in the cook-off while I'm serving lunch."

Sherry pinched her lips shut tight awaiting Amber's response. To see this discussion play out before her eyes was fascinating and terrifying at the same time. Losing Amber from working at the family's store would be a major blow. Sherry knew how much her father depended on Amber. If Amber reduced her hours, Sherry may have to sacrifice an activity she adored to fill in for lost personnel at the Ruggery.

"Tell me more," Amber said.

"As you know, when Charlotte and I relocated back to Augustin, I pitched a book proposal to a number of publishing houses. The premise would be the how-tos of running a profitable food truck business. The ins and outs, from soup to nuts, A to Z. The proposal was complicated, as I included a two-year research period where I do the legwork in real time, while writing the chapters. I roped in three interested publishing parties and those were whittled down to one after the initial vetting process was complete. I signed the contract and the clock is ticking. If I ask for any extensions on the numerous chapter deadlines I've committed to, the deal is off. Sure would be a great addition if I had a sous chef."

"Wow. That's a very interesting and unusual offer." Amber paused while shifting her glance from Pep to Sherry then back to Pep. "But, I can't do that. I'm the manager at the Ruggery. Your dad depends on me. As a matter of fact, he would love nothing more than for you to join us at the store so he could reduce his hours," Amber said with a serious insistence.

"Okay. I understand. If you have a change of heart the offer stands."

"Thank you for the offer. It's nice to be wanted," Amber said with a smile.

"By the way, I'm not counting out working at the Ruggery," Pep added. "I have some items on my bucket list I need to strike off first before I settle in long-term."

"I understand," Amber said. "If I were starting a family I'd want to get a few items checked off my bucket list before I'm too tied down. You have a good head on your shoulders."

"Thanks," Pep said. "Changing the subject, you two want to join us for dinner?" He held up his food container.

"I can't tonight. I'm going to a low-key contestant dinner being held at the lodge," Amber said. "Only contestants are invited. I suppose they don't want us schmoozing with the judges and sponsors in case any untoward connections are made." She winked.

"Ha. Thanks for the offer, but not me tonight either," Sherry said. "Don's at his sister's for dinner. I bailed out on joining him. It's been a long day. I might get in my jammies and watch a good movie."

"I'm being rejected all over the place," Pep said as his lower lip jutted forward.

"I'm leaving you a serving for dinner, Sherry. To enjoy when you're dressed in your jammies. I'll take the rest of the noodles home," Amber said. "I know eventually I won't have much of an appetite for the lasagna rolls after binging on them for days, but right now they're delicious. I still have yesterday's trial run stocked away. My refrigerator smells like an Italian restaurant. I'll see you both tomorrow at the lunch. Sherry, I'll see you at the cook's orientation. Pep, I can't wait to sample your food truck menu. I'll call Erno and remind him I can't unlock the store in the morning."

"Oh, no," Sherry groaned. "Speaking of unlocking, I forgot to return Rickie's key to her. I better call her and see if I should run it over to her right now."

"I have Rickie's number if you need it," Pep said.

Sherry didn't respond. She was already dialing Rickie's cell phone. As she looked up from her phone Amber tossed a wave and headed toward the front door. She watched her friend let herself out of the house. After a few words with Rickie, Sherry was satisfied she hadn't lost the woman's trust in her ability to act responsibly.

"Rickie said she'll lock up with her key and I can return the key tomorrow when I go over at lunchtime." Sherry paused. "Wait, I have a better idea. If Amber's still here." Sherry trotted to the front door and swung it open. "Amber," she shouted when she saw her seated in the driver's seat with the car door still open.

Amber looked up from her phone. "Yes?"

Sherry cupped her hands around her mouth to amplify her voice. "Can I give you this key to return to Rickie at your dinner tonight? I'm sure she'll be attending." Sherry didn't wait for Amber's reply. She ran down her front path, feet adorned only in socks, and handed Amber the key. "Thanks so much. Have a good time."

"Sure," Amber said.

"Hope that text isn't bad news. You have a concerned look on your face," Sherry said.

Amber looked up from her phone. "Do I?" She glanced back down at her phone. "I received a text from someone I've only had sporadic contact with over the last couple years. He had expressed interest in coming to watch the cook-off. He's already bought a ticket. It'll be good to see him."

"A love interest, perhaps?" Sherry teased.

"A working relationship I never considered crossing the boundaries to test. More importantly, I was married. We were in therapy practice together. He's all business. He was quite a good friend of my husband's at the time. It'll be good to see him again," Amber said.

"Any chance your ex-husband would be coming down with him?" Sherry asked. Amber's forehead pinched tight, giving Sherry a good indication what her feelings on that subject might be.

"Stranger things have happened." Did Sherry detect a coy note in Amber's reply?

"Just thought I'd ask. I wouldn't mind meeting the man who once stole your heart."

"And ripped it to shreds," Amber added.

Sherry winced. "Are you going to the contestant breakfast in the morning? Another meal on the cook-off's dime. It's usually a casual buffet-style meal where people drop in and fill a huge plate with goodies before they realize they're too nervous to eat much."

"It starts at seven a.m. That's a bit early for me," Amber said.

"Have a good night. See you tomorrow. Oh, and be sure to return the key."

Back inside the house, Sherry found Pep helping himself to a container of smoked trout dip. "Have you settled on your food truck's theme?"

"That's the beauty of the trial run serving the contestants and others tomorrow at the cook-off orientation," Pep said. "I'm going to present the two food themes I've settled on. Charlotte will take an unofficial survey of their reactions. All these steps are going into the book I'm writing about the process, so I have to follow a well-thought-out-game plan."

"Amazing that you have a publisher who's willing to back the two-year proposal."

"That was the easy part, I'm afraid. Speaking of new ventures, how was your trip on Don's boat? Does his venture seem like a viable business?"

"Nothing's a given, but I thought the trip was lovely. The passengers seem to enjoy the water commute as an alternative to driving. Whether he can sustain the business year-round is yet to be determined." Sherry's smile was timid.

"Did anything present itself as a challenge on the voyage?"

"There were a couple of hiccups."

"Like?" Pep asked as he placed the empty dip container in the sink. "That dip was delicious, by the way." Pep's trait of being easily distracted by good food was as strong as ever, Sherry noted.

"Thank you. Flaked smoked trout fillet, cream cheese, yogurt, lemon, capers, dill. Easy." Sherry thought of how good the dip would have tasted as an hors d'oeuvre that evening prior to Amber's roll-ups. "There's more traffic on the sound than one would imagine. We had a run-in with a jet skier."

"Run-in? As in, you ran into him?" Pep's eyes widened.

"No, thank goodness. Close call, though. And one of the passengers was late arriving, which is something Don needs to set boundaries for. Don needs to construct either a strict or loose policy depending on the clientele. Some folks adhere to timetables, while for others it's a mere suggestion. Don's also learning what needs to be better secured on the boat in case of speed and direction changes. All in all, that was the reason for the trial run and he should pencil in a few more to be fully informed.

"Sounds like Don, Amber and myself are all on the same page about trial runs. I hope my truck's trial run tomorrow goes alright."

"What are you serving?" Sherry asked. She was pining for the smoked trout dip Pep consumed, while mentally creating a shopping list for the next trip to the grocery store to recreate the briny spread.

"I've narrowed the menu choices down to bowls and toasts as I try to settle on my truck's theme. I'll offer a limited menu tomorrow. I don't want to go down in flames by being in over my head on the first go-round. Either choice is a quick prep with so much possibility. I'm not the world's greatest chef, like you are, but with the right recipes and practiced consistency I know I can get this venture off the ground."

"Good attitude. I'm sorry I can't pitch in. As you know, I can't work in any food-related industry or I'll lose my amateur cook status in recipe contests. The biggest rule no-no. But I might be able to provide recipe advice, here or there."

"Not sure I'd be comfortable having you as my sous chef. That would be like having Tom Brady as the backup quarterback for my weekend touch football team. Overkill."

Sherry pondered Pep's analogy, and even with her limited sports knowledge she knew that meant she was overqualified.

"Thanks for the dinner, and I'll see you after the cook-off orientation over at the lodge tomorrow. About midday," Pep said as he headed toward the door. "Aw, heck," he added. He put his container of food down on the front hall table and picked up Chutney's leash. "I can't resist that cute face and wagging tail. Sher, let me give your hand a rest. Come on, boy. It's time for a Pep-style walk."

Chapter 5

Sherry was thrilled the sun was shining through her bedroom window Tuesday morning, until she stood and took in the full view. The new day brought a thin layer of snow blanketing the lawn, trees and crocuses in her front yard. New England never ceased to surprise her. Spring one day, winter's return the next. Sometimes both in the same day. She noted the driveway was clear so the weather must be relatively mild. Mother Nature dictated Sherry's shoe choice, all-weather and functional, to her dismay not the ones she had laid out last night with her chosen outfit—fun and fashion-forward. A necessary modification, as there would be mud everywhere when the morning thaw took place.

Sherry arrived at the lodge half an hour before the scheduled contestant orientation was to begin.

"Pep," she called out.

Pep halted his trek around the front of the truck. "Hey, Sher. Where have you been? I thought you'd be here a little earlier."

Sherry closed in on Pep. "Dad phoned me last night and asked if I could pop into the store for two hours early this morning. Rickie didn't need me until now anyway, so it all worked out for the good. I have to go find her. I'll see you after the orientation, okay? The volunteers and the cooks are only meeting for an hour at the most, then everyone's heading for the food truck for lunch, so prepare yourself."

"Looking forward to the orderly chaos," Pep said.

Sherry walked to the hotel. The lobby of the lodge was buzzing with a group of cooks in their cook-off aprons. Sherry spotted Rickie on the fringe of the crowd talking with one man in uniform and another casually dressed in blue jeans and a sweater. Hoping to not interrupt important proceedings, yet eager to receive her volunteer apron, Sherry sidled up to the conversation circle.

During a pause she interjected, "Sorry to interrupt. I'm looking for my assignment when you have a second, Rickie." Sherry smiled at the men, who appeared somewhat taken aback by her statement.

"Sherry, this is the lodge's security officer, Officer McCaw."

"Nice to meet you," Sherry replied.

"And this is Walter. We were putting out a small fire," Rickie said.

"Nice to meet you." Sherry's busy thoughts were centered on two items, her orientation assignment and seeing Amber somewhere in the crowd. Her reply was half-hearted at best.

"Walter is having some issues Officer McCaw is nice enough to address because I really am at a loss for time," Rickie said.

Sherry faced the officer. "I hope it's nothing bad." She shifted her gaze to Walter. He shook his head.

"Not sure, ma'am. We're hearing about the claims from the individuals involved right now."

"I maybe shouldn't have come on so strong with Gray first thing in the morning," Walter said. "Who knew we both like an early morning walk? I couldn't resist checking out the beautiful beach below. I don't see why he had to be there."

"I'm sorry. I'm sure things will get straightened out. Maybe the tension of the cook-off is getting on people's nerves," Sherry said.

"He had some help from a pretty red-haired lady who seemed to know how to talk down his temper. She reasoned with him and he left with a smile on his face."

"Red-haired?" Sherry asked as she pictured Amber. "Where is Gray now?"

"Don't know, don't care," Walter said. "If I don't see him again that will be too soon for my taste."

"Sherry, my assistant, Gigi, has the assignments for the volunteers. She's also handing out aprons." Rickie pointed to the lobby entrance.

A tall woman with a tightly wound, frosted topknot was handing aprons out to accredited volunteers.

"Check in with her and head over to the convention hall. The cooks will be heading over there in about twenty minutes. You're going to be in charge of cook stations number seven, eight, nine, ten, eleven and twelve. I think six stations per volunteer is doable. Tomorrow you'll be running errands, answering questions and other various what-nots. Monitoring six stations doesn't sound like much until you're in the thick of it and everyone needs your attention."

"I agree one hundred percent," Sherry said. "I remember not being able to find my runner at a particular cook-off because he was spread too thin and never available. When time came to present my dish to the judges, my recipe's garnish was nowhere to be found. May have cost me a prize."

"That's an example of the words of wisdom I'd like you to impart upon the contestants today. The more educated the cooks are, the smoother the contest will run," Rickie said. "Each has different equipment provided, based on their recipes, as I'm sure you already understand."

"At my first ever orientation I recall being nervous and having to concentrate so hard to retain the provided information. Turns out it was invaluable."

"You'll have a roadmap of where to find whatever they need." Rickie checked her phone. "The other volunteers will be heading over to the convention hall in about ten minutes. Security has hopefully unlocked the building. It's going to be a full house. Organization and communication are essential. The goal is to minimize the fear of the unknown for the cooks. That way they can focus on putting out the best version of their recipes. If that's achieved, everyone's a winner. And the Kitchen Royalty company is happy, and that's paramount."

Sherry admired the smooth delivery Rickie maintained as she was being pulled in many different directions.

"I'll go see Gigi and I'll be on my way," Sherry said with a sudden rush of enthusiasm. Before she was out of earshot, she overheard Officer McCaw strongly suggest Walter "stick around until the issue is cleared up." She stole a look back at Rickie, who had a steely glare fixed on Walter.

After speaking with Gigi, Sherry made her way down the lodge's driveway. The convention hall was across the street, and depending on the chosen footwear would be a pleasant walk for the cooks. She didn't think many of the contestants would opt for the short shuttle bus ride to the event unless they wanted a few more minutes of footrest. Sherry gave herself a moment to take in the scenery as she neared the convention hall. The breeze rising from the shore bluffs enlivened her senses. By the time she arrived she was excited to take in the cook-off atmosphere from an entirely new perspective, as behind-the-scenes volunteer rather than cooking contestant.

Instead of going through the convention hall's front entrance Sherry walked around the side of the building in search of stray contestants or volunteers who may have followed the sidewalk in the wrong direction, which seemed to her an easy mistake. Finding no one, Sherry heaved open the side door. Half expecting the door to be locked by security, Sherry tipped backward when it swung open with ease. Her foot squished down in a puddle.

"I made the right shoe choice," she said as she silently thanked her waterproof booties. Inside the door the long hallway was empty of people and the floor painted in watery footprints. "Rickie's not going to like this mess," Sherry said as she surveyed the puddles on the linoleum floor.

Sherry entered the huge room, which held fifty cook stations. In her estimation the first station she approached was about six feet wide by six feet deep, containing a prep area, an oven, cooktop, and various bowls and utensils. She located the dry goods supply station with bags of ingredients lined up, each marked with a name and station number. She neared the oven and was happy to discover the brand was one she was very familiar with. Nothing as fancy as the prize package appliances, but adequately functional.

"Sherry? That *is* you. This place is humongous," Amber said breathlessly. "I ran all the way here when Rickie told me where you were. I'm getting nervous and could use the sight of a calm face. I wanted to see you before anyone else was here."

"No one's ever accused me of being calm," Sherry said and laughed. "But I'll gladly take the compliment. Do you know what your assigned cook station number is?"

"Rickie just finished giving preliminary instructions to the cooks back at the lodge. She'll read the list of who gets what station when everyone arrives here in a few minutes. I don't suppose there's much chance I'll be in your group."

"I don't think so. Rickie knows you and I work together and felt people wouldn't see us collaborating as fair."

"I've never seen so many ovens together in my life."

Sherry followed Amber's gaze around the room. "I have. The biggest cook-off I've been in had one hundred cooks, and that means twice as many ovens as you see here. Two home cooks were chosen from every state. That was so amazing to see the recipes that represented each region."

"And I thought fifty contestants was a huge amount," Amber said. She hugged herself. "It's cold in here. I think I'll keep my coat on under my apron for a while."

"Cook-offs always start in a cold room. You can imagine once all the ovens are fired up and the room is chockablock with people, the temperature rises steadily until you can't peel off layers fast enough."

"Makes sense," Amber said.

"Did you have any problem getting the key back to Rickie last night at the contestant dinner?" Sherry asked.

Amber squeezed her eyes shut. "Ugh." She reached in her quilted coat pocket and pulled out the key. "I'm so sorry. Here, you take it back. I brought it today because I forgot last night. I'm letting nerves get to me, so I'll surely forget again." She placed the key in Sherry's healthy palm. "How's your other hand, by the way?"

"A lot less sore today, but I think I made the right call not participating in the cook-off. I still have limited mobility until the stitches come out. It's up to you to carry the Augustin torch to the finish line."

Voices outside the open doorway caught Sherry's attention. "Here comes everyone. I hope I've calmed your nerves."

"You did until you mentioned the fate of Augustin's reputation rests solely in my spatula-laden hands." Amber chuckled a cautious laugh. "Where are the grand prize appliances? I was told they'd be on display in here. That would give me lots of incentive to win, win, win."

Sherry scanned the surroundings. Rows of cook stations filled the core of the room sandwiched between rows of audience chairs at one end and a stage at the other. Sherry pointed to the stage. "Behind that curtain. No peeking. Suffice it to say, what's behind the curtain will charge everyone's senses."

"I brought along my knife set. I mean your knife set." Amber held up the folded knife carrier.

"I saw that you were holding them. Why?"

"I'm not exactly sure. It makes me feel more confident, like I'm a veteran. Maybe I thought it would present an intimidation factor to my fellow competitors."

"Can't hurt, and yes, you do look like an experienced veteran."

The prior quiet of the cavernous convention hall had been replaced by the din of an increasing number of people entering the room.

"I better join the other contestants. I'll see you after the orientation. We'll grab some lunch from Pep's truck," Amber said.

"Absolutely," Sherry said as she watched her friend blend into the group.

Sherry made her way over to the gathered cooks. She hovered near the back listening to Rickie explain the upcoming cook-off schedule. Sherry was introduced along with the other volunteers. The volunteers were given a round of applause by appreciative contestants before the crowd split into specified groups.

When Sherry's six assigned cooks assembled, she went to work describing the hows, whens and wheres of the two hours the cooks were given to prepare their recipes.

"You'll find your perishable supplies in the refrigerator located behind you and the remainder of your recipe ingredients in labeled grocery bags alongside the back wall. Use the time today to check whether every single ingredient you asked for is here, in the amounts you require. Don't worry if something is missing. It will be there tomorrow if you let us know. I'll be here to assist with any necessary troubleshooting, so you won't have to worry about unforeseen disasters sabotaging your success." Her audience was wide-eyed and homed in on her every word, just as she always did when she went through her own contestant orientations.

A woman raised her hand.

"Yes?" Sherry asked.

"If we finish before the allotted time can we bring our food to the judges immediately, before it cools down? My dish is very temperature-sensitive. As it cools it isn't as tasty and there go my chances."

"You can bring your finished dish to the judges at any time you consider it complete. My personal advice would be don't rush, take your time. That way silly errors of omission are less likely to creep in."

"You sound like you've done this before," the woman said.

"Don't you know who she is?" a man asked. "Sherry Oliveri practically invented the cook-off. She's been winning for years."

Sherry's cheeks warmed. "Thank you for the shout-out. I've loved this hobby for years, yes. I admit, if I hadn't had my own knife accident, I'd be out there with you competing, but helping you all is second best."

"Happens to the best of 'em," the man said with a sympathetic tone. "We are all one misdirected knife cut away from tragedy."

Sherry grimaced. "Maybe not to that extreme but I know what you're saying. Any other questions?"

The cooks exchanged glances, but no one spoke up. "Okay, then we're done here. If you'd like to take one more look at your supplies, I would highly recommend that," Sherry said. "Best of luck tomorrow and have fun tonight at the playhouse."

The cooks dispersed, clearing Sherry's view of the stage. She considered the dramatic scene when the winner's name would be called and the prizes revealed.

"How did your instructional go?" Rickie asked as she crossed the path of Sherry's vision. "Other volunteers reported some contestant nerves, but overall they were brimming with excitement and enthusiasm."

"I can confirm the same," Sherry said. "It's so interesting to see it from this vantage point. I admit I was nervous for them. Do you need me for anything else here? Otherwise, I'm going to check out Pep's lunch offerings."

"Nope. Thank you. I'll hang around until everyone is gone," Rickie said as she scanned the room. A few cooks were taking last looks at the equipment. "I'm going to blow my whistle soon to round up the stragglers. And I better alert the janitorial services to mop up these floors before the cook-off."

Sherry left the convention hall, along with others she assumed to be press or sponsors, crossed the street, and made her way toward Pep's food truck in hopes of finding Amber. Not seeing her, Sherry sat down on a bench a few yards from Pep's truck and watched those in line for lunch get served. After some time, the line shortened and Sherry saw her chance to jump in.

"Hi, Pep," Sherry said as she made her way to the front of the line. "How's it going? The line is moving nicely along. You seem to have the system down."

"Phew, so far the nearly nonstop four-hour race to prepare, take orders and serve in a timely fashion is presenting itself to be a challenge. The main takeaway thus far is I definitely need a sous chef. I don't know what I was thinking going it alone, even at a small venue like today." Pep dabbed his forehead with a towel. "Thank goodness I had the sense to offer a very limited menu."

"What's been the most popular item?" Sherry asked as she studied the menu written on a chalkboard beside the serving window. "I'll have a smoked trout toast, please."

"You've hit the nail on the head. The toast toppers are the most popular. I'm really happy about that because they're fast to prepare. They make a great presentation with a spring greens salad. Not just your grandmother's avocado toast I'm hawking here." Pep laughed at his perky wit.

"No, your sister's smoked trout, ha-ha. You're on to something, little brother," Sherry said as she watched him assemble her order. Peering behind her she saw no one waiting in line so she continued the conversation. "Is Charlotte here? I thought I saw her a while ago."

"You missed her. She snuck around back of the truck and went home. She had to relieve the babysitter. She was in charge of keeping track of sales trends, so the tracking ended prematurely. I have a good feeling about the toasts being the winner, though."

"Was this location a good one for you?" Sherry asked.

"It was, but the lodge has an issue with me staying here for more than a short amount of time. The security guard keeps coming out and subtly asking me if I'm almost done. I get the impression someone is urging him to move me along."

"Officer McCaw is his name."

"That's the one."

"Wonder why? I think you're a perfect addition to the lodge's ambiance," Sherry said. She panned the area with a judgmental eye. "I don't see any mess around here. Everyone is doing a great job cleaning up after themselves."

"The lodge isn't interested in providing me with the ability to add my refuse to theirs. I'll bring my garbage bags home when I close up soon. Waste management is part of the process." Pep leaned across the counter.

Sherry could see his shirt was stained with work sweat and his face was flushed. "I understand. The lodge isn't a huge place and they probably get dinged extra fees by the refuse removal company if they go beyond a certain amount."

"I agree."

"I'm happy for you. Sounds like a winner, either way." Sherry peered around again. She only saw scatterings of people. "I have to go find Rickie and see what my next assignment is. Have you seen Amber?"

"She and a man she introduced as Tig were one of the first to come by the food truck. Not sure if he was a cook or a friend. They ordered toasts, and as far as I could see from in here, they enjoyed the food."

"Sounds like she connected with her old friend. I'll see her at the orientation. Here come a few stragglers," Sherry whispered.

"Good afternoon, Sherry," Livvy said. "You remember my friend Bart."

Bart dipped his head in a greeting. "Hi, Sherry. Good luck in the cook-off," he said as his gaze lowered to Sherry's cook-off apron around her middle.

"Rickie O'Dell gave the volunteers these wonderful aprons to help us stand out from the cooks. I'm also supporting my friend in the cook-off, Amber Sherwin. From the sidelines, that is."

"Sherry was the one to beat, before she hurt herself," Livvy explained.

"I would have thought Amber Sherwin was the one to beat," Bart said. "Didn't she win the last cook-off she was in?"

"She's been in only one cook-off," Sherry said, "and she did very well. So, you've been researching the cooks. Makes for a more knowledgeable viewer. Are you from the same area?"

"Boston, yes. We met in the small world of premium appliances. All very boring, really." Livvy brushed her hand through the air in front of her face.

"Oh, okay." Sherry felt the stilted reply warranted no further probing. "Amber has a great recipe in tomorrow's cook-off. I agree, she might be the one to beat."

Bart nodded.

"Is your husband having lunch?" Sherry asked. She jutted her head in Pep's direction. "That food truck is my brother's new venture, and I highly recommend you all give it a try." She wanted to introduce him, but he was occupied with new arrivals.

"We're planning on it. Last I heard, Gray was stuck in a teleconference meeting with the Boston store, although that was hours ago. He never made it to breakfast, at least while I was seated. I'm waiting to hear from him," Livvy said.

"You didn't see him at the orientation?" Sherry asked. Her thoughts wandered to Walter's description of his early morning encounter with Gray.

"I didn't see him. Easy to miss anyone in there. Too many people milling around," Livvy said. "The plan was to meet up at lunchtime." She lifted her sights over Sherry's shoulder. "Just as well he's not here. Here comes Walter Hemphill. It's best they stay away from one another." She accelerated her words. "Bart and I will give your brother's food a try. I'm sure it's delicious. We'll be back in a few minutes. Let's go, Bart." Livvy set a quick pace in the opposite direction of where Walter was heading. Bart trotted to stay by her side.

Sherry turned back to Pep. She caught his attention with a hand gesture. "Got to get a move on. See you later," Sherry said as she headed toward the main building. Pep waved back. After a few steps she paused and looked Pep's way. "Oh, and the toast was a winner."

Pep gestured a thumbs-up. "From one winner to another, thanks."

Back at the lobby, Sherry received her assignment for the following day after finding Rickie. "I'll arrive around eight in the morning." Sherry slung her purse over her shoulder.

"I have a favor to ask of you," Rickie said. "Would you mind accompanying me back to the convention hall?"

Sherry considered Rickie's request, at the same time attempting to suppress her desire to go home and put her feet up. "What are you going back for?"

"I'm going to check on the merchandise. I didn't have two minutes this morning to check the space up on the stage behind the curtain. I have a sneaking suspicion we didn't leave ourselves enough room for the awards podium to be wheeled up in front of the curtain. We may need to rethink the logistics of the prize unveiling. These are the details that keep me up at night. I need a second opinion, if you wouldn't mind."

"Of course," Sherry said, putting forth a less than effusive show of enthusiasm. Her wish for a caffeine-laden drink was driving her lack of motivation at the moment. On the other hand, she had similar tendencies toward overthinking details and could empathize with Rickie's dilemma.

"I have another reason to check on the prizes. And I hope I'm wrong about this one."

"What's that?" Sherry asked.

"Walter Hemphill was giving the cook-off officials such a hard time about being paid for his time, which was really minimal. Unfortunately, there's a loophole in the contract we signed with Hemphill Appliances that gives him a right to take legal action under certain circumstances. We're on shaky ground, thanks to too much goodwill."

"Walter Hemphill?" Sherry asked. "Hemphill luxury appliances? Was that the man I met earlier who was talking to the security guard? The Walter Hemphill you were talking about on the commuter boat ride?"

"The very same," Rickie said.

"I should have made the connection when you introduced me. Although I don't think you provided his last name. Why is he even at the cook-off if his working relationship with you ended?" Sherry asked.

"We invited him, never in a million years thinking he would accept the invitation. Burning bridges is not an option in my public relations world. When a sponsor, current, former or future, is unhappy, that takes priority." Rickie's mouth drooped. "The process can be exhausting."

"Sounds like you have to smooth his ruffled feathers. Is that what you were discussing with security?"

"In part." Rickie laughed. "I need one more thing to think about like I need a hole in my head." Her laugh had a sarcastic edge. "There's a whole other issue. He told security he thinks someone connected to the cook-off is out to get him."

"Out to get him? In what way?" Sherry asked.

"He claims someone may have rummaged through his suitcase after he parked it in his room on arrival. He's staying at the Nutmeg Motor Inn. The hotel staff on duty was questioned but all were cleared. A short investigation led to the conclusion he was a messy packer."

"From what you've described he's acting like the squeaky wheel. Maybe his way of righting what he considers a wrong against his company. Who knows?" Sherry said. "What does this have to do with making a visit to the convention hall right now?"

"I want to make sure Walter doesn't pull some sort of retaliatory stunt in order to get back at the Washingtons and me. Intuition is telling me to check on the prizes."

"Okay then, let's do it," Sherry said. "But I think you're being overly cautious."

"I hope so. In the meantime, we have to treat the man with kid gloves because he had the gall to bring the cook-off contract with him and wave it in my face. Yes, the lawyer's wording wasn't strong enough to head off any compensation he may seek over and above his time in the most unusual circumstance of his product being recalled by a third-party watch group. Which is exactly what happened. I mean, who would ever have seen that coming?"

"Do you really believe he'd do something to sabotage, for lack of a better word, the cook-off, now that he's no longer a sponsor?"

"It's my job to make sure nothing like that happens. I'm also worried about the hallway that was a mess this morning, and it's given me pause. Who made all that mess before the contestants even arrived?"

"When the appliances were delivered the men did traipse in through the grass."

"I only hope someone didn't enter the convention hall overnight, looking to do some damage. The cleaning crew was not happy when I gave them the extra job of mopping up the puddles. Pray for no rain or snow tonight or the slop in the hall will be back in no time when the crowds flock in. Ready to head over there?" Rickie began to walk away.

"Oh, Rickie, wait," Sherry called out as she strode after her. "I forgot to return the convention hall key." She dug the key out of her pocket and handed it to Rickie.

"Thank you." She studied the key. "If any of the appliances are missing, I'll know who's enjoying them." Rickie winked. "See you down there." Suddenly, she stopped in her tracks and turned on her heels. "It wasn't you who went into the convention hall overnight, was it? I mean, you did have the key."

"No, no. Of course not. I'll meet you down there in a few minutes. I'll drive so I can head home directly from there," Sherry said. She caught herself sighing at the thought of not being able to go home and rest her hand.

Sherry made her way to the parking lot, her steps dragging as her energy was dipping. Her first day out after her accident was proving to be a busy one.

"Sherry? Are you done for the day?"

Sherry rotated and caught sight of Amber approaching. The smile on her friend's face brought her adrenaline up a notch.

"I thought I was done but I have one more job to do with Rickie before I can head out."

"Watch out. Volunteering can become a full-time job."

"You read my mind." Sherry laughed.

"Did you have lunch from Pep's truck?" Amber asked.

Sherry inhaled a deep breath. "Yes, I had a smoked trout toast and salad and I loved it. Pep's concept is a good one. Tasty toast toppers. No utensils required. How about you? I heard you and your friend from Boston bought lunch from Pep. How'd you two like it?"

"I loved the Southwest Avocado Toast Topper and Tig had a Ranch Steak Bruschetta Toast. He went bonkers for it. We ate at the picnic tables with Jean and Curt McDonald, who also were loving their lunch choices," Amber said. "I agree. Pep has the beginnings of a grand idea."

"Tig is the friend who wanted to come to watch you compete?"

"That's right."

"I'd like to meet him. Is he around?" Sherry asked with a suggestive note in her question.

"He went for a walk. I had a few things to tend to after we had lunch, so I sent him on a nature walk."

"Tig is such an interesting name. Is it short for anything?"

"Thomas Ignatius Glover. T I G are his initials. He's gone by Tig since I've known him," Amber explained. "He's still very good friends with my ex, Jeff. I haven't seen either since I moved to Augustin."

"Interesting," Sherry said. Again, her tone was suggestive.

"Just stop right there. Dating your ex-husband's good friend is a textbook way to say you're not over your past relationship and I certainly am."

"Okay, no need to get defensive." Sherry smiled. "What are you doing this afternoon?"

"I'm going to head home to change and then stop at the Ruggery to check on Erno," Amber said. "Tonight, we have another contestant dinner. Tig's going to join me for that. This evening's more formal. It's being held at the private dining room at the Augustin Playhouse, which only rents out to high rollers. The highlight of the evening is a tour of the playhouse and a short performance."

"You're a high roller. How exciting. That sounds like so much fun," Sherry said.

Amber bowed her head and took a step closer to Sherry. "I have a confession to make. I'm so sorry, the strap on your knife storage bag snapped at some point." She held up the canvas carrier with the dangling strap. "Looks a little worse for wear but still does the trick. I think someone knocked it off my counter during our orientation rounds. I shouldn't have left it unattended. The counters are so tiny, doesn't take much to overcrowd them."

"No worries. Carriers are a dime a dozen," Sherry said with a smile. "As long as the knives are still sharp, all is well. That, too, can be fixed, but it might take a while." Sherry walked Amber to her car, which was parked a few spots from hers. "See you later. If you go to the Ruggery, I'll most likely see you there. Dad will have plenty of company."

"See you then," Amber said as she unlocked her car door.

Sherry relocated her car to the convention hall lot, then left her car and made her way to the front entrance. She found the door locked. She wound around to the side delivery entrance, where the door was propped open with a cinder block. The windowless hallway was dark, navigable only by the shafts of light streaming in under a few doors on the left side of the building. Sherry poked her head through the open doorway leading to the enormous cook-off room. There were no windows in the room and the overhead lights were switched off. The ambient light of the oven consoles was enough to spread a warm glow throughout the room.

"Hello? Rickie? Are you in here?" Sherry called out before setting foot in the room.

"Back here. Up onstage." Rickie peeked out from between the curtains. Her phone's flashlight was beaming. "Hope you brought your phone. You'll need the flashlight. I wasn't able to unlock the light control panel. This place is like Fort Knox with all its security. You need a key for this and a key for that. Watch your step."

The warning came a moment late. Sherry stubbed the toe of her shoe on a mat used to designate a cook's work area. She pinched her lips tight to trap any irreverent word she might inadvertently release. She tiptoed over the countless snaking electrical cables powering each workstation.

"Sherry, come quick!"

"Coming," Sherry called back. She set each footstep down with extra care as she made her way across the room. "I have to keep an eye out for where I'm going."

Rickie parted the curtains again. "My intuition was right. Someone's been into these appliances. Greasy fingerprints everywhere."

"There were no prints when we left the convention hall yesterday. The Washingtons and I wiped them all spotless after the deliverymen finished positioning each. You're right. Someone was here after that. What a mess."

Rickie faced Sherry and held her gaze with steely steadiness. "I know you were one of the first volunteers to arrive here before the contestants this morning. Did you notice anything suspicious?"

"I think I might have been the very first volunteer to arrive. I went in the side door, down the hallway and into the cook-off room. That's where I ran into Amber."

"She was inside? Amber shouldn't have been here. I saw her over at the lodge with the other cooks," Rickie said.

"I don't mean she was there before me," Sherry scrambled to say. "She came down early before the orientation to find me. To say hi. I didn't know she was coming." Her tumbling words betrayed her attempt to steady her growing anxiety. What if Rickie thought she was doing a terrible job? If she was fired from her volunteer position she would be so humiliated.

"Did you use the key to get in?" Rickie asked.

Sherry was suddenly caught in a white lie. Her mind was bombarded with guilt. Maybe she hadn't heard Rickie correctly. "Did I use the key?" Sherry repeated the question back to Rickie with as much calm as she could muster. What if this mess was all her fault?

"That's what I asked," Rickie said. It sounded as if her patience was waning.

"When I went in the side door this morning the door was unlocked, which was lucky because at that point I didn't have the key in my possession. I'm sure security unlocked it for the orientation."

"Where was the key?"

Sherry glanced at her shoes to buy herself some time to think. "What happened was, I gave the key to Amber to give back to you last night at dinner because I wasn't going and I didn't want to lose the key."

"She didn't give me the key." Rickie's words were delivered with severity.

"No. She told me she forgot. Today she gave it back to me and I gave it to you," Sherry said.

"Well, no harm. At least I hope no harm." Rickie raised her index finger high. "The security camera at the side door will have caught anyone who entered the building during the night."

Sherry squeezed her eyes shut while gathering her words. "Didn't Gray or Livvy tell you what happened to the camera?"

"Apparently there's lots people haven't told me. Is there something wrong with the security camera?"

"It was smashed during the delivery. The big refrigerator was quite unwieldy. The dolly the delivery crew used to leverage the appliance up off the ground smashed the camera mounted over the outside of the door. It fell down to the ground. Not sure what Gray did with it." Sherry shrugged her shoulders.

"There goes that idea. I'm going to think optimistically. Someone was just curious about the prize package and decided to take a look-see. No harm done. If this is the only thing that goes slightly askew during the cook-off, I consider myself very lucky."

Sherry stepped up onstage and parted the curtains. As they closed behind her the stage darkened. She held up her phone light and located Rickie. She gathered the cloth Rickie offered and got to work.

"Let's check each one for any evident problem and wipe them clean. Be careful, they're connected to power because we will have a surprise in the refrigerator for the winner. A gorgeous bouquet of flowers."

"A tiny part of me is wondering if Walter Hemphill has anything to do with this shenanigans," Rickie said. "He was adamant that he deserved the right to substitute the appliance package for his next lower-level set, but that ship had sailed. I didn't want to make the same mistake twice and have his product recalled. Yes, we will compensate him for his time, but that's where we put a period on the deal. I'll start with the dishwasher if you can work on the oven smudges."

Knowing she had little to contribute to Rickie's speculation, Sherry remained focused on her inspection of the oven. When the exterior was spotless, she placed her hand on the oven door handle. A wave of prickly heat consumed her for a split second. She blinked and the morbid image of the body from her dream the previous night dissolved. She pulled the door open and with an extensive exhale examined the empty interior. Spotless. Relief.

A piercing scream knocked Sherry backward.

"Sherry! Help! There's a body in the refrigerator!"

Chapter 6

"Did you say a body? In the refrigerator?" Sherry's voice cracked as she said the words. "Did Amber tell you about my dream? Are you pulling a prank on me?"

"I don't know what you're talking about, but I did find a body. Not in the refrigerator, behind. When I opened the door, I caught a glimpse of an arm through the door gap. I went around the back and there was the body. Facedown. Dead. One look and I could see right away the poor man was lifeless."

"We need to call security," Sherry said when she shone the light on Rickie. The woman appeared paralyzed with indecision. Her mouth hung open and her eyes were bulging as if she'd seen a ghost. And she almost had.

Rickie shook her head. "Right, yes. Come with me. You shouldn't be alone with the body. I didn't look at him for more than a second, but he was stone cold when I touched his hand. His dark skin had an odd translucent tint." Rickie motioned for Sherry to follow her off the stage and toward the entrance. She raised her phone to her mouth with a shaky hand and instructed security where to come, without mentioning the reason for their summoning. She managed an even tone, devoid of trauma. After the short call she turned to Sherry. "They should be right here."

The two women stood in silence until footsteps could be heard tapping down the hallway.

"What can I do for you, Ms. O'Dell?" Officer McCaw asked.

Rickie whispered in the man's ear. The man swallowed hard. "Yes, ma'am," he said. "If we can clear the building the proper authorities will be notified." The security officer lowered his voice and spoke into his phone. "They're on their way. No sirens, as you requested."

"No one else to clear out of the building. Sherry and I are the only two here." Rickie scanned the surroundings. "That we know of."

Moments later, when the police arrived, two Hillsboro County police officers requested Sherry and Rickie wait outside the hall's side entrance before they took their statements. After debriefing the women, the police had one more piece of information for them.

"The documents in the man's wallet identify him as Gray Washington. Do either of you know him?"

Rickie and Sherry exchanged solemn glances.

"We both do," Rickie said. "He was associated with the cook-off. Tell me. Did he have a heart attack? I couldn't make out in the dark whether he was clutching his chest or just fell. After I touched his cold hand I called for Sherry. Didn't want to take any more looks."

"Rather not speculate, ma'am. I'm not a coroner and the information would be questionable at this stage."

"He was on the boat from Long Island we were on yesterday," Sherry added. "I didn't talk to him much. I had a longer conversation with his wife, Livvy. Poor Livvy. How horrible for her."

"What would he be doing in there? Behind the stage curtain." The police officer nodded his head in the direction of the cook-off room.

"His company provided a wonderful appliance package for the grand prize winner of tomorrow's cook-off. I imagine he was checking his product. Just as Sherry and I were." Rickie's gaze shifted toward Sherry. "If he was out for a walk and found the door unlocked, he may have taken advantage of the situation." She leaned toward Sherry. "He's the one with the wet shoes, I suppose."

"Maybe, ma'am," the officer said. "To my eye there were more than one set of footprints. Who locks and unlocks the building's doors for the cook-off, Ms. O'Dell?"

"We may have had some confusion concerning that assignment. I hired the hotel's security to cover the days we rented the convention hall. Whether the door was locked or unlocked overnight is something I'm not sure of right now," Rickie said. "Officer McCaw may have that answer."

"McCaw?"

"Head of security for the lodge."

"Right." The officer continued with his line of questioning. "Do you know who has copies of the building keys, besides the hotel's security team?"

Sherry examined her shoes.

"I do, as I am the cook-off's organization head," Rickie said. "And we have a few copies floating around. I can double-check that for you."

Sherry winced. If her negligence had led to Gray entering the convention hall in the early morning she shouldn't blame herself. If he had a pending medical trauma it may have played out anywhere. She wasn't to blame for him dying next to his appliance package.

"Thank you, ladies. We have your contact information. Appreciate your time." The police officer turned to reenter the building.

"Officer, before you go, I have one more question," Rickie began. She paused until he faced her. "Will we be able to continue with the cook-off as planned? And in the same facility?"

"I have every reason to believe, yes, you can. If the scene can be documented in its proper entirety this facility can be used tomorrow for the cook-off," the officer said. He didn't wait for a reply. "Most unfortunate for the deceased but the scene will be cleared, and you may proceed if you wish."

Rickie lowered her voice. "We have to keep this under wraps as best we can. The man has passed away in an untimely fashion, but where the body was found must remain a secret. Promise me, Sherry." Rickie spoke with a steely seriousness.

Sherry held her gaze on Rickie's face until the woman's expression softened. "Yes, of course." She dipped her head in tribute to Gray.

Rickie lightened up her voice. "I feel guilty saying this, but we need to consider a substitute for Gray Washington in tomorrow's awards ceremony. He was slated to be the presenter for the appliance prize package."

Sherry wasn't sure of the correct response. "You seem the obvious choice. Or his wife."

"Oh, yes, thank you for pointing that out. As you can tell, I'm not thinking completely straight at the moment. I'm thinking about how I'm going to have to speak to his wife, and that's not going to be easy after such a heartbreaking shock," Rickie said.

On her drive home, Sherry decided to take a few detours to detangle her spiderweb of thoughts. She drove the longer, more scenic route by the water's edge in an attempt to quell an uneasiness growing in her core. Even after one of her favorite diversions, parking by the public beach and observing the progress the local osprey pair were making while renovating their monstrous nest above the protected marshlands, she still needed more reassurance everything was all right with the world. She steered the car home, picked up Chutney and proceeded down Augustin's Main Street toward the Ruggery.

"Good afternoon, everyone," Sherry announced as she entered the Oliveris' family-run hooked rug business. The hinges of the antique front door whined as she shut it behind her, accompanied by the tinkle of a brass bell overhead. It was difficult to enter unannounced. "I came to offer my one good hand, should anyone need help."

"Hi, honey," Erno called out. "Pep beat you here. Did you see his truck parked out back?"

"I did," Sherry said. "He's taking up all the parking spots in the alley. I'm not sure the lingerie shop next door will be happy about that. Evette's car is completely blocked in the shared space. I know because I made the mistake of thinking I could park next to you behind the shop. I had a harrowing time backing out."

"Evette will be fine. She never leaves before six," Erno said. "We're long gone before that."

"I was thinking, as I was reversing and pulling forward and reversing trying to squeeze past, Pep needs to give his food truck a name very soon. That way people will start to recognize the logo as he's driving around and subliminally want what he's serving."

Pep stepped out of the stock room. "Hey, sis."

"I was saying you need to name your truck," Sherry said.

Pep walked over to the yarn storage wall holding a skein of yellow yarn. He stood staring at an empty cubby. "You're right. I do. I'm almost ready to commit to the menu and then it's time for the name game. What shade of yellow would you all say this is?"

"That would be daffodil yellow," Sherry said.

Pep hesitated. "Dad?"

"No. Buttercup yellow," Erno said. "A touch of cream dye mutes the yellow. The shade is best used for a background flower to give the illusion of depth."

One of Sherry's favorite pastimes was historically lengthy debates with her father about color shades. She loved to challenge his experience and was never disappointed with the pearls of wisdom stored in his artisan brain.

Sherry removed her jacket and hung it on the row of hooks by the front door. "Amazing how we had a burst of snow last night and now it's nearly sixty degrees."

"If you don't like the weather in New England, wait a minute," Erno said. "What are you up to, sweetie?"

Sherry considered sitting on the bad news for a while. "Just finished cook-off orientation volunteering. I have a great group of contestants that I'm also the runner for tomorrow."

"Remind me what a runner is again," Erno said.

"A very important job. Whatever the cooks need to make their allotted two cook-off hours more productive, I'm there for them. If they need a clean bowl, I can run the soiled offender to the utility sink and give it a one-handed wash. If a cook drops a mixing spoon, I can run and replace it. If a glass of water is needed for dry mouth, I can rush to the fridge and get a bottle of water. I do most chores for the cooks, short of actually doing the cooking for them." She laughed at her quip. "What's going on here?"

"Slow morning. Filling some orders from yesterday. We were discussing the cook-off. Pep heard a rumor there was a death at the convention hall," Erno said.

Sherry's mouth fell open. "Where did you hear that, Pep?"

"I was curious how my food truck was received. Charlotte said everyone loved the food, but she's my wife. She has to say that. Despite the fact I promised myself I wouldn't bother Rickie O'Dell, at what must be her busiest time, I ran into her as I was packing up the truck. I couldn't resist getting a read on what she's heard from the cooks about my food, if anything. I had a moment of insecurity and needed some positive feedback. I should have waited. She blurted out she had no time to talk because there had been a death of one of the cook-off sponsors."

"Wow. She didn't heed her own advice about keeping the word mum for as long as possible," Sherry said.

"I guess not."

"I'm surprised she told you where the body was found," Sherry said.

"She didn't. I put two and two together about the location when she called out to someone in the middle of our conversation and told whoever it was to make sure the hall was locked when they were finished with the cleanup," Pep said. He beamed a broad grin. "Was I right? If so, you may not be the only amateur sleuth in the family."

"Yes, you're right. Rickie doesn't want the news to become widespread so as not to detract from the cook-off, but I'm not in complete agreement with that decision. I hope his wife is okay."

"It was a man?" Pep asked. "I didn't hear any other details."

"Gray Washington," Sherry said.

"One of Don's passengers. I'm so sorry," Pep said.

"The cook-off will continue on as planned?" Erno asked. "We haven't had a chance to tell Amber the news. She just got back and we weren't sure if the news extended to the cancellation of the cook-off. She'd be awfully sad if that were the case."

"The cook-off will continue as planned," Sherry said. "Rickie is bound and determined to carry on if possible. It would be best if Amber doesn't hear about the death from us. We are her support system right now. We need to keep things positive."

Across the room Amber poked her head out of the kitchenette doorway. "Did I hear my name? Hi, Sherry. Making some tea back here. Want to come join me?"

"I'm on my way," Sherry called back. She lowered her voice and directed her attention to Pep. "Do me a favor and please hold off telling Amber for a bit. She's having so much fun participating in the cook-off and I don't want to spoil the mood. I'm sure she'll hear the news at the contestant dinner tonight."

"I hear the voice of my big sister loud and clear," Pep said in a solemn tone that brought a smile to Sherry's face. Her little brother always had a way of diffusing a tricky situation with lighthearted humor. She wished she had the same set of skills to manage adverse times.

"Okay, there's something you're not telling me," Amber said from across the room. "I detect sidebar whispering."

Sherry considered whether Amber was a lucky guesser or a clairvoyant. "What makes you say that?"

"You do this thing where you fiddle with your hair and search the ceiling for something that's not there when you have a nugget of information you're considering whether or not to share with me. More often than not, you share."

Sherry dropped her fingers from her hair at the same time her phone rang. She dug the device out of her pocket. "Perfect timing."

"Huh," Amber replied.

"Hi, Rickie. Is everything alright? I don't think I'm supposed to be anywhere until the morning," Sherry said before Rickie had a chance to explain the reason for her call.

"You're right. That's not why I'm calling." Rickie cleared her throat. "A Detective Ray Bease, from the Hillsboro County Police, made a visit to the lodge and called me down to a meeting in the lobby."

Rickie paused, but Sherry had no words. She bit her upper lip.

"He said, in no uncertain terms, Gray Washington's death was no accident," Rickie said. "Despite the new development we've been given a firm go-ahead for the cook-off. I may be kidding myself when I say most will be none the wiser for the immediate future. All I can do is move forward with the current schedule. Livvy Washington has taken the news relatively well. Her friend Bart seems to be a comfort to her."

What exactly was their relationship? Sherry pondered. Whatever it may be, good that Bart was here when Livvy needed comfort.

"Is there anything you need from me today? I'm at the Ruggery helping out but could change my plans if need be," Sherry said.

"No, we're sticking to the printed schedule. Oh, and Detective Bease is fully aware you were with me when the body was found. That's really why I'm calling. He may be in touch with you soon."

"Thank you," Sherry said. The tone of her words fell short of their intended sentiment.

"I was surprised the detective seems to know you," Rickie said.

"We do know each other." Sherry pushed the words out with difficulty. "I was involved in the investigation of a few murders that he led."

"A few? Murder investigations?" Rickie said incredulously. "How involved?"

"There's a lot to go into on that subject. When you have time one day, I can fill you in on the details." Sherry could see Amber was watching her intently from the kitchen doorway.

"Sounds fascinating," Rickie said. "At the convention hall the stage has been cordoned off and the curtains will remain drawn. The detective and his team are performing all the immediate necessary steps and he said they will be out of there by this evening. The appliances will be moved to the side of the convention hall, so unfortunately the drama of unveiling the shiny new prizes to the winners in real time is lost without the curtain, but that's a small price to pay to keep the cook-off happening."

Sherry turned her back to Amber, lowered her voice to a whisper and asked the question she feared the response of. "Detective Bease is okay with the cook-off continuing?"

"More than okay. He thinks over the next twenty-four to forty-eight hours the killer will reveal his or her identity in some fashion if the contest continues. He seemed adamant about letting the event carry on. He's an interesting man. Oozes confidence while at the same time is very short on words. Gets right to the point, no time wasted. I like that in a person."

"He is a very nice man, quirky and set in his ways, but admirable. He would go to any lengths to get the job done and done well."

"I gave him all the contestants' names, provided him with my staffs', volunteers' and sponsors' contact info. I don't suspect any one of them of any wrongdoing, of course, but I didn't know how else to help."

"That's all you can do for the time being," Sherry said.

Rickie agreed.

"I'll see you bright and early," Sherry said in her cheeriest voice. She tucked her phone next to the register at the sales counter and made her way to the kitchen, where Amber was preparing tea.

"Really?" Amber drew out each syllable of the word.

"Really, what?" If Sherry's lips were pinched any tighter she might pop a blood vessel.

"Sherry, spill the beans. What was that phone call about? Who would go to any lengths to get the job done? You were speaking in hushed code. Something's up with the cook-off and you were told not to say anything." Amber bobbed the remainder of her sandwich to emphasize her words.

"I'm so bad at this," Sherry said as she shook her head. Her fingers snaked through her hair and wrestled out a tangle. "Okay, okay. A man connected to the cook-off died today."

"That's awful. I'm so sorry," Amber said.

"That's not all. It happened at the convention hall. I don't have any details, but Rickie says the cook-off will continue."

"Anything else?" Amber asked.

"The man was . . ." Sherry added without making eye contact with her friend.

"Was what?"

"The man was married and I hope his wife copes with the news." Sherry's words were hesitant. She kept her gaze everywhere except on Amber.

Amber coughed and appeared under distress trying to swallow a bite of sandwich. When she managed to push the food down her throat she said, "Wow. I'm so sorry. Why would the cook-off continue? It's going to be difficult to keep the death from dominating the press coverage."

"Rickie was told by the police the event can continue as long as the family agrees. Rickie said she spoke to his wife and she thinks her husband would definitely want the event to continue."

"I have to say I'm relieved the cook-off will continue. My sympathies to the family," Amber added. She cupped her hand around her ear. "A phone is ringing."

Sherry stepped out of the kitchen and caught sight of Pep near the sales counter holding up her phone.

"For you," he called out.

Sherry trotted over to Pep. He handed her the phone.

"Thanks," she said before she addressed the caller. As the phone passed across her sights, she saw the name of the caller on the screen. She checked to see if Amber was out of earshot. "Hi, Ray. I'd like to say it's nice to hear from you but I'm never sure whether it is or not." Sherry's thoughts scattered in different directions as she tried to guess the reason for the detective's call. One certainty, murder was on his mind.

"Good afternoon, Sherry. I hope all is well."

"Not everything. I did hurt my hand recently, which is why I'm not competing in this year's cook-off, even though I did qualify for the finals." Sherry glanced at her hand, which felt surprisingly good despite overusing it during the orientation.

"Sorry to hear that." Ray cleared his throat. "I'm calling in regard to the cook-off."

"I figured," Sherry said.

"The lead organizer, Rickie O'Dell, recounted the finding of the body. She said you were with her at the time."

"To be precise, I wasn't with her when she found the body."

"So, she is fabricating you were a witness to the discovery?" Ray asked.

"I'm sure she was nervous being questioned by you and misspoke. *Fabricate* is the wrong word. I was in the enormous room with her in the convention hall after the contestant orientation concluded. We were the only two people in there. She found the body and screamed out my name."

"What were you two doing there in the first place? Why only two of you?" As Ray spoke Sherry's neck began to prickle with discomfort. What was he getting at?

"Rickie asked me if I'd accompany her back to the convention hall to check on the appliances."

"Did she anticipate there would be a problem?"

Sherry considered Ray's question. Historically Ray's questions, even the simple ones, sought a multitiered pile of information that may come back to bite. She had to give his simple question a lot of thought, not because it was difficult, but because the implications may be more subtle than meets the eye.

"I don't think so," Sherry said. If she could take those words back and replace the phrase with a simple "no" she wouldn't leave the door open to further probing. But since the answer was, in actuality, "yes," she probably should have just said that one word. Why was he flustering her? They were friends, not adversaries.

"But maybe?" Ray prompted. His patience came as a surprise.

"She asked me to join her because she didn't have a chance during the busy orientation we went through this morning. She has to escort the contestants to and from the hall."

"Okay, so no particular reason to check on the merchandise other than to refresh her memory of the prizes. Something like that."

"Yes. Isn't that what she told you?"

"She mentioned a Walter Hemphill might be holding a grudge against the cook-off. He lost the appliance sponsorship. Did she talk to you about that?"

"Yes, but I didn't want to get involved in speculation. I learned that from you. I don't know Walter Hemphill so I can't comment on what he's capable of." Sherry smiled to herself. She recalled the many times Ray advised her not to assume or speculate during a murder investigation. Hard facts and evidence were what the investigation was all about.

"Right," Ray simply said.

"After she asked me to accompany her, Rickie went on ahead, leaving from the lodge. I went to the parking lot to relocate my car to the convention hall parking lot for a quick exit when we were done. I was looking forward to going home and walking Chutney before helping Dad at the Ruggery. By the time I got there and let myself in the side door, Rickie was behind the stage curtain."

"So you could *not* see her at that point when you first entered the room?"

"Right. Besides the fact the lights were off. Rickie didn't have access to the light panel to turn them on. Only light in the room was from the ovens and our cell phones. I called out to her and she answered. While back there, Rickie found the appliances had been soiled and smudged. She called me over to help her clean them up. I was wiping down the oven while she was working on the refrigerator. I wasn't looking at her at that point."

"You wiped away all the fingerprints. You two did a very good job removing some key evidence," Ray said. His words were delivered without emphasis, but they stung.

"We didn't know," Sherry said. "We were putting a shine on the prizes. How would we ever know we were wiping away evidence? You know that."

"Of course."

"We were deep into cleaning when suddenly Rickie screamed out my name. She said she found a body inside the fridge, then corrected herself and said the body was behind the fridge. When I ran over to her, I saw an arm. Rather, I saw a hand extending from a shirtsleeve. She told me she saw more of the body when she opened the refrigerator door. Through the gap at the door hinge. I wasn't interested in seeing any more than the arm. That was enough." Sherry winced. "She told me she touched him and she knew instantly the man was dead."

"Okay," Ray said. "Did you know the man? Gray Washington?"

"Only met him for the first time yesterday. My friend Don is starting up a commuter boat back and forth to Long Island and Rickie arranged for a few of the contestants and sponsors to be among the first to take the ride. I was on the trip, as was Rickie, and Gray's wife, Livvy, and another couple, the McDonalds. He seemed like a pleasant man, maybe a bit stressed but that's to be expected."

"Oh? Why's that?"

"His appliance company was called in as a last-minute replacement and he was having trouble getting the logistics straightened out. He and his wife may also not be on the best terms." Sherry thought for a moment. "They had a friend joining them. His name is Bart Foster."

"Also staying at the lodge?"

"I met him briefly at the lodge's front desk, where the Washingtons are staying. He mentioned he was staying at the Nutmeg Motor Inn. He was very interested in joining the Washingtons for any cook-off activities they could get him a ticket for," Sherry said.

"When was the last time you saw Gray Washington?"

"Last time I saw him was in the lobby of the lodge. Yesterday. I ferried passengers from Don's boat to the lodge. The Washingtons checked in with a bit of attitude because Livvy wanted separate rooms and Gray didn't want to pay for the extra room. The cook-off only covers the expense of one room per contestant. The budget isn't unlimited." She paused to check her thoughts. "I didn't see him after that. I'm not sure he was at the orientation today, to be honest. He didn't need to be."

"Excuse me, Sherry. I have to take this call. I'll be in touch." With that, Ray ended the call.

Knowing she was talking to dead air, Sherry bid Ray goodbye. "Par for the course. He almost always ends a conversation with a mad dash." She shook her head.

Sherry returned to the kitchen, where she found Amber cleaning up.

"Your tea is getting cold," Amber said and laughed.

Sherry sat down and helped herself to a napkin. Before she took a sip, she said, "The death at the cook-off. That's what I wanted to tell you but wasn't sure how you'd take it."

"Such a shame. I'm sorry for his family," Amber said with a shake of her head. "Do you think the man's death will cast a dark cloud over the day tomorrow?"

Sherry swallowed. "Rickie says the organizers will work around the situation and pay tribute to him at the appropriate time during the event. I don't want you to worry too much, there's nothing that can be done at this point. This cook-off is still yours to win."

"I'll take your words to heart. Why don't we get back to work and put the negative out of our minds as best we can," Amber suggested.

"What can I do to help out?" Sherry asked.

"With your one good hand would you be able to check off the inventory list while I go through the new yarn delivery?" Amber asked. "I always do that with Erno as he is the yarn shade expert. I tried sorting the yarn in their cubbies one day and I nearly went blind trying to differentiate the minute differences in colors. Hand-dyed wool batches have such subtle variations. Erno has the system down pat."

"Two more sips and I'm all yours," Sherry said. "Sounds like Dad's with some customers." Sherry made fast work of her tea, wiped her mouth and left Amber. Her eyes widened as she recognized the couple who were chatting with Erno.

"Sherry, so nice to see you again. We were getting the history of the hooked rug industry from your father."

Erno beamed a broad smile.

"I saw you at the orientation, but you were deep into answering contestant questions at the time," Jean McDonald said. "I wish I were in your group." Her husband, Curt, raised his hand and gave Sherry a wave from behind his wife.

"Hi, Jean. Hi, Curt," Sherry said. "Thank you for coming into the store. Let me show you around."

"Thank you so much," Jean said.

Sherry led the couple to the rug display area, where they admired the spring-themed rugs in vivid greens and various colors true to nature awaking after a cold New England winter.

"These are beautiful," Jean said. "We need one by the fireplace, right, honey?"

"Absolutely," Curt said. "I'll check out the choices while you have that chat with Sherry."

Curt began flipping through the neat stack of rugs.

Jean turned to face Sherry. "Sherry, one of my knives is missing from my carrying case. From the knife set we talked about on the boat. My heart is broken."

"Oh, no. Are you sure? You probably left it at your cook station after the orientation. Call Rickie. Anything found at the convention hall would be returned to her or the lodge's lost and found."

"Even a knife?"

"I'd assume so. If you misplaced it or someone picked it up for some reason, what else would they do with it?" Sherry asked. "When is the last time you had the knife?"

"I brought the set to the orientation so I could get a feel for my working space, and when I unzipped the carrier my best knife was missing. Your friend Amber Sherwin was in my group and she had the exact same knife set. Do you think she may have picked up my knife by mistake? I can't think of any other way I would have misplaced it."

"You know the knife was in the case to begin with?" Sherry asked.

Jean's eyes darted toward the ceiling before returning to Sherry. "Come to think of it, I never unzipped the bag since we left Virginia. It was definitely in there when we left home. I didn't open the case at all at the orientation. Didn't need to."

"Did I hear my name being bandied about?" Amber asked as she approached. "Jean, I'm so happy you came in. Sherry, Jean has all but adopted me into her family since we met at orientation. She sensed my nerves and took me under her wing."

"Lucky you," Sherry said.

"Yes, hi, Amber. We accepted your invitation to visit the Ruggery," Jean said with a grin. Her fleshy cheeks were rosy and she exuded maternal warmth. "I was telling Sherry I've lost one of my knives. The six-inch one I was counting on using to trim my chicken breasts for my recipe. The cuts are so uniform and precise. Looks like something the chefs on TV produce." She put her finger perpendicular to her lips and whispered, "And I know those celebrity chefs have people behind the scenes doing all their prep work."

"I'm sure it'll turn up, if you lost it at either the lodge or the convention hall," Sherry said.

"I wouldn't worry," Amber said. "Are we allowed to share? You're certainly welcome to use mine during the cook-off."

"Such a nice offer. If I don't find mine, I may take you up on it if we're allowed. I know we have similar, actually, exact knives. I'm grasping at straws that you may have picked up one of mine when I unpacked them at my cook station this morning. Any chance of that?"

Amber waved her index finger. "One minute. I have the set in the back room. I'll go check, but I don't want to give you any false hopes. The set is Sherry's and I've been meticulous about keeping an eye on it. I would never forgive myself if something happened to one of them. Be right back." Amber hurried away to the kitchen.

"I found the rug we should purchase," Curt said as he held up an Erno Oliveri lambswool masterpiece featuring a cornucopia of spring root vegetables. "For the spot in front of the fireplace."

"Honey, you have a great eye," Jean said. She turned toward Sherry, her smile slightly dimmed by the concern on her face. "We don't use our fireplace much, being we're from Virginia. The spot is kind of neglected." Her head dipped slightly.

"Try not to worry. We will do everything we can to get your knife back." Sherry smiled warmly in hopes of changing the mood. "If you've settled on the rug, we can bundle that up for you at the register. The artist himself can ring you up. He drew the design." She pointed toward Erno, parked by the sales counter. "Unless you prefer his handsome son." She directed her sights toward Pep stuffing something into a storage drawer next to the design table.

"Can't go wrong with either of those choices," Jean said with renewed enthusiasm.

Mission accomplished. Jean was in bright spirits once again.

On their way to the front of the store Amber called Sherry's name. She reemerged from the kitchen with her eyes fixated on Sherry. "One of the knives is missing."

Chapter 7

"Excuse me one second. I'll be right back," Sherry said. She turned her back on the McDonalds knowing they wanted to be part of the upcoming conversation. She intercepted Amber halfway across the room. "Are you sure?"

Amber presented the knife carrier, open, with a glaring empty slot where Sherry's favorite six-inch knife would reside.

"I just unzipped the carrier and the knife was missing." She pointed to the indentation where the knife once lay. "Just like Jean's. What's going on?"

"Remember you and Jean were nervous yesterday. You said so. I know I don't think straight if I'm overly nervous. To be expected. You each could have misplaced the knives not far from your stations. If no one knew who they belonged to they would be taken to an official. We need to find that official."

"Could someone be shopping for a new knife, admired our brand and helped themselves?" Jean asked as she arrived at Sherry's side. Her round face was flushed.

"Let's not speculate," Sherry said. "The convention building is locked now. If the knives are inside the building, they're safe. The cleaning crew may come and go but they're trustworthy. I'm pretty sure."

"I hope you're right," Jean said.

"I'll call Rickie and see what she suggests. That's the best idea, don't you think?" Amber said. The uncertainty in her voice wouldn't convince anyone.

"I didn't notice mine was missing until I got home. Of course, I was very careful packing up my knives before I left orientation." Jean's eyes lost focus for a moment. "I did leave the set on my counter when we had a final collective meeting with the organization team to go over plans for tomorrow. I may have visited the ladies' room at one point, also. When I returned, the groups were taking turns walking to the stage and back to get a feel for the presentation ceremony. An ingenious motivator for the cook's best performance. Well done, Rickie." Jean paused as if letting the idea sink in. "There was plenty of movement between stations." She shook her head. "Anyone could have helped themselves."

"Very strange," Sherry said. "Rickie will know what to do. I can't say she'll be thrilled with one more item on her agenda to take care of."

"I do have a Plan B if the knife doesn't turn up. I'm going to have to use my smaller paring knife to prepare my chicken breasts for my Tidewater Smothered and Stuffed Chicka Noodle Casserole. Problem is, that makes the prep procedure more delicate and time-consuming. I'm sure you've had to adjust your technique under duress at cook-offs, haven't you?" Jean asked Sherry, as if seeking consolation.

"Of course," Sherry fibbed. Of all the situations she'd been exposed to during cooking competitions, she had never misplaced one of her favorite knives. She considered for a moment how much that equipment substitution may have thrown off her game. There was a reason the best chefs took extra care with their favored equipment. "Let's ring up your rug purchase and then call Rickie. That'll put everyone's mind to rest."

"Did I hear someone say they were calling Rickie? I was on the phone with her two minutes ago," Pep announced as he made his way from the drawing table.

"What did she have to say?" Sherry asked. "Are you asking her again if people liked your food? She's very busy. I would give her a break and believe her when she says they loved your toasts."

Pep peered up from reading his phone. "No. Actually, Rickie would like me to bring my truck around after the cook-off tomorrow to feed the starving masses. That's very good news. Dad, I may have to cut out early again today to load up on truck supplies."

"I'm very impressed. On the other hand, letting your son pursue his passion is one of the downfalls of hiring him part-time," Erno lamented. "Relatives can get away with murder if you let them."

Sherry cringed at her father's choice of words. "Dad, can you ring the McDonalds' rug up, please?"

"Step right over here," Erno instructed. Curt followed his direction.

Sherry was relieved Pep had introduced a new subject. Before she could reply to his good news, Jean spoke up.

"Do you think something nefarious is going on at the convention hall? Is security doing their job?"

Sherry and Amber exchanged glances. Sherry considered Jean may not know about the death of Gray Washington yet. Even Amber didn't know the identity of the victim. Following Rickie's instruction, she withheld the breaking news. Amber frowned, while Sherry put on a happy face, masking her uncertainty. The convention hall key was forefront on her mind. Was any of this due to the fact she took a shortcut returning the key to Rickie and the convention hall door ended up unlocked the entire night?

"Security's doing their job. Those knives will turn up. I'm sure there's a funny story to go along with their disappearance," Sherry said. As she scanned the group, hers was the only face wearing a smile.

"Maybe contestant sabotage?" Curt said.

"Only in books and movies," Sherry said with a surge of confidence. "I have yet to come across any bad sportsmanship on that level in cooking competitions."

"Wouldn't you call murder bad sportsmanship?" Pep asked.

"Murder? You've seen murder at a cook-off?" Curt was incredulous.

"Sherry's seen it all," Erno said. His nonchalance seemed to take Curt and Jean by surprise. They mirrored eyebrow lifts.

"Anyway, go see what else Augustin has to offer in the way of entertainment. I'll call Rickie. I'll take down your number on the sales slip and reach out when she has some good news about your knife. Sound good?"

"Fingers crossed," Jean said. "Right, Amber?"

Amber forced a smile and nodded in agreement.

"Thank you, Oliveri family, for sharing your artistry with the McDonald family," Curt said as he held up his new rug. "We are off to explore more of Augustin before tonight's activity over at the playhouse. We haven't seen the marina or the historical society yet. We hear the newly renovated library is quite something. Even your dog park is written up in the Northeast's guidebook as being a gem. How lucky you are to live in such a quaint town."

"Yes, we are. I'll see you later at dinner," Amber said. "I hope we have some good news about our knives to share by then."

After the McDonalds left the store Sherry tried to reach Rickie by phone. The call went to voicemail. Sherry left a message explaining the knife situation.

"She's probably not answering her calls right now in the eleventh hour. She'll play the message soon, I'm confident." Having no other recourse on the matter, the two got down to the business of checking off new inventory. When they were done Sherry offered to spot Amber her remaining hours if she wanted to go home early to prepare for her night out.

"I might take you up on your offer," Amber said.

"Are you making friends with the other contestants?" Sherry asked. "Knowing people makes the evening that much more fun."

"I spent a good amount of time with the group of cooks on either side of me on the cook-off floor at orientation. I'll probably be seated with them tonight. I had hoped Tig could join in, but I didn't realize tickets were required. I would have preregistered him if I had known he was coming. That's what spouses did. I need to make a few phone calls to see if I can finagle a ticket. I would feel pretty bad if I had to rescind his dinner invitation."

"Good news," Sherry said. "Rickie put a ticket in my hand when I left the lodge today. I tried to tell her I wasn't going but she had already moved on to addressing another issue across the room. Don would like to have dinner at his place. I haven't seen him since yesterday. The ticket is all yours." Sherry found her purse and fished inside for the ticket. She planted the paper in Amber's hand.

"Fantastic, thank you."

"Tig wants to go tonight even though he doesn't know anyone besides you at the dinner and isn't participating in the cook-off? I don't think Don would go with me under those circumstances," Sherry said.

"Of course Don would. He's your guy. Tig didn't mention that would be a problem," Amber said with a shrug.

"I bet there are a number of people from Boston down here this week," Sherry said. She paused, waiting for Amber to offer up any acquaintances. She stayed silent. "You'll have a nice time. See you tomorrow."

After Amber left the store Sherry pulled up a stool behind the sales counter. Pep joined her, leaning up against the long wood table. "So you're leaving early, now that you have to prepare for tomorrow's lunch."

"You're spot on. I have grocery shopping to do," Pep said.

Sherry studied the face of her younger brother. "How is the idea of the food truck commitment for the next two years sitting with Charlotte? It's going to be a lot of work to make a profit."

"Charlotte is my rock. We don't have the typical husband-provider, wife-child-rearer marriage, but who really does these days? I do admit I'm probably testing her patience with this venture."

"I really admire your enterprising spirit. I like to think the trait runs in the family."

"Speaking of enterprising spirits, you remind me. Marla is in a class by herself when it comes to enterprising spirits. I pale in comparison." Pep laughed.

Bringing up Marla struck Sherry with a twinge of compassion for their sister, who was living in Oklahoma and going through a "thing" herself.

Sherry knew Marla would figure out her current midlife crisis. Being the older sister, any problems her siblings confronted caused her protective side to emerge. Along with her sister's state of personal uncertainty, Pep beginning this new phase for himself and his young family gave her cause for concern. Both were situations Sherry wanted to keep a close eye on, but only one sibling was within arm's reach at the moment.

"Remember, I'm your ride-or-die sister. Your highs are my highs, and likewise, your challenges are my challenges."

"Thanks, Sher. I appreciate the support," Pep said.

"You're a lucky guy to have Charlotte and Mimi," Sherry said. Her voice was mellow as her heart swelled with love for her brother. "What will you serve after the cook-off tomorrow?"

"Charlotte thinks the toast toppers were more popular than the bowls, so I'd like to narrow the menu down to that theme for the day. I can't name the truck until the theme is finalized so tomorrow is important. The challenge is to fill stomachs and offer enough variety that people will make a return visit."

Sherry nodded. The pride in Pep's voice brought a smile to her face.

"Were you happy with the location you were given at the lodge today?"

"I'm going to ask Rickie if I can relocate my truck closer to the convention hall. The lodge's parking lot was fine for today, but as I told you, I wasn't allowed to use their refuse facility because of the agreement the lodge has with the town of Augustin. The hotel is required to sort and recycle to such an extent they don't have the capacity for any additional. They were watching me, too. I had to bag and bring home all the garbage produced. The convention hall will have different regulations. When I brought up the subject initially Rickie wasn't sure she wanted the truck that close to the cook-off location. She didn't want it confused as one of the sponsors. So much to think about."

"More content for your book," Sherry added.

"By the way, you did a great job not telling Amber the full details about the murder at the convention hall. I'm proud of you. She doesn't need to be stressed out about it right now," Pep said.

"I didn't tell Amber any details about the murder. She doesn't even know there was a murder, only an untimely death. And I feel awful withholding the full truth."

Heads turned when the bell over the front door tinkled. A man dressed in an iconic eighties-era bomber jacket strolled in. His tan hat was marginally askew, dipping one side toward his ear.

"Detective Ray Bease. How have you been?" Pep said. "Last time I saw you I was a prime suspect in a murder investigation."

"Hello, Pep. I've been well. How about yourself?" Ray asked.

"Very well. I was on my way out. Sherry and Erno are here to serve. Bye, all." Pep let himself out, only to return before the door closed completely. "Oh, Sherry, I forgot to ask your permission to use your fig, goat cheese, pesto dip as one of my toast toppers tomorrow. I know I have to have it on the menu. What do you say?"

"Of course. My recipes are your recipes," Sherry said as she waved a goodbye.

"Thanks. So long," Pep said as he slipped out the door again.

Sherry turned her attention to Ray. "Hi, Ray," she said as she stood up. "What can I do for you?" Sherry's gaze drifted to the kitchenette doorway. She was glad Amber had gone home early, so she wasn't burdened with whatever Ray was bringing Sherry's way.

"I'd like to ask you about your coworker, Amber Sherwin, before I speak to her directly," Ray said.

Erno poked his head around the corner from the entrance to the storage room. "Hi, Ray." He waved his hand and disappeared.

"Hello, sir," Ray replied.

"Amber is in the middle of a very prestigious cook-off. Can this wait?" Sherry said with a preemptive strike against Ray's next topic.

"I am in the middle of a murder investigation." The seriousness in Ray's voice made the hair on Sherry's arms stand on end. "I'll get right to the point. Does your friend know the victim, Gray Washington?"

"Absolutely not. And she doesn't know he was murdered, either. She only knows a man died who was involved with the cook-off."

"If she doesn't know, which may be your personal assumption, she will soon. That's a fact."

"She doesn't know Gray. I only met him yesterday on our boat trip across the sound and Amber wasn't aboard. Amber's obviously a local and not staying at the hotel, so she doesn't have as much interaction with others outside of event activities. I suppose she may have met him at orientation in passing. There wasn't much time to socialize outside the small groups we were assigned to. I'm not sure whether Gray even attended. His wife said she had lost track of him before breakfast, which he never showed up to."

"He did attend for a short while."

"Well then, the fact I didn't even see him may answer your question."

"Doesn't really. Unless Amber was in your group? Was she? Then you'd have had your eye on her."

Sherry's definitive tone softened. "No. She wasn't."

"In other words, you really aren't absolutely sure whether Amber met him or not," Ray said. The corner of his mouth drooped ever so slightly.

"Right. Listen, I was hesitant to tell her about the death in the first place because I didn't want her to be distracted from the task at hand, the cook-off. But she sensed I was sitting on a secret and drummed the information out of me."

"You wouldn't make a good poker player," Ray said.

"Funny."

Ray glanced in all directions. "We're not getting anywhere. She's not here?" A note of frustration crept into his voice.

"She went home to get ready to go to a contestant event tonight. Dinner and a behind-the-scenes look at Augustin Playhouse's current production, *Scrambled*."

Ray mumbled something inaudible before raising his voice. "What's Pep up to these days?"

"He and his wife and baby moved to Augustin for at least the next two years. Besides putting in some hours here, he's taken on a very interesting project. Starting a food truck and writing a book about the experience. He has a backer and a publisher. His mission is to make the most out of his next two years serving delicious lunches out of his truck while documenting the journey. He served lunch at the cook-off's orientation and everyone enjoyed his food."

"At the Sound Shore Lodge?" Ray asked.

"That's right. Why are you asking about Amber knowing the man who died?"

Ray shifted his weight from one leg to the other. "She's a contestant, he served as a sponsor in the cook-off she's in. That's all I'm willing to say. The investigation has begun, and if we can work all angles in a short amount of time while the case is hot, chances are very good we will find the killer quickly. That's the reason I pushed for the cook-off to continue as scheduled. My gut tells me the killer will hang around, and if he does, we will nab him."

Sherry shuddered. "Will he strike again?"

"If he hasn't gotten what he wanted he will."

"How did Gray die?" Sherry asked.

"Knife in the back. A very fancy chef's knife."

Sherry pinched her eyes shut and the imagery of her knife set danced across the darkness. She didn't want to ask about the variety of knife because she feared she already knew the answer. The question lay unasked on her lips.

"I'm told the size and brand of the knife is one most chefs would kill to own," Ray added before Sherry opened her eyes. "Hunziker. Have you heard of it?"

Sherry slowly lifted her lids. "Yes. The very best."

"The weapon has yet to be recovered. The victim was stabbed and the assailant had the forethought to lay the body, wound side up, raincoat draped over the top, on one of the soft tarps behind the refrigerator so the blood soaked in, rather than pooled."

"That's why Rickie didn't know he'd been murdered. With the lack of light behind the curtain, no evident blood spillage was visible."

"The knife was gone. The wound was very telling though. Not many knives could have made such a huge incision with one stab," Ray said. "That's all it took."

Sherry grimaced as the imagery of the scene she hadn't even witnessed trudged across her mind.

"How did the investigators figure out the type of knife used?"

"That's the science of forensics. Or should I say the art of forensics. Hunzikers have a very distinct serration pattern. Their trademark, I'm told. The knife left its distinct marking in the man's flesh."

"Hunziker. That's the best chef knife available," Sherry said. She willed her voice to remain steady and strong.

"Interesting," Ray said. He left Sherry longing for elaboration, but none was forthcoming. "Okay, well then, I'm done here."

"Wait. We're friends, right?"

"Right."

"Off the record, Gray Washington seemed to have troubled relationships with a few people, including a bumpy marriage as far as I could make out. There's also a man named Walter Hemphill who was not at all happy the contest had replaced his sponsoring appliance package for the Washingtons'. He blamed the Washingtons in part. Even a couple from Virginia who Don and I transported from Long Island was upset with the

Washingtons for swapping out the appliances they longed to win. Amber doesn't enter into any of those scenarios."

Sherry knew Ray heard her, but his mastery of the emotionless face concealed any reaction to her revelations.

"The Virginia couple who owns a set of Hunziker knives," Ray said. "I've spoken to them. They would like me to find their missing knife. The cook-off organizer, Rickie O'Dell, would like me to find their knife. I certainly would like to find the knife that took Gray Washington's life, and if it's their knife one piece of the unsolved puzzle has been set into place."

"Knives are going missing everywhere." Sherry's attempt at levity went unnoticed by the detective. For only a moment.

"What do you mean knives, plural. Is there another knife missing?"

"Knife. The knife is missing and Jean McDonald was counting on using it at the cook-off."

Ray squinted a hard glare in Sherry's direction.

"The McDonalds didn't tell me you had spoken to them. They were in here a while ago shopping."

"They didn't tell me they'd spoken to you, either."

Sherry nodded.

"I imagine I'm not someone people boast about having conversed with when I'm on duty. Doesn't always bode well for their innocence. Mrs. Washington gave me their names as persons who had displayed an adverse reaction toward her husband."

Sherry stayed silent but nodded. "Not adverse so much as disappointed. Jean McDonald was hoping to win the original custom appliance package. That's all."

"Hmm. Last question. Do you know where Amber was between, say, dinnertime last night and midmorning today?"

"She went home after we practiced her recipe yesterday afternoon. She wanted to relax before a contestant dinner. We didn't see each other until the orientation."

"No sighting of Amber from late afternoon until the next morning?" Ray asked.

Sherry mulled over her choice of words. "Not by me, but she was somewhere."

"Yes. I'm quite certain she was somewhere."

"I must repeat, she's nervous. She hasn't been in many cook-offs and this is a very prestigious one. Fifty home cooks from all over the country are preparing their best noodle recipes and she's one of them. That's why I don't want you to burden her with silly questions."

Ray's gaze lowered to the floor.

"To finish my answer, this morning Amber was at the Sound Shore Lodge, before we all congregated at the convention hall for contestant orientation." She stared at the detective for a moment. "Has the time of death been established?"

"What we're going on is that when the police arrived, the convention hall floor in one path to the stage was wet with watery puddles, not mud. In another path, most likely taken by the later visitors, mud was everywhere. That's important because the murderer couldn't have trudged through the thawed ground later in the morning without tracking in mud. From very early in the morning, the ground was covered in a fresh blanket of snow. Gray must have been murdered by midmorning. Probably much earlier. After that the temperature rose quickly, producing mud."

Sherry began to speak but reconsidered.

"Thank you. You've been most helpful," Ray said. His words were clipped.

"You're welcome, I think," Sherry said. "I wish I knew what you were getting at. Amber needs to relax today, so if you're determined to speak to her, would you wait one more day?"

"Sherry, this is a murder investigation. I have a job to do. That's all I have to say for now, and I say it as a friend," Ray said. He tipped his tan hat and let himself out.

Sherry took a moment and stared at the closed door.

"What'cha looking at, sweetie?" Erno asked.

Sherry backed up and faced her father. "The air of uncertainty Detective Bease left in his wake."

"Identifying air types might be a specialized skill."

"Ray was asking about Amber and whether she knew the man who was murdered. I'm not one hundred percent certain but I don't think she knew him. Although he was from Boston and Amber used to live in Boston when she was a practicing marriage and family therapist. Maybe she bought her appliances from the Washingtons? How would I know that nugget of information? I can't ask her before the cook-off. The matter will have to wait." Sherry shrugged.

"You know best," Erno said.

The afternoon passed with many browsers dropping into the store.

Sherry assumed more than a few were associated with the cook-off, judging by the rug themes they were interested in. While the number of purchasing customers was quite a bit lower than the looky-loos, she and her father managed to sell some big-ticket custom rugs to out-of-towners. She was glad she dropped in to help him out.

Twenty minutes before closing time, a man and a woman walked through the door. Sherry left the text she was crafting to Don unfinished. "Good afternoon," she greeted them. As soon as the door closed Sherry hopped off the stool and made a move forward.

"Hello, Sherry." Livvy extended her hand and shook Sherry's. "You know my friend Bart Foster."

So many thoughts rushed through Sherry's brain she didn't know what to say next. The momentary silence became awkward until finally Livvy and Sherry began to speak over one another.

"I'm sorry, you go ahead," Sherry said, in hopes Livvy would steer the conversation out of the clumsy territory it had found itself in.

"I was going to say I'm sure you've heard about my husband's passing," Livvy said.

"Yes, I'm so very sorry for you and your family's loss," Sherry said. The elephant still loomed large in the room.

"He was murdered," Livvy added.

The elephant was named. "Yes, I did hear that, also," Sherry said. "I'm so sorry."

"My friend Bart is a private investigator Gray and I hired because we strongly suspected someone was following us, harassing us intentionally and closing in on our private lives to no good end. And that's exactly what happened."

Sherry considered the obvious fact that Bart may not be doing such a great job if whomever he was hired to prevent acting out against the Washingtons had since done so under his watch. Before she was able to put the words together to express her thought Bart spoke his mind.

"I realize you're inclined to label my job performance inadequate. There's more to it than meets the eye," Bart said.

"None of my business," Sherry said. "What you're hired to do for the Washingtons and how well you do it is none of my concern."

"Livvy is keeping me on to continue the good work I have already amassed," Bart said. He plunged his hands into his pants pockets.

"I'm sure she knows what she's doing," Sherry said. "If you've been on the case for a while you must have plenty of evidence leaning in a certain direction."

"See?" Livvy said. Smile lines emerged around her eyes as she glanced at Bart. "She is as good as people say she is." Livvy redirected her gaze toward Sherry. "We've been told you have solved a few murders in your time."

"Not exactly solved. I've aided in investigations and been lucky enough to have dug up some vital clues certainly, but I've only done so because someone I know and or loved has been high up on the suspect list, when he or she shouldn't have been."

"Spin it any way you want, it does sound as if you're a great amateur sleuth," Bart said. "At this point, I've run into a bit of a roadblock. You see, Livvy herself may be on the suspect list. That complicates matters tremendously."

"That's right. Gray and I are in a rough patch in our marriage. He drives me absolutely batty when it comes to being late, mood swings concerning our business and his continually casual approach to what I consider crucial strategies to the success of our business. Recently I've reached my breaking point. We're only spending time together when business requires it. Like at this cook-off. The vacation we were just on was an attempt at compatibility. Wasn't going too badly, I admit."

"You can understand how the timing of his murder is most unfortunate," Bart added.

"A murder is unfortunate any time, I'd say," Sherry said. "Sounds as if you've spoken to the investigators from Hillsboro County."

"Yes. A Detective Bease had a few questions for me. I played the part of grieving widow, but in all honesty, I am still in shock over the whole ordeal. My grieving emotions haven't kicked in. I'm in go mode to find who did this. Can you think of how we could go about doing that while I am also being watched closely by the authorities?"

Sherry studied the ground while her thoughts sorted themselves out. "I don't really have any valuable information to offer. All I can say is how sorry I am for your loss and if there's anything I can do to make your stay in Augustin as pleasant as could be expected under this type of situation, please ask."

"I was hoping you'd say that, Sherry," Livvy said. "Right, Bart?" She encouraged a reply from the man, engaging a lengthy stare in his direction.

"We sought you out in hopes you would keep your eyes open for any behavior, chatter or clues as to who took violent action against the Washingtons. Livvy is not safe by any means and, while she and Gray hired me to find who was harassing their business, the situation's now taken a turn in the worst direction possible," Bart said. "Livvy may be on the detective's suspect list, and worse, the killer's hit list."

"Did Detective Bease come out and name you as a suspect? I mean, all married couples run into bumps along the way. Not many take aggravation to the next level and murder their spouse."

"Why else would he question me about the state of our marriage, our financial standing, our business relationship, all questions directed at uncovering an animosity between Gray and me?"

"That's what he does. Don't read too much into it until he comes right out and labels you a suspect," Sherry said. "I know. I've been in your shoes."

"I assure you I had nothing to do with Gray's demise. Bart and I will stick to the planned schedule and proceed with the cook-off. Gray would have insisted on it, if he had a say. All we can do is wait and see what develops."

Sherry shifted her sights to Bart, who was nodding with each word Livvy spoke. When Livvy concluded, Sherry expected Bart to chime in, but he remained silent with his eyes trained on Livvy. *What if Bart were having an affair with Livvy and wanted Gray out of the way? What if Livvy wanted her husband gone and somehow was covering up the murder with a premeditated plan involving hiring a private investigator to promote the appearance of innocence?*

"Like anyone else, I would report any information to the police I might stumble upon." Sherry faced Livvy. "I didn't know your husband until yesterday and that's the extent of my involvement with him. Beyond that, if you need any recommendations for Augustin sights, my family has lived here for ages and has lots of insight into how to get to know the town's history. Did you know Augustin was at the top of the country's onion production a century ago?"

Bart smiled. "Amazing."

"Very interesting," Livvy said. "Fitting, the town has such a foodie past and hosts a national recipe contest. Thank you. We will certainly be in touch. Let's go, Bart. Sherry needs some time to consider our request."

"I really don't," Sherry said. "I don't know any more than you two do. Probably a lot less."

Bart was holding the door open for Livvy. Livvy made no move through the doorway.

"I'm sure if I don't pressure her, she'll come around," Livvy said to Bart, as if Sherry weren't three feet away. "She knows what's right. Especially since Gray was, in fact, her friend Amber Sherwin's close confidante. Sherry will want to ensure Amber isn't mistakenly added to the suspect list due to past indiscretions."

"Wait!" Sherry blurted out. "Amber was Gray's close confidante?"

"Anyone's therapist should be considered someone to confide in safely. When Gray had sessions with Amber at the Back Bay Therapy Center he would come home renewed and full of hope. I didn't probe him on what their sessions covered, but safe to say I was one of the main topics. I wish Amber had been able to convince Gray I had fallen out of love with him. Chances are we wouldn't be having this conversation if she had."

Rather than be baited into a discussion she couldn't be certain she knew anything about, Sherry shrugged.

"Your store is beautiful," Livvy said. She led Bart out the door.

Chapter 8

Don passed a basket of warm corn muffins to Sherry, followed by the small crock of orange rosemary compound butter.

"Thanks." Sherry spooned the savory spread on a mini muffin and set it on her dinner plate. She proceeded to flake the lemon caper cod with her fork. Her garlic smashed baby potatoes were almost gone and she was savoring the crispy salty skin from the last bite she took. "Are you sure you've never been in a cooking contest? This is delicious. You could crush the competition with this recipe."

"Only the cook-off where we met and, as you know, I wasn't even the cook, just my sister's sous chef. Since then, my joy is to follow your cook-offs and cheer for you. I cook for the sheer pleasure."

"You always know the best way to butter me up," Sherry said. She swallowed the last bite of her baked cod. She studied the lone potato morsel on her plate and popped the spud into her mouth. A moment later her fork came to rest on her plate.

"I wish you looked at me with the same loving reverence you eyed that potato with," Don said with a broad smile.

Sherry ignored Don's remark, knowing that would be more of a tease than if she replied. "I don't have a dessert for us tonight. I was running a bit late after spending the afternoon at the Ruggery."

"No problem," Don said as he patted his stomach. "This has hit the spot. How was business today? Lots of out-of-towners in Augustin, judging by the variety of license plates I've seen on the road. the Ruggery is always on visitors' lists of desired locations to visit."

"You're right. Lots of customers in the store this afternoon. Most notably, Gray Washington's widow, Livvy."

"To think he was on the boat yesterday. I'll be darned. Such a shame. Any idea who murdered the poor fellow?"

"Your guess is as good as mine. Livvy had a motive, as do others. Livvy even made a suggestion about Amber. Amber. Can you believe that? She claims Gray had been in Amber's therapy practice and there may have been circumstances beyond the typical patient-therapist relationship."

Don's jaw dropped open. He ran his fingers through the short auburn stubble that once was a curly mop of hair. Captains needed a well-shorn head for easy all-weather maintenance, he had explained to Sherry when he shocked her with his new haircut. She was still getting used to the severity of the cut. "Murder investigations can uncover some sorted details. Don't give them life by encouraging the woman to vent."

"What do you think about Livvy?" Sherry asked.

"What stood out about her was her irritation with her husband because he was running late. Come to think of it, I wasn't happy about that either. Hope that doesn't put me on the suspect list," Don said as he raised his eyebrows for emphasis.

"If you haven't heard from the investigators by now, I'd say you never made the list."

"There was an undercurrent of tension between the two spouses and also between Gray and Rickie O'Dell. Even the McDonalds joined in and gave Gray a little what-for about replacing the appliances they preferred. And there was something about a Hemphill fellow who was hovering about, grumbling that his appliance package was removed from consideration. When you consider all that, Gray was stepping into a hornet's nest of animosity on the boat. He should have taken his car instead."

"Wow!" Sherry said. "I didn't think you were tuned in to the small talk in the slightest. Was I ever wrong."

Don pursed his lips and the dimple on one cheek showed itself. He gave Sherry the look that melted her heart. "Observing details is my strong suit."

"So much to learn about you," Sherry suggested. "I'm worried about Amber's connection to Gray. This is new to me. She has never uttered a word about this."

"I'm sure a lot of folks knew him. If she was his therapist she won't want to divulge the content of any of their sessions. Imagine a therapist sharing all your inner worries and insecurities."

"Don't even go there," Sherry said. "Something Livvy doesn't know, I'm guessing, is Amber had the same brand of knife used by the murderer."

"If you're talking about the Hunziker . . ." Don pushed back his chair, left the room and returned with a massive knife in his hand. ". . . I purchased the very same after I used yours last week. It's a beaut. Another reason I might be on the suspect list."

"Hers, well, actually it's mine that she borrowed, is missing."

"Sher. You're getting ahead of yourself here. Yes, it doesn't sound great for Amber but she just has to provide an alibi and she's home free. We know she didn't kill Gray Washington. She has to stand up for herself and tell the investigators she was asleep or walking Bean or whatever she was doing at the time of his death."

"She was with me for the afternoon while we practiced her recipe. Then she was out at a contestant dinner. Where she went after she left there, I'm not sure. Home, I would venture to say. If she has a witness to her whereabouts, no worries."

Don grimaced. "Details. Amber needs to provide concrete details. Let the subject rest. There's nothing we can do right now except enjoy this lovely dinner."

Don placed the knife down on the table with the utmost of care. Sherry eyed the shiny instrument that could make quick work out of the toughest of meat cuts.

"Do you think this knife would kill with just one plunge?"

"No doubt in my mind. If you think about it, you're lucky you only came away with a few stitches when his little brother, the paring knife, slipped from your hand. That knife was just as sharp, though can't penetrate as deep as this guy." He tipped his head in the direction of the carving knife.

Sherry sighed. "Speaking of details," Sherry began, her voice soft, "when we were at the urgent care facility the night I hurt my hand..."

"Say no more," said Don. "I know where this is going."

Sherry sat up straighter.

"I came on too strong, talking about our future together. I regret spilling my emotions like a teenage crush. You have every right to think I'm too pushy. I didn't like seeing you in discomfort and suddenly the words that are tucked in my subconscious came out. Of course, I would love our future to be together but we've only known one another for a relatively short while. I can't expect you to be on my love timetable. I moved to the area to be near you, my sister and the boat facilities that are superior in this county. All of those are very important to me. Enough said." Don puffed out his chest. "I'm ranting, stop me."

Sherry's head was spinning. He was saying he didn't mean to express his devotion to her the other night, she realized. She misunderstood any underlying intent. Her heart sank. She opened her mouth to reply. A sense of relief set in when she was interrupted by her ringing phone.

Sherry answered on the first ring. "Hi, Amber. Is your evening over already?"

"Sherry, can we talk? In person? Are you home?" Amber was breathless, and if she spoke any faster Sherry was going to have to ask her to repeat every word. Judging by the concern on Don's face, Amber's excited tone was coming through the phone loud and clear. He glanced at his watch and made a gesture they were finished with dinner and Sherry was free to exit whenever.

"I'm at Don's townhouse. We are finishing up dinner and I can be back home in, say, twenty minutes if that works. He was the cook and I'm the one-handed dishwasher, and I mustn't neglect my duty."

"I'll be there," Amber said. She clicked off without so much as a goodbye.

"Pre-cook-off jitters, don't you think?" Don said.

"She wasn't in such a state earlier in the day. I wonder what set her off. Maybe being around the other cook-off finalists at the dinner made the whole thing a bit too real."

"You go on and give her support," Don said as he collected the dishes from the table. "I can clean up. You'll just owe me big-time."

"I wouldn't dream of living on credit. Let's get these dishes washed," Sherry said. She suddenly wasn't interested in pursuing the subject of her future with Don. Things were as they should be. She shouldn't push the relationship in any direction it wasn't going in naturally.

After the dishes were loaded into the dishwasher Sherry and Don shared a good-night kiss that lingered far beyond her expectation. A sense of reassurance filled the spot in her heart left wavering after their unfinished conversation.

"Will I see you tomorrow?" Sherry asked when they separated from their embrace. "The cook-off will be very exciting. You should stop by."

"I have a few items on my agenda, like a visit to Town Hall for a check of my business credentials, but I'll do my best to be there after that. I want to try Pep's lunch offerings, too. I hear he's looking for a sous chef and I have experience in that field," Don said. "Always good to have a Plan B if my boat gig doesn't pan out."

When Sherry arrived home, Amber was sitting on her front steps.

"How was dinner and the playhouse tour?" Sherry asked as she approached her friend.

Amber stood. Her linen pants were wrinkled as if she had been seated for quite some time. "The playhouse tour was spectacular. The play is a murder mystery titled *Scrambled*. Two chefs become enemies and one ends up dead. But things aren't as they appear. We saw a few scenes being rehearsed and that really whet my appetite to buy tickets for the full performance. Plan on attending with me and together we'll solve the whodunit."

"Perfect. The play must have been written with us in mind," Sherry said.

"What a coincidence you should say that," Amber said. "That's why I'm here."

"Not sure where this is headed," Sherry said.

"The night was going well until we sat down to dinner. At the playhouse there wasn't much interaction between all of us because we were audience to a riveting presentation. Conversation was kept to a minimum. When we moved to the private dining room there were smaller groups per table. The conversation flowed. The contestants were kept distant from the sponsors and organizers. I didn't see the three judges but supposedly they came just in time for dinner. Wasn't long before the topic of the man who passed away came up."

"You were with your friend from out of town?" Sherry asked.

"Yes, Tig. We sat together along with three other couples and a single. Anyway, did you know the man's name?"

Sherry pulled her key from her purse. "Shall we go inside? Would you be more comfortable?"

"No, let's just sit out here, if you don't mind. I won't stay long. It's turned into such a mild evening for this time of year after the snow we had overnight. Spring is a season of weather emotions in New England. Mother Nature can deliver winter conditions one hour of the day and T-shirt weather a few hours later."

"My favorite time of the year." Sherry sat on the top step and Amber took the step below her. "What did you hear about the man?"

"His name. Gray Washington."

If Amber saw Sherry cringe she didn't react. "That's right. I only knew of him because Gray and his wife, Livvy, were on Don's commuter boat from Long Island. That's where I met them. They were cutting short a vacation in the Hamptons to join the cook-off. A last-minute addition."

"Right. But in our conversation about the man, you never mentioned his name. And you certainly didn't mention he was murdered."

"I didn't, no. Never thought you'd know him. Did you?" Sherry asked. She already knew the answer but not the full story.

"Turns out I did. From my days in Boston," Amber said.

"I'm so sorry. Were you and Gray close?" Sherry twirled a lock of her hair with her good set of fingers.

"Acquaintances. Such a small world." Amber shook her head. "Wonder what happened to the poor fellow."

"I don't know many details. So sad for his family."

"It set a somber mood for the night but we managed to have a good time." Amber studied Sherry's face. "You're twirling your hair. You know more than you're willing to share. I get it. I don't need to know right now, and at the moment I have too much on my mind."

"Too soon for any real answers. That's one thing I've learned from a past murder investigation or two. Facts will fall into place when the right people step forward. Ray Bease is on the case." Sherry was interested in steering the conversation in a lighter direction, which was difficult when she had questions she'd love answered as soon as possible.

"That's it?" Amber paused and Sherry let the silence linger. "Oh, no. Something happened. Did you discuss your dream with Don?"

"You're very good at reading people. I brought up the subject, and before I even told him about my dream, he apologized for anything he may have said the night of my injury about any possibility of our future together. He hoped the topic didn't upset me. He basically retracted any reference to happily ever after."

"I'm sorry. Hope you're not too disappointed."

"No, no, don't worry about me. This moment is about you. We need to make sure you're feeling confident about your cook-off chances. That's why you're here."

"You caught me. Yes, I'm a little shaky."

"Some nerves are normal and necessary. They give you energy and focus, so embrace them."

"You're the best, I feel better already. What about you?" Amber said. She gave her friend a quick hug.

"All is well. Don and I are happy and the relationship is moving forward in a great direction. I couldn't ask for anything more."

"I don't believe you but I'm too tired to argue. See you tomorrow." Amber bid Sherry good evening before heading home.

"See you tomorrow," Sherry called after Amber. She was relieved Amber made no mention Ray had called her. He had listened to Sherry's request and kept his distance for the time being. Whatever it was he wanted to speak to Amber about could wait until after the cook-off.

• • •

Wednesday morning, the day of the cook-off, was one of the finest Sherry had seen all spring. Gentle lukewarm breezes, sparse puffy clouds and newly sprouted greenery overwhelmed her senses as she walked from her parked car to the Sound Shore Lodge to accept any last-minute instructions she'd be given. Inside the lodge, cooks dressed in casual attire, functional shoes and the contest-logoed apron were milling about the lobby. On the far side of the building, she joined her fellow volunteers in a holding pattern by the lodge's side door.

"Good morning, everyone," Rickie said as she neared the group. "In a few minutes we will head over to the cook-off, ahead of the cooks. They will follow about ten minutes later in a procession so that the audience gets a good look at who is competing. Reminder to mute your phones. If you have any last-minute messages to send or receive, now's the time. Thank you again for all your hard work."

Before muting her phone, Sherry took the opportunity to read a text that had come in from Pep.

Stop by the truck at lunchtime. Sample the fare.

She confirmed she would. Her voicemail indicated she had one unacknowledged message. She clicked on the phone number to have the transcript of her message pop up.

"Sherry, Ray here. Call me back. It's about Amber. I left a message with her, too."

"He didn't!" Sherry growled. "He said he wouldn't!"

Sherry crafted a scolding message to Ray. Before she hit the Send button the group of volunteers began to leave the building. She left her emotional text unsent. Knowing the rules prohibiting electronic devices, Sherry set her phone on mute and tucked it in her pocket.

On the walk to the convention hall Sherry lagged behind the others. The stroll across the street meandered close to the bluffs overlooking the rocky beach below. As she neared the edge the wind picked up. Cooled by the ocean winds, Sherry hugged her arms across her chest.

"Cold?" a voice behind her asked.

Sherry turned and saw Bart Foster gaining ground on her.

"Amazing how the water can lower the air temperature," he said.

"I love the feel and the smell of the salty breeze," Sherry responded.

"I was at the dinner last night on behalf of my clients, the Washingtons," Bart said. "With Livvy."

Sherry stepped away from the edge of the bluff. "I'm sure she appreciated that. I heard the evening was very nice, and Gray was on everyone's minds."

"Very nice, indeed, with the exception of one man's behavior. Walter

Hemphill was temperamental and clinging to the idea he was wronged. I'm keeping a close eye on him in order to keep Livvy safe. Doesn't he have respect for lost life?" Bart scanned the surroundings. "I'll be in the audience this morning. Livvy will be presenting the grand prize package and I want to make sure the ceremony proceeds without incident."

"Again, she'll appreciate your efforts," Sherry said. She watched her colleagues move nearly out of sight ahead of her. "I need to get going."

"One more thing, Sherry." Bart lowered his voice. "Your friend, Amber. Would you say you trust her implicitly?"

"With my life," Sherry said with a touch of aggravation in her tone.

"Okay, thanks." Bart turned on his heels and strutted away.

When she entered the convention hall, Sherry located the cook stations she was assigned to. Name placards adorned the work counters, and since the contestants had yet to arrive, she took the opportunity to find the row Amber's station was situated in. An oven, a cutting board, a small countertop. No sign of a stray knife having been returned. Rickie hadn't returned her call about the knives. Whether the woman was too busy or had no news to share was unclear. Sherry checked the oversized clock on the distant wall at the front of the room. Twenty minutes until go time. She wouldn't have a chance to talk to Amber before the cook-off horn blew proclaiming the start of the contest, nor did she wish to, for fear the news about the detective's call was negative in any way.

Sherry returned to her assigned group's stations. She mentally acclimated herself to the paths from the cooks' ovens to the mini refrigerators containing their perishable ingredients and the bins filled with presorted dry goods. Moments later, murmurings circulated that the procession of cooks was on its way down the hall.

The line of cooks was halted at the door until the audience seats were filled. The cooks entered the cook-off room in a double line accompanied by an upbeat soundtrack played through overhead speakers. Clapping signaled the cooks were manning their stations one by one and the cook-off was imminent. Sherry was energized by the charged atmosphere. She caught sight of Amber walking in. Not far behind her was Jean McDonald. Both ladies wore a fragile smile while clapping an enthusiastic beat, as Rickie had instructed the cooks to do. Amber glanced Sherry's way but didn't seem to see her, which was understandable considering the intense sensory overload occurring.

When the cooks found their assigned stations, Rickie made a short introductory address to the room, followed by a horn blast. The cook-off was underway. At the start signal half the cooks raced to collect their supplies from the refrigerators and bins while the other half appeared shell-shocked and frozen for a split second. Sherry knew that feeling well, and also understood the panic would pass in an instant, leaving everyone on a level playing field.

It wasn't long before Sherry had requests for refrigerated ingredients, cups of water and information on how often cooks were allowed to use the restroom. If the assistance required two fully functional hands, Sherry asked for reinforcements. To her surprise, she was an accomplished multitasker using only a hand and a half.

The constant motion on the cook-off floor was intoxicating and Sherry's adrenaline never ceased to flow. The time allotted to the cooks to prepare their recipes would pass in the blink of an eye. With Sherry's help the cooks would put out their best efforts and not be bogged down with miscues. As the cooks settled down to work Sherry was rewarded with a moment of relative calm and made a silent wager to herself as to which recipe within her group had the best possibility of garnishing one of the prizes. That was the last moment of calm Sherry experienced until the cook-off was over. She changed her mind four times during the first ninety minutes of the cook-off as to the winner within her group. Interesting ingredient combinations swayed her opinion one way, before aroma tempted her in another direction. Later, the completed presentation of another dish changed her opinion. Another reason she would never want to judge a cook-off. She had only judged one cookie bake-off and that had ended in murder.

With about a half hour left to go, Sherry settled on Gloria Evans's Penobscot Seafood Ramen, a recipe prepared by a well-seasoned veteran cooking contestant from Maine, as the most likely to collect a prize from her group. Her silent wager was if the recipe she chose won she would ask the cook whether her brother, Pep, could use a variation of her recipe as an item on his truck's menu. The seafood-laden sauce over a piece of sourdough toast would be heavenly. Thirty minutes to go until Sherry would find out if she was on the right track. If Sherry couldn't compete in the cook-off with her culinary skills, she'd settle for silently competing with her culinary know-how.

When the horn sounded for the completion of the two hours allotted to the cooks, all dishes had been presented to the judges. Sherry was thanked by her cooks for the help she gave. With her duties complete, Sherry headed to Amber's cook station to congratulate her on what she was sure was a job well done.

"How'd it go?"

"I surprised myself," Amber said. "My presentation was as good as I could have imagined. No burnt edges, nothing was runny, presentation was eye-catching. I might have a chance." She held up two crossed fingers. "I made do with the smaller knife." She frowned. "Sorry, but there's no sign of the missing knife. Jean said hers remains vanished without a trace, too."

"Please don't worry about it. It can always be replaced," Sherry said. "Ray said he left you a phone message."

Before Amber could respond the loudspeaker crackled to life.

"Ladies and gentlemen, may we have your attention, please. Cooks, I know you're exhausted, but if you'd stay by your workstation for a few more minutes we are ready to announce the five prize winners."

"Only a voicemail. Didn't say much," Amber whispered. She and Sherry remained poised to listen for the reading of the winners' names.

As each of the five winners was called up, one by one, to the stage at the front of the room and awarded progressively more valuable checks, Sherry kept her hopes alive Amber's name would be called. She heard Jean McDonald called for fourth place and heartily applauded for the woman's Tidewater Smothered and Stuffed Chicken Noodle Casserole. Sherry made a mental note to execute Jean's recipe at home to uncover its winning components, as the title gave no hint as to what the dish was made of, besides chicken and noodles.

Third prize was called, which made Sherry a winner in her private competition. Taking pride in her ability to spot a winning recipe, she would speak to the cook from her group to see if she could obtain permission to serve a variation of Penobscot Seafood Ramen on Pep's truck. The tomato, basil, shrimp and cod concoction would make a perfect nod to New England's local seafood bounty. Swap out the ramen and serve it on toast. Sherry already had changes to the recipe in mind to make it her own, so as not to step on the owner's rights, which was the contest's once the recipe was named a winner.

"Gloria Evans was in my group. I had a good feeling she would pick up a prize," Sherry whispered to Amber.

"I knew you'd make a good judge," Amber said.

"Nope. I'm a cook, not a judge."

"Do you have that same feeling for my recipe? Two prizes to go."

Sherry nodded yes, but she wasn't on board with Amber's recipe being a winner after she saw many of the other recipes. Amber's was great but lacked a simple complexity Sherry knew was hard to obtain. Only the winning recipes reached that level of perfection. Second prize was announced, and it wasn't Amber's to claim. The grand prize was Amber's last hope. It was not to be. A woman from Colorado, Rosie Janson, won the grand prize of ten thousand dollars and the appliance package worth twice that amount. As the woman made her way up to Rickie at the podium to accept the check, Sherry stole a glance at Amber. Amber was smiling for the woman and applauding her competition with full conviction.

"I remember her recipe when I walked around the contest floor. She took a Denver steak, seasoned it with a homemade smoky blend of spices, grilled it to perfection. She topped the thin slices with blue cheese and served them on flat egg noodles with a Ranch horseradish sauce of her design. Less really is more. That seems to be a theme in this contest," Amber said. "At least I have the talent to recognize a great recipe. Now I just have to up my game to concocting one."

Sherry smiled. "You're a good sport. Sounds like you've got the bug," Sherry said. "Here comes Livvy Washington to present the prize package." Sherry's gaze tracked Livvy ambling from the front row of seats to the stage. She was striding in a full-length flowing day dress requiring a slow deliberate gait so as not to catch the material underfoot. By the time she reached the stage the audience had begun a low chatter. Livvy had to put up her hands to regain the audience's attention.

"Good morning. Congratulations to all the fine cooks here today at the Kitchen Royalty Use Your Noodle Cook-off. I will be presenting the winner with a set of Washington Appliances. My husband passed away yesterday, as most of you are aware, and I am here to represent him and our business. He was so honored to be part of the cook-off. Rosie Janson" —Livvy looked at the woman to her left—"has made a recipe that has won her royal status in the kitchen. Before we unveil the prizes, located to everyone's right, I do have an announcement to make. Washington Appliances will again be sponsoring the Kitchen Royalty Use Your Noodle Recipe Cook-off next year. We are so happy to partner with Rickie O'Dell and her fabulous team to bring the contest the best appliance prize packages the industry offers."

The audience gave Livvy a round of applause as the silky tarp was lifted off of Rosie Janson's prizes. Everyone oohed and aahed a chorus of admiration. As Livvy stepped aside she was met by Bart. Sherry paid close attention to the interaction between the two and tried to interpret their facial expressions.

"The body's still warm," Amber whispered to Sherry. "She didn't have much of a mourning period. I guess business is business."

"I wonder. Was this all planned?" Sherry thought out loud.

Chapter 9

"You'll get 'em next time, Amber. I have no doubt," Pep said as he handed Amber her lunch order. The line in front of his truck was long and he was hustling to keep up with orders. Sherry watched him from behind Amber with admiration as he maintained constant motion to keep up the timely customer service.

"There's a picnic table over here," Sherry said when she received her order. She carried her recycled paper plate to a wooden table with bench seating. Sherry didn't wait for Amber to sit down to start her lunch. She attacked her tuna niçoise toast with abandon. "Pep has outdone himself."

"Yours looks so good," Amber said. "I thought I would go the healthy route and try his Cowgirl Avocado Toast." She took a bite of the toasted multigrain bread, chunky avocado and black bean creation. "Such a lovely beach overlook."

"Isn't it?" Sherry said. "Reminds me of my childhood."

Amber dabbed her mouth with a napkin. "Maybe I should join Pep's truck and become his sous chef. I think he's on to something here."

"If you think you can spare the hours, maybe you should. It might be a gold mine for both of you. Sure seems like he would benefit from another pair of hands."

"Now that the cook-off is over, I have some time to give the matter more thought. Is the knife set safely back in your car?"

"Safe in the car. I slid the case under the driver's seat and locked the car." Sherry licked an errant tuna chunk off her lip. "Can I change the subject? Want to talk about what Ray said to you? Or will it spoil the mood?"

"You seem to think he gave me bad news." Amber squinted and held her gaze on Sherry. "You know something, don't you?"

Sherry produced a slight grimace. "What did he say?"

"His voicemail said to call him after the cook-off because the investigation team found something in Gray Washington's hotel room that has some relation to me."

Sherry savored her last bite before swallowing. "That's all he said? Relation to you? In his hotel room?"

Amber nodded before taking another bite.

"How well did you know Gray Washington?"

Amber kept her sights on her lunch. "I told you. Not that well."

Sherry considered how Amber did a good job of switching topics last time this subject was brought up.

"I'm sure it's not a big deal. What they found may be associated with me. If it is, I wouldn't worry too much about it. Since it's a murder investigation, nothing is out of bounds in terms of evidence consideration early on."

"I don't think it's a big deal either. What do you think they could have found?"

"When I was living in Boston, I was a marriage and family therapist, as you know. It's not unheard of to have an old business card of mine from my practice or even a referral of some sort. I'll let you know exactly what it is they found when I talk to Ray." Amber took a long look at Sherry. "Are you concerned for me? Your forehead is screwed up pretty tight."

"Hey, you two," a familiar male voice called out from the food truck. "How are you liking your lunch?"

Sherry grinned when she turned and saw Pep leaning out of the truck's pass-through window. She and Amber gave him the thumbs-up.

"Get back to work, little brother," Sherry said. "You're holding up the line of hungry lunchers."

A man in shorts and a T-shirt strolled up to the table. His angular face was strong and attractive. His prevalent cheekbones lifted his mouth into an inviting smile. "What a view," he said. "You're lucky to live in such a beautiful area of the country, Amber. The Boston winters are way too long and the summers are way too short."

"Hi, Tig. Augustin isn't that far from Boston," she said and laughed. "Our weather's pretty similar. Glad you could make it for lunch."

"What is it you two ladies ordered? I'd need a forensic scientist to figure the answer out from what's left on your plates. Looks like you ate every morsel," Tig said. He leaned toward Amber's plate. "Wait. I see one crumb we can work with."

Sherry broke out into a broad smile at the man's colorful humor.

"Sherry, this is my friend Tig," Amber said. "He came down from Boston to watch the cook-off. He wants to enter a cooking competition someday. He's also my ex's great buddy. They share the same silly sense of humor."

"The famous Sherry Oliveri. Amber speaks so highly of you. I wish I could have watched you compete today. I can see why you weren't able to," Tig said as he gazed at Sherry's bandaged hand. "Amber did a good job today, don't you think?" He held up his thermos. "Care for some iced tea? I brought my own in case the food truck didn't have any. It's my drink of choice."

"She certainly did. I can't stop complimenting her," Sherry said with a nod. "And no, thank you, to the iced tea."

"I'm learning from the best," Amber added.

"I'm going to check in with Livvy Washington this afternoon if I can locate her," Tig said. "I can't imagine what she's going through." He turned to face Sherry. "Her husband was in our practice for a while. I think I owe her at least the effort of asking her how she's coping."

"That's a nice idea," Amber said.

Tig made a move toward the food truck. "I'm starving. I'll be back in a few. Anything you two need?"

"No, thanks." Both women declined his offer at the same time.

"There's a whole Boston contingency here." Amber laughed.

"Tig's a nice guy. Handsome, too," Sherry said. "Are you sure there aren't any romantic undertones between you two?"

"You get right to the point," Amber said with a laugh. "No is the short answer. Just friends." She pulled her phone from her pocket. "Mind if I call Ray while you're with me? Just in case the conversation takes a turn."

"Please do," Sherry said with more vitality in her words than she'd intended.

"Hi, Ray. I'm returning your call," Amber said when Ray picked up. "What can I do for you?" She clicked the phone's speaker button.

"Thank you for returning my call, Amber. I'll be brief. The investigation team searched the room Gray Washington was staying in at the Sound Shore Lodge. What we found was a bundle of letter paper and envelopes addressed to you here in Augustin. Have you received any correspondence from Mr. Washington?" Ray asked.

Sherry saw Amber's expression freeze. She kept her gaze on her phone and made no effort to reply.

"Amber? Did you?" Sherry prompted.

"Hello, Sherry. I didn't know you were with Amber." Ray had adhered to Sherry's request not to burden Amber before the cook-off, and for that she was grateful. At the same time, a cold chill went through her core when he addressed her. He was inflecting his voice with the seriousness of an investigation, meaning his patience was shorter than usual.

"Hi, Ray. Yes. We're having some lunch after the cook-off," Sherry said.

Amber began to speak but her voice was garbled so she cleared her throat and began again. "Yes, one note. I was his therapist years ago. He knew I lived in Augustin. Nothing newsworthy."

"Were you aware he would be attending the cook-off?" Ray asked.

"No one was aware until a few days before the event," Sherry said. "He was a last-minute substitution."

"Amber? Were you?"

Sherry winced at her dismissal by Ray.

"Yes, I knew," Amber said.

"He meant did you know before the cook-off," Sherry corrected.

"I know what he meant, and yes, I did know," Amber said without making eye contact with Sherry.

Sherry lowered her gaze to the ground.

"Amber," Ray began, "how well did you know Gray Washington?"

"We shared a client-patient relationship. He came to a number of sessions to work on his marriage difficulties. Beyond that I'm not willing to break patient-therapist confidentiality. I'm sorry, Ray."

"While you're on the line, Sherry, I'd like to ask you a question." As Sherry braced for Ray's words, Tig rejoined the ladies. He sat down beside Amber and began working on his Ranch Steak Bruschetta toast.

"Okay," Sherry said with hesitation.

"Why didn't you tell me you had a set of Hunziker knives when we were discussing the benefits of owning such a superior cutlery set and yours went missing?"

Sherry released a slow breath. "I assumed you knew?" The statement came out as a question. She visualized Ray shaking his head in frustration.

"Me, assume?"

"Oh, right. Never. Forgot who I was speaking to." Sherry took a moment to take in Tig enjoying his toast. The contentment on his face spoke volumes. "Out of fifty contestants were there only two sets of Hunziker knives?"

"Only two went missing that I'm aware of," Ray said.

Amber lowered the phone below the table. "Did you tell him your knife went missing?"

Sherry shrugged. "Not exactly," she whispered. The phone reappeared above the table.

"But he knew two knives went missing. Who told him?"

Before Sherry could speculate, Ray continued.

"Rickie O'Dell told me Amber used a Hunziker six-inch knife and it also went missing," he said. "I was told she borrowed it from Sherry and felt awful about misplacing it. I should have learned those facts from you, Sherry."

"You taught me not to answer questions that aren't asked. I'm a good student."

"Hmm."

"I had a strong feeling we would stumble on my knife somewhere before I needed to report it missing to you. It has my initials on the handle, making it easily recognizable. How can anyone feel they can get away with stealing it?" Sherry explained.

"Did the knife materialize?" Ray asked.

"Not yet."

"I'm getting her a replacement," Amber said.

Sherry relaxed her clenched jaw. "Please don't worry about the cost."

"You say that, but I can't rest until I either repay you for the cost or buy you a replacement. Either of which I will do as soon as I can," Amber said.

"Ladies, ladies, would you mind settling your issue after this call. I have to keep moving," Ray said. "I have one last question for you, Amber." There was silence on both ends of the phone until Ray cleared his throat. "Was there any part of your relationship with Gray Washington that you would categorize as outside the patient-client boundaries?"

Without hesitation Amber said, "Yes." She turned to Tig beside her. "I'm not sure I should say anymore. I'll get a lawyer if I need to, but I'm worried about breaking my oath as a former mental health-care provider by disclosing my patient's information."

Tig nodded.

"What about Walter Hemphill?" Sherry asked. "That man had reasons to seek revenge on Gray Washington. He's the one who lost the sponsorship and his business's reputation may have been sullied. He's the one you should focus on, Ray."

"I am aware of Mr. Hemphill's situation," Ray said. "My job is to check out all leads."

Sherry faced her friend. "Amber, you don't have to say any more."

"It's okay. What I am at liberty to say is the truth and I stand by my words. What I can elaborate on is already public knowledge."

Tig wiped his mouth and leaned in close to Amber. "Are you sure you want to say more?"

"I'm sure. My clinical, and amicable, relationship with Gray

Washington went off the rails when he threatened to sue my practice, which in many ways led me down a slippery slope, ending in my business filing for bankruptcy. The suit was never actually filed, but there was an extended period of lawyering up, threats and posturing by both sides."

"I see," Ray said.

Sherry closed her eyes. She opened them when she made the abrupt decision Amber should end the phone call. She gestured to Amber, swiping her bandaged hand across her throat to suggest cutting the phone call off.

Amber gave Sherry an agreeable nod. "Ray, I have to get going. I'd like to say goodbye to some cooks I became friendly with during the last few days and they're beginning to disperse."

"Sure," Ray said. "I know where to reach you."

Amber pocketed her phone and turned to Sherry. "I don't like talking about that time in my previous career. The memory is a rough one for me. It affected my marriage also. Tig knows that as well as anyone. He was a good friend to both Jeff and me during those trying times. Even dog-sat our Jack Russell, Titan."

Tig mugged an angelic expression. "He was small but mighty."

Sherry scanned the surroundings. She lowered her voice. "We don't have to talk about it right now, but at some point, you need to tell me where you were when Gray Washington was murdered with the knife that may or may not have come from the knife kit in your possession. What you've told Ray could come with consequences if we don't clear your name. What's your alibi?"

"After I saw you, I went home, I walked Bean, I made one more run to the grocery store, I walked Bean again. Then I went to the dinner. Afterward, I knew I wouldn't sleep much so I tried to keep busy. In the morning, I had a change of plans. I wasn't going to the contestants' breakfast, which is a freebie offered those staying at the hotel, but at the last minute I decided to go rather than pace my front hallway. I was so early the doors hadn't even opened to the buffet yet, so I took a walk around the lodge's grounds. A lovely blanket of snow had fallen overnight. I knew it would melt soon with the rising temperatures." She lifted her arm and pushed up her shirtsleeve.

"Rickie found Gray's body after the orientation, but he may have been there all night as far as I know. Let's cover every base as to your whereabouts, to be extra sure. Did anyone see you walking the grounds?"

"I did," Tig said. "I came over from the inn to find her when she texted me. I couldn't talk my way into the breakfast, so I left to find a bagel store. By the time I returned she texted she was at the beach on a walk. I wasn't brave enough to conquer the snowy bluffs that early."

"I was restless. The other contestants got to return to their rooms but I had nowhere else to go," Amber said.

"So far, so good. You were seen by many people. Except for the time on your walk." Sherry's eyes widened. "Did you see Gray and Livvy Washington at the previous night's dinner?"

"Yes. They were seated at the sponsors table with Rickie, the Kitchen Royalty reps, and Rickie's cook-off team members."

"You spoke to them?"

"Not at dinner."

"You were home by nine?" Sherry asked.

"Not exactly," Amber said as she lowered her chin.

"You went out with Tig afterward?"

"I didn't even ask her if she was interested in meeting me after dinner. I didn't want to be responsible for keeping her out too late," Tig said.

"Okay." Disappointment crept into Sherry's tone. "Where did you go, if not home?"

"At the end of dinner when everyone was leaving, I searched for Rickie to return the key you gave me. I didn't want to do it in front of others at dinner in case anyone thought I had an unfair connection to the cook-off organizer. Before I found her, I was approached by the Washingtons after the sponsor table broke up. That was my first mistake, letting myself be distracted from the task at hand. I didn't recognize Gray until he reintroduced himself. It's been years since I've seen him and definitely out of context from the sessions we had in the office. He's put on a substantial amount of weight and lost a fair bit of hair up top. I'd never met his wife. After I spoke to the Washingtons, a man named Walter Hemphill came up to me," Amber said.

"He's the man whose company was the prior sponsor of the appliance package," Sherry said.

"Yes. That surprised me. What was he even doing there?"

"Long story. What did he want? Just being friendly?"

"He wanted to know what I was speaking to the couple about. On the contrary, I thought he was quite rude and I made him understand I had no intention of sharing a private conversation. He grumbled about being excluded from the sponsor table. Hemphill may have known I was the one who . . ." Amber's words died out.

"Who what?" Sherry asked.

"I was the one who reached out to Gray as a nice gesture. Unfinished business doesn't sit well with me," Amber said.

Sherry opened her mouth to speak. Only a puff of air came out.

"That was very nice of you after what Gray put you through," Tig said.

"And you, too," Amber said. "He really put us under more pressure than the Back Bay Therapy practice could withstand."

"You reached out to the Washingtons to suggest they become the next appliance sponsor?"

"I did."

"You're a good person," Sherry said.

"Or a fool."

"Not a fool at all," Tig said.

"Then you went home that night?"

"No. The Washingtons asked me for a favor. Then they went off to the powder rooms to freshen up, that's when Walter appeared."

"Favor? Not sure you owed them a favor. Maybe the other way around," Sherry said.

"The story is a lot more involved than that. But, in the end, I'm always willing to forgive and forget."

"What did he want from you?" Tig asked.

"He said his wife wanted to change something about the appliance display over at the convention hall and did I know who would unlock the door for them. Rickie had made a quick exit from dinner and was nowhere to be found. I think they thought since I knew you, a cook-off volunteer, I could help them."

"Interesting," Sherry said. "So Livvy initiated a trip over there that night. She would be able to corroborate the fact you weren't with them at that time. That's all you need. You have your alibi."

Amber rolled her eyes toward the sky, as if mulling over Sherry's assertion.

"Unfortunately, I was with them, as was their friend Bart Foster," Amber said.

Sherry opened her mouth to speak but thought better of interrupting Amber's train of thought.

"I offered to open the convention hall door for them since I hadn't found Rickie to return the key. What could it hurt was my feeling at the time. The decision may have been fueled by a glass or two of wonderful Chardonnay at dinner."

"You're way too nice," Sherry said. She knew Amber did not enjoy this scenario. She was a proud pragmatist and never relished in being proven wrong after she had considered every option and made her choice. Sherry, on the other hand, often made decisions based on emotions and was familiar with those consequences. "How is it that Bart Foster tagged along?"

"He jumped into our conversation. He appeared out of nowhere," Amber said. "The Washingtons invited him to join us."

"You let the group into the convention hall and maybe they moved the appliances around a bit, which wasn't hard because each sat on a palette on rollers," Sherry said. "That's all?"

"I didn't hang around long enough to see what they did because Rickie walked in. I hadn't gotten behind the curtain. She was curious as to what I was doing there. Said she saw some lights on outside the building. It looked as if I was all alone when she first caught sight of me. I was so embarrassed. I couldn't let her know I had the key and used it to let a group in. I felt like a teenager caught sneaking a smoke behind the shed. She was kind enough to accept my explanation that I was invited by the Washingtons to accompany them to the hall to shuffle their products around to their liking. I told her I didn't feel comfortable taking a look at the prize, which was why I was all alone in the huge room while everyone else was up onstage behind the curtain."

"I didn't tell you the key only fit the side door. Did you have trouble unlocking the building?"

"When I tried the front entrance, you're right, the key didn't fit. Livvy suggested the side door. She said that entrance was used to move the appliances in. I took the suggestion and ran around the side of the building. Kind of scary in the dark. Plus, it was beginning to snow and the footing was slippery. I wouldn't do that again. I was spooked when something rustled in a bush to my side. I made it and didn't even need to use the key, as the door was unlocked."

"Really? But no one saw you open an unlocked door?"

"That's right. No one did. That won't help me if the investigators don't believe I didn't use the key," Amber said with a groan.

"The building was open to anyone who wanted in," Sherry said.

"You're right. But if no one was aware of that fact and I was holding the key . . ." Amber paused. "Come to think of it, it wouldn't help me if they thought I used the key in my possession." She hung her head. "Guilty in both scenarios. Wrong place at the wrong time."

"Don't worry. We'll figure this out." Sherry let her sights drift over to Pep's truck while she gave the matter more thought. "Once inside, you didn't go behind the curtain at all?"

"No, I didn't. Probably the only thing I did right. I would think everyone's fingerprints except mine would be all over those appliances, reenforcing my story, right?"

Sherry sucked in a deep breath. "Unfortunately, no. Rickie and I spent a good amount of time and effort removing prints and smudges from the stainless steel surfaces so the newness shone through. Thinking back, she was quite adamant about a thorough wipe down," Sherry said as she recalled Rickie's sense of urgency.

"So, you're saying there's no proof my story is an accurate portrayal of the truth unless Livvy, Bart Foster and Rickie give their sides of the story and all the pieces of the puzzle fit together in a time line that tracks my every move?" Amber threw up her hands. "There were gaps where I didn't see anyone."

"Okay, let's go down another avenue. You said you had a history with Gray. How was your perceived rapport with him that night? Did people see you two laughing and joking and sharing positive words? That's something," Sherry said with a nod of her head.

Amber took a moment before answering. "We started out on pleasant terms. He sought me out. He was chatty at first. As soon as Livvy and Bart joined us the tone of the conversation turned combative. Livvy launched into a topic I wasn't privy to. Definitely a disagreement between the two. And Bart was on Livvy's side."

"But Gray wasn't upset with you specifically?" Sherry asked.

"No. When he asked, I agreed to accompany them. Maybe not immediately, but as I said, the Chardonnay clouded my better judgment. Gray went on ahead while Bart looked for his coat. He was very eager to go on ahead of the rest of us even though I had the key. Of course, it turned out he didn't need the key. The side door was unlocked." Amber nodded her head.

"You met him there?" Sherry asked Amber. "You, Livvy and Bart?"

"I never saw him there. When I got there I was spooked by noises along the pathway and regretting every moment of what I had originally considered a good deed, taking them all to the convention hall. Especially when Rickie appeared. I begged off and left for my car, back at the lodge."

"Rickie could have locked the door when she left the hall that night, except we had her key. She probably called security to come lock up." Sherry paused while she considered the scenario. "None of that's going to convince Ray you have an alibi. I understand he has to do his job and follow the clues, but we have to nudge this along in the right direction," Sherry said.

Amber tossed her hands up in the air. "We can't do anything about this right now. Let's go check in on Pep. I want to say hi to Charlotte and baby Mimi." She pointed to the tall blonde cuddling a baby. "Then I'm going home to change and get over to the Ruggery. I promised Erno I'd spot him for a few hours before closing time."

"Okay, sure."

"Come on, Tig. Let's go see that cutie," Amber said with vigor.

The trio trotted over to the food truck, where the line was thinning out.

"Charlotte and my favorite niece." Sherry whisked baby Mimi out of her mother's arms and gave her a noisy kiss.

"I think she looks a lot like you, Sherry," Amber said as she stroked the baby's wispy hair.

"If only I were half as cute," Sherry said.

Tig was introduced to Charlotte and Mimi. He gave a rave review of Pep's Steak Bruschetta toast.

"I'll pass that along," Charlotte said. "I'm feeling very good about the success of his truck. I have to admit I was a skeptic at first. His entire plan is really growing on me."

"Last call," Pep called out.

"I think you're done," Sherry called back. There was no longer a line and the picnic tables were nearly empty.

Pep disappeared from the window and reappeared out the back of his truck. He gave baby Mimi, then Charlotte, the same brand of noisy cheek kiss Sherry delivered. "How is everyone doing?"

"Pep, do you know Tig? He's eaten at your truck twice. Not sure he's introduced himself," Amber said.

"Not formally, no." Pep shook Tig's hand. "Nice to meet any friend of Amber's. She's a special friend to the Oliveri family."

"Is this a family affair?" A couple holding hands approached the food truck. "You look as if you are all related."

"Most of us are, Jean," said Sherry. "This is my brother, my sister-in-law and my favorite niece. Amber is an honorary family member. And her friend Tig. You two on your way home?"

Jean and Curt exchanged glances.

"Either Friday or Saturday," Curt said. "A Detective Bease has asked us to stay local for at least one more day since Jean's knife may have been the murder weapon used to kill that poor man, Gray Washington. No skin off our nose. We love this town."

Sherry and Amber exchanged glances before Amber returned her sights to the McDonalds.

"I texted your friend Don about riding his water taxi back to Long Island to pick up our car," Curt said. "He's so nice to be flexible. Rickie O'Dell says the contest will pick up the tab for the extra night's stay at the lodge and the transportation under these extraordinary circumstances."

"Wasn't that just so awful about Gray Washington?" Jean asked. "To think, we were all on the boat together, alive and well. Bet his wife is sorry she laid into him so hard on what was to be his last day on earth."

Everyone agreed with a nod of the head and a soft yes.

"Did you two have a chance to spend any more time with him before he passed away?" Sherry asked. She could feel Amber's sights linger on her long after she asked the question.

"No, well, actually Jean did. Right, honey?" Curt said.

"That's right and I'm glad of it, with one exception," Jean said. "After the dinner, he came up to me and asked whether I had seen his prize appliances in person. He remembered I was unhappy about Hemphill Custom Appliances being pulled in favor of his. He wanted to prove a point that his were just as fabulous. His question caught me by surprise and all I could say was the truth, no. He wanted to take me down to the convention hall and show me how wonderful his appliances were. He was adamant about it."

"I don't think going with him would have been a good idea," Sherry said.

"I said yes to going with him, actually," Jean said. "I told him to go on ahead and I would tell Curt where I was going. I excused myself, gave the matter some more thought and never went down to meet him."

"Oh, and he mentioned Amber was letting folks into the hall with her key."

"Oh, no. I'm getting the feeling I'm being blamed for an explosion of events, ignited by my bad judgment," Amber said.

"Not at all, dear," Jean said. "The missing knives, the change of sponsors, the murder may have all happened without your involvement."

"Not necessarily," said Amber. She tucked in her chin and rubbed her forehead.

Chapter 10

"Sherry, if anyone can figure out what's behind Gray's untimely death, it's you. I've heard some fascinating tales of your sleuthing prowess," Curt said. He yanked on his wife's elbow. "You ready, dear?"

"We're off to explore Augustin," Jean said as she backed away. "I think we'll check out the historical society. Have a good day, everyone. Tell Don we'll firm up our departure very soon." She hooked arms with Curt and they strolled away.

"Amber, what did you mean when you said your involvement may have had something to do with the missing knives, change of sponsors and Gray's murder?" Sherry asked.

"I can't deny, I was the one who suggested Gray's company take on the sponsorship role when there was an opening. I knew it would be good for his business, which was struggling. I had been in contact with him recently and the timing worked out in his favor," Amber said. "Who would have predicted the outcome of my actions?"

"A generous referral, I'd say," Tig said. "I'm sure the Washingtons were grateful."

"No good deed goes unpunished. Now Sherry insists I need to come up with an alibi. I have the impression she isn't fully convinced of my innocence," Amber's words caught in her throat.

"You're tired, Amber. Don't misinterpret Sherry's concern for you for anything other than that," Charlotte said. "We all need to go home and take a few minutes for ourselves."

"You're absolutely right, Charlotte," Sherry said. "Amber's taking my concern the wrong way."

"I'm not tired. I'm frustrated by this crazy situation," Amber said. "Best thing for me is to head over to the Ruggery to get back to work and lick my wounds for not placing in the cook-off. See you all soon." She kissed Mimi on the head and walked away.

"I'll walk you to your car," Tig said. "Bye, all. Thanks again for lunch."

"I haven't been in on this conversation for very long, but I don't like what I'm hearing. What's going on between you and Amber?" Pep asked. "The tone in her voice was a bit defensive. Not the usual animated banter."

Sherry sighed. Baby Mimi cooed and closed her eyes. "She's in Ray

Bease's crosshairs. Not only was Gray Washington killed with a Hunziker knife, and the one she used in the cook-off is missing, but she has a past with him, not devoid of animosity. Plus, letter paper and envelopes addressed to her were found in Gray's hotel room. To make matters worse, Rickie and I inadvertently erased the evidence that may have proved Amber wasn't at the scene. Amber wasn't anywhere near the appliances and the lack of her fingerprints on the stainless steel surfaces would have helped substantiate that claim. Now nobody's prints are on them."

"Amber has a past with the murdered man?" Charlotte asked. "In what way?"

"Gray was a patient at her therapy practice," Sherry said.

"Along with many others, I'm sure," Pep said. "Was there a specific incident that occurred that would make them adversaries?"

"Yes, a pretty significant one. She wouldn't offer many details. The short version of the story is Gray began a lawsuit against her practice."

"That qualifies as an adversarial act, most definitely," Charlotte said.

"When she began to open up about that time in her life, I think I pressed too hard and she tightened up like a clam out of water," Sherry said with a pout. "I feel bad about that. Like I broke the girlfriend code. Don't pressure me and I won't pressure you. That's what friends do."

"You were only trying to help her," Charlotte said. She reached over to Sherry and stroked her baby's pink cheek.

"If anyone can help, it's you, Sherry," Pep said. "Now, unless you're interested in helping me with my cleanup, I need to get a move on. The lodge wants me out of here in a timely fashion. Oh, and I think I've made up my mind on my menu for the opening of the food truck to the general public. The cook-off crowd has spoken, and if I trust anyone's opinion of food it would be cooking contestants. Next, I have to come up with a clever name for the operation." He returned to his truck before taking any questions or comments.

Sherry kissed Mimi's cheek and handed the baby back to Charlotte. Charlotte held her gaze on Sherry, prompting her to ask, "Anything else you want to talk about?"

Charlotte snuggled closer to Mimi's face. "How well do you think you know Amber? I mean, the Amber we didn't know, prior to moving to Augustin?"

Sherry rotated away from Charlotte while collecting her thoughts. She turned back after a moment. "I only know what she's relayed to me, and visa versa. Of course, she hasn't told me every single detail. Which is to be expected, except now might be the time. She and I are both pretty good judges of character and I'm very secure in my feeling Amber isn't sitting on something that will blow up in all of our faces. On the other hand, knowing what's coming would be a plus."

"From what you've described, she is sitting on something. Wouldn't you agree?"

"Seems like it. There's something between Amber and Gray she either thinks isn't pertinent or, more likely, she's protecting him for some reason. I need to help Amber. She's a very proud person and may not be seeing the gravity of the situation."

"I think she does and she's still locked up tight," Charlotte said. She rocked her baby to soothe the fussy gurgles she began making. "I'm worried you're not seeing the forest for the trees. Maybe you're too close to the situation to get a good perspective."

"Too close to Amber?" Sherry asked. She knew the answer.

"From my vantage point, a bit removed admittedly, I don't think you should be so focused on Amber if you're looking into the murder. Rather, circle back to the squeaky wheel, that man Walter Hemphill. From what Pep has told me he has reason to see Gray Washington dead, even though Amber has the attention of the investigators at the moment."

"She has so many reasons to be concerned and I want to help her."

"The truth will come out. If she can't tell you everything there must be a good reason why."

"It has to be she doesn't trust me," Sherry said. Her voice trailed away, along with her hope for her friend to rely on her proven ability to aid in murder investigations.

"Then trust yourself," Charlotte said. Mimi's eyes closed. "I need to get this little nugget home for her nap. We'll see you soon, and good luck. Oh, and be careful."

"Bye, Pep," Sherry called out. He emerged from behind the truck's delivery window and tossed Sherry a wave. "See you later. Good job today." She made her way back to the lodge's parking lot.

As she fished her car key from her purse, she felt the presence of someone in her personal space. She wheeled around and dropped her car key in the process.

"I didn't mean to startle you," Bart said as he bent down to retrieve her key. "I saw you across the parking lot and wanted to catch you before you left. Any chance I could get you to come over to the Nutmeg Motor Inn with me? Walter Hemphill is there. He went back after the cook-off."

Sherry accepted the key from Bart. "What's the purpose of the visit exactly? I don't think ambushing him unannounced will go over very well."

"Livvy's in danger as long as Gray's murderer is roaming free. Walter has the highest likelihood of guilt. If the investigators can't see that for themselves, I need to provide them with the evidence." Bart clenched his hands into fists.

"I don't see how my going with you will be of any help," Sherry said.

"Gray had envelopes in his hotel room addressed to your friend Amber Sherwin."

"I know. No one is sure what the envelopes were doing there."

"Did you know she's received emails from Gray?"

Bart had a smirk on his face Sherry didn't like. "I know they had some communication prior to the cook-off, but that's their business. He and Amber were acquaintances in the past. People reach out to one another. I don't know the full story. In any case, what does all this have to do with Walter Hemphill?"

"If we can prove Hemphill is trying to frame Amber for the murder of Gray Washington to deflect the spotlight from himself, we've killed two birds with one stone. Your friend is off the hook and Livvy can breathe a sigh of relief that her husband's murderer is tagged."

"And my role in coming along is?"

"If you come along, I have a witness to whatever he might admit. You can throw some of your sleuthing expertise my way. If nothing comes of our visit, at least you can strike his name off the suspect list. I'm catching the shuttle as soon as it arrives."

Sherry checked the time on her phone. She had some time to spare before stopping in at the Ruggery to check on Erno. "Okay. I'll see you in the inn's parking lot in a few minutes. Want a ride?"

"No, thanks. I need to gather up some belongings and talk to Livvy. The bus runs from the other side of the building and that's where I'll be. See you at the inn."

Sherry watched Bart disappear around the corner of the building.

"Sherry? Sherry, is that you?"

Sherry took her hand off the car door handle and scanned her surroundings to locate the voice. A woman scurried toward her.

"I thought that was you. I didn't want you to leave without your bag of thank-you goodies. Here you go." Rickie handed Sherry a logoed canvas bag. "Open it. There are lovely items in there you volunteers deserve wholeheartedly."

"Thanks, Rickie. With your help, please," Sherry said as she handed Rickie back the bag to hold. With her good hand she pulled out the first item, an apron.

"I realize you must have quite a few contest aprons but maybe this is your first cook-off volunteer apron."

"My second. I have the apron I wore this morning around my waist under this coat. I couldn't untie it with one hand to return it. I'm so embarrassed you caught me red-handed."

"Please, take it." Rickie tipped her head toward the bag in her hand. "There's more. Let me hold the apron."

Sherry handed over the apron and went in for more. She pulled out a jar of chutney, a jar of tomato jam, pesto and a seasoning packet, all products from the sponsor, Kitchen Royalty. "I will put all of these to good use. Thank you so much."

She replaced the items one by one before Rickie stopped her.

"Wait a minute. There should be an envelope in there. Do you see one?"

Sherry reached in and pulled out an envelope with a printed return address in the top left corner. *Washington Appliance Center*. She carefully lifted the unsealed flap with the fingertips of her bandaged hand. "Two tickets. To *Scrambled*. That's fantastic. Everyone I spoke to who saw a snippet of the play was enthralled." She studied the tickets. "Oh, they're for Thursday night. I better find my plus-one immediately." Sherry helped Rickie repack the gift bag before thanking her again for the experience over the last few days.

"You are most welcome. Everyone learned from you as well. It was a win-win situation having you on the team." Rickie held her gaze on Sherry. "I know you'd have rather been at the oven preparing your recipe but there's always next year."

"I'm already looking forward to entering," Sherry said with a broad smile.

"One more thing. I think I know who killed Gray Washington. I don't want to speak to that investigator, Detective Bease, about my suspicions until I'm fully confident. I know you're someone I can confide in and get feedback from."

"Who are you thinking killed him?"

"Hear me out. I'd like to find the killer because the cook-off's reputation and longevity may hang on cracking the case as soon as possible. To have lingering doubts about the safety and security of the event is a very poor reflection on my leadership skills and my ability to deal with worst-case scenario problems that arise. That being said, I don't want anyone falsely accused of the murder."

"No one does. Rest assured, Detective Bease is the best. He's very thorough." Sherry rechecked the time on her phone.

"Problem is, he may take longer to get to the punch line than I'm willing to wait." Rickie became more insistent as she spoke. "The night of the murder Amber Sherwin was convinced by the Washingtons to go over to the convention hall. I saw her there. Later, Gray was found murdered there by a brand of knife she once had in her possession. You're her friend. Would she do a thing like that? Kill the man, I mean?"

"Livvy Washington and Bart Foster were there, too. Why not them?" Sherry's voice trembled. "Why not Jean or Curt McDonald. They also owned the brand of knife used." Sherry narrowed her eyes. "Why not you? Amber said you were at the convention hall, too."

"I understand your reaction. I've hit a nerve," Rickie said.

"Yes, you have. Amber did not kill Gray. And I will prove it," Sherry stated in no uncertain terms.

"You may want to find out why she was the one who contacted me about Washington Appliances as a substitute for Hemphill Appliances when the news broke the cook-off had lost one of its main sponsors."

Sherry's breath caught in her throat, then she gasped as she tried to regain her composure. A deep inhale did the trick. "Are you sure about that? I mean, I know Amber reached out to Gray before the cook-off, but to go as far as contact you?"

"She did just that," Rickie said.

"Okay, well then, why don't you consider that a nice gesture to help out an acquaintance?"

"I did at the time. Finding and suggesting a substitute sponsor was a lifesaver for the cook-off, as well as a great bonus for the Washingtons. No conflict of interest because Amber wasn't in any way connected to Washington Appliances. All was well in the arrangement. I placed my stamp of approval on the idea and thanked Amber by email. At that point she was out of the loop."

"How did Amber reach out to you with her suggestion to use Washington Appliances?" Sherry asked. "Wonder how she knew you had lost Hemphill Appliances?"

"She emailed me. The finalists were all given my email address for any last-minute changes or questions. This personal touch, I thought, would make the cooks feel more at ease. Amber wrote me saying she'd heard on the news Hemphill Appliances were being recalled pending an investigation of spontaneous electrical fires caused by possible faulty connections."

"That's true. It was on the news," Sherry said.

"She robustly recommended Washington Appliances if we needed a last-minute fill-in. The cook-off organization committee had to double-check Amber had no business or family ties with the Washingtons that would make them illegible."

"Sounds aboveboard," Sherry said.

"When I called Gray's store, he was terribly excited and astonished at the same time."

"Sounds like Amber did both you and Gray a favor. I don't see a problem."

"That's true. Make no mistake, she expected nothing in return. Nothing. But it still doesn't override the fact she was the push behind the man coming here. He was killed, possibly with her knife, at a scene she was at. He had envelopes addressed to her in his hotel room."

"Maybe Gray was sending her a thank-you note?" Sherry shrugged. Even as she said the words she had a hard time believing them. "But why more than one envelope addressed to Amber from Gray?"

"The icing on the cake is the letter I received the day before I traveled to Augustin. At the time I didn't give the letter much credence. Now, looking back, I get the shivers."

"A letter? Like, in the mail?"

"Yes. Postal service. Amazing, right? I haven't received a postmarked handwritten letter in forever, only bills and junk mail. My excitement quickly turned sour when I read the contents."

Sherry checked her phone again for the time. She shifted her weight from one leg to the other when she considered Bart would be wondering how she could be taking so long. "What was the letter about?"

"It was an angry anonymous letter," Rickie said. "Whoever wrote the letter said it was sent as evidence, should something bad occur."

"Was the change in prize packages solidified a week ago?"

"Longer than that. Just not made public. That's the reason many of the contestants weren't happy when they arrived and found the change had been made. Gray was very unhappy with the cook's reactions. They wanted the gold standard Hemphill Custom Appliances brings and they only got the runner-up. Some call that bait and switch. We had our backs against the wall. Unfortunately, we had all the print material set in stone. Too late for revisions. We decided to correct the information in person when the cook-off began."

"After you took Amber's suggestion and Washington Appliances came on board, did you advise Amber? She never spoke to me about the issue before the cook-off."

"I didn't." Rickie seemed to be watching something behind Sherry. Absentmindedly she repeated, "I didn't. I simply thanked her for her suggestion. That way she wasn't directly connected to any further action we took. I certainly did appreciate her help in the throes of an impending crisis. I never gave it a second thought as to her motives. Why would I?"

Sherry shook her head. "She had no motives other than kindness. Sounds like the author of the letter was grasping at straws. In my opinion, someone with a grudge, say, Walter Hemphill, wrote the letter as a last-ditch effort to salvage his company's name by casting doubt on others." Sherry made a slight head turn to pinpoint what or who Rickie's wandering attention was on. She did a double take when she spotted Ray Bease looming in the background.

"I hope you're right. For Amber's sake," Rickie said.

The back and forth was beginning to wear on Sherry's patience. "Rickie, I have to run or I'll be late for an appointment." She also wanted to avoid an impromptu chat with the detective that could delay her longer. "Can you tell me why you think the letter you received implicates Amber? I don't understand." Sherry's temples were beginning to pound.

"Don't you see? I didn't take the letter seriously when I read it for the first time. Even if you don't believe Amber may have inadvertently taken Gray's life, the pieces of the puzzle are coming together in a way you might not be willing to accept. The person who wrote me suspected there might be foul play, but did plans go awry? Gray may have snapped when he received too much criticism for the appliances he provided. Imagine if Gray went after Amber for putting him in a humiliating position on the national level. Yes, it very well could have been Amber who killed Gray in an act of self-defense."

Sherry wasn't even able to conjure up an image of Amber's anger taking her where Rickie was suggesting. "No. You're wrong about that theory."

Rickie ignored Sherry's answer. "And what about Walter Hemphill?"

"What about him?" Sherry asked. She gave Rickie a look of intense interest. If Rickie had any reservations about Walter's innocence, that would confirm Sherry's growing suspicions of the man.

"He's the scapegoat here."

Sherry screwed up her face. "I'm not so sure I agree."

"Consider this scenario: with no time before the cook-off to have the claims against Walter's company proven, one way or the other, Hemphill Custom Appliances finds its lost credibility beyond repair. The adverse publicity has been broadcast everywhere, thanks to the national cook-off press coverage. Whoever was out to discredit Walter was successful."

"Yes, and that's why he may have been so angry he retaliated," Sherry said.

"Someone knew exactly how low below the belt to hit Walter. Attack his highest-end products that give his company the highest return. And the timing was perfect. The Kitchen Royalty cook-off is one of the most prestigious in the nation and Walter's disgraced products made the national news outlets in no time."

"That's not what I thought you were going to say about Walter Hemphill. From the information I've heard here and there, he should be right up on top of the suspect list. Yes, he took the fall thanks to whomever initiated the product recalls, but a scapegoat can also be a murderer if pushed too far."

"Amber may have been pushed too far."

"One thing I've learned," Sherry said and glanced in Ray's direction, "is speculation doesn't equal fact. Neither does assumption." Sherry pulled her door handle, leaned in, placed her goodie bag on the passenger seat and stepped inside her car. "I really have to get going."

"Think about what I said. Amber is a wonderful cook, a very nice woman, and may be in trouble. She needs help to clear her name. Or the alternative may happen. I need help clearing the good name of the cook-off if I'm to count on its continuity. You'd be helping the cooking competition world, too, if this case were wrapped up sooner rather than later."

Sherry placed her hand on the door pull. "Believe me, I'm thinking about everything you said and more. Thank you again, Rickie. I'll be in touch."

"I hope so. I'm here for a few more days winding up event details."

On her drive to the Nutmeg Motor Inn, Sherry dialed Amber. She wasn't sure what she wanted to say, but she was sure she wanted to hear her friend's voice providing some sort of reassurance. By the first ring, Sherry settled on telling Amber again she had done a great job in the cook-off and already had another one in mind for her to enter. After the fifth ring Amber's voicemail greeting came on. Sherry declined to leave a message. Amber would see she had a missed call and return the call at her convenience.

Bart was not going to be happy. When she glanced at the time, Sherry saw she had made him wait at least twenty minutes for her arrival. He couldn't still be in the parking lot. If she'd missed him, she was fine with that. When she arrived, he was nowhere in sight. She made her way up the sparsely landscaped walkway to the single-level building. Between the uninviting grounds to the minimalist décor of the façade, the Nutmeg Motor Inn didn't offer the lodge much competition when it came to enticing guests. Unless creature comforts weren't a consideration and budget prices were. Sherry approached the entrance. This was not the place to stay if automatic doors and grand carpeted valet-staffed lobbies were a priority.

Inside the lobby Sherry scanned the hallway up and down for any sign of Bart. A moment later the tapping of his shoes on the scuffed linoleum announced his appearance.

"Sherry, you made it. I was getting worried you'd changed your mind about coming."

"Sorry about the delay. Where is everyone?" Sherry asked. "This place is deserted. Not even anyone tending the main desk." Sherry glanced at the twisted expression on Bart's face. "Everything okay?"

"Walter Hemphill's been taken to the hospital. They were wheeling him to the ambulance when I arrived. Sorry to make you come over for no reason."

Even in the aftermath of delivering such upsetting news, Bart took no time adjusting his downturned lips into a smile.

For a split second, Sherry thought he might say he was only kidding. "What happened? Is he going to be okay?"

"I'm sure he'll be fine. The manager of the inn said something about a gas leak of some sort in his room that caused him to pass out. A chemical or toxic cleaner combination was considered the most likely culprit," Bart said.

"Only *his* room was affected?"

"As far as I know. A hotel-wide evacuation was put into effect but quickly lifted when nothing else was found. Most guests are back in their rooms. The staff has nearly completed checking the building. Last person I spoke to said only one room was involved and Walter happened to be staying in the unlucky room. There were plenty of emergency vehicles around back to handle the situation if it were any more widespread. You have a great fire department here in Augustin. They were here in minutes I'm told."

Bart seemed a bit cavalier about the situation. A man Sherry held very high on a murder suspect list was being rushed to the hospital under odd circumstances and Bart didn't seem ruffled.

"You said when you pulled up they were wheeling Walter out?" Sherry's question didn't change Bart's relaxed expression.

"That's right. It was quite a chaotic scene. That's all I know. Anyone with more information is very busy right now."

"In that case I'm not needed here," Sherry said.

"I'm staying at the inn so I'll be at the scene of the crime, so to speak, if any updates are warranted. I'll be in town as long as Livvy needs me, if you need to find me." Bart handed Sherry a business card. "So long." He walked to the doors, waited presumably for them to automatically open, and grumbled when he had to open them manually. "Cheap hotel," he said with a head turn in Sherry's direction.

Chapter 11

Before she left the inn, Sherry texted Don, inviting him to the play Thursday night. He wasn't quick to respond, which meant he was most likely tinkering with his boat's mechanics, driving his boat or otherwise dealing with boat matters. Should he decline she would try Amber. There was also a possibility Charlotte would enjoy a girls' night out. Erno preferred afternoon matinees to evening performances so as not to miss his coveted nine p.m. bedtime.

Seated in her car, Sherry crafted a text to Amber. She followed that up with one to Charlotte, deciding she'd act on a first-come-first-served basis as to who would be her date. In the meantime, she needed to get home and love up her dog, Chutney, who had only been walked by her neighbor, Eileen, in the morning and must be waiting anxiously for her return. When she arrived home and thrust open the front door, her pup barely stirred. He was very content lounging on the couch in the sunny warmth streaming in through the front picture window. After a moment, Chutney yawned, stretched and lumbered down from his perch. He made Sherry wait while he ambled over to the leash she let dangle from her hand.

"Let's go, boy," Sherry said with an enticing change of her shoes to her walking sneakers. Chutney perked up and wagged his short stump of a tail. On the stroll down the sidewalk Sherry checked her phone. No one seemed to be in a hurry to get back to her concerning the play invitation.

"Good afternoon, Sherry." A singsong greeting traveled across her neighbor's front yard. "Hope you had a nice time at the cook-off. Heard there was another murder."

Leave it to Eileen to get straight to the point. "I had a very nice time. My creative juices are already flowing for my next cook-off entry. Can't wait to get back to cooking."

"Try not to slice your hand again when you do," Eileen suggested.

"I'll take your advice to heart."

"And the murder, dear? Any details you wish to share?" Eileen held a garden trowel in her gloved hands. She had a palette of what looked, from a distance, like baby purple and blue pansies ready to plant.

"A man who was a sponsor of the cook-off was stabbed. No witnesses as of yet."

"Are you and that Detective Bease fellow on the case?" Eileen punctuated her words with a wag of her trowel, spraying dirt chunks left and right. Her cat, Elvis Purrsley, scattered toward the bushes when the dirt rained down on him.

"I'm sure he and his team have things well in hand," Sherry said. She couldn't change the subject fast enough. "Thank you for walking Chutney."

"One of my favorite things to do. He helped me with some planting in the back. Pansies love this cool weather. Hope I didn't tire him out too much. You know, he's not a spring chicken anymore."

That was the reason the dog was so content to remain prone on the couch. He'd had a busy morning. Eileen gave Chutney the very best treatment. She was like the most wonderful grandmothers Sherry had ever had the pleasure to know. The quality over quantity of time Eileen spent with Chutney made a world of different to the dog's overall wellness, Sherry was certain. Not to mention the fact Chutney and Elvis were growing fond of one another. "Thanks again."

"My pleasure, dear. Keep me posted on the murder."

"You know as much as I do," Sherry said with a wave. "Bye, Elvis, wherever you are."

Continuing on her way, Sherry paused to see who was texting her. Amber wrote back she wasn't able to accompany her to the play because she was already committed to going with her friend Tig. Apparently, cooks had received performance tickets if they were staying in the area for an extended visit. Amber was the sole local and included in the ticket handout.

"That's nice," Sherry told Chutney, who was deeply involved with a scent on a boxwood. Before she replied, another text came in. From Don.

If you can find someone else, I'll take a rain check. I'll call you later.

"Two strikes," Sherry said. She coaxed Chutney to give up his sniff and turn back toward the house. The effort and creativity Sherry had to put forth to lure Chutney from whatever scent he was obsessed with was a reminder, he was always in charge of the walk. Sherry was merely along for company. By the time she made it back to her house she had a text from Charlotte.

"A yes. Yay. For that you get a biscuit." Chutney gave Sherry a quizzical stare and was rewarded with a crunchy biscuit.

Sherry found a sheet of paper and a pen and took a seat at her kitchen table. With her left hand she shakily wrote the initials *A.S.* on the first line. On the next line she began a list.

Facts:

Knife missing
Was Gray's therapist
Gray threatened to sue Back Bay
Recently reconnected with Gray
Recommended Gray's biz to cook-off
One of the last persons to be with Gray

She skipped a line and added,

Questions:
Can she provide a concrete alibi?
Why the unsent addressed envelopes from Gray?

Sherry put down the pen and shook out her exhausted hand. She scanned the list. "Starting points. Now the first thing to do is go straight to the source." She reached down and stroked Chutney's head. "Come on, boy. We're going to the Ruggery."

A short drive later, Sherry and Chutney entered the old wooden building that housed the Oliveri family business. There she found Amber and Pep sending Erno on his way out the door for the afternoon. As soon as Chutney caught the scent of his best dog pal, Bean, he scampered across the wide plank floor to join Amber's dog in their favorite hangout under the hooked rug demonstration table.

"Sorry I didn't return your call," Amber said. "You didn't leave a message. I figured it wasn't urgent and that I'd see you later. Then you texted about the play. Was that what you were calling about?"

Sherry recalled the conversation she envisioned having with Amber. The timing was off. The questions, still unanswered, about Amber's involvement with Gray Washington would have to remain so for a while longer. "Yes, that's it."

"You could donate the ticket," Amber said.

"Charlotte said she'd like to tag along." Sherry turned to her father. "Dad, I'm seeing the doctor in two days and the stitches should come out. Then it's back to work for me. I owe you all lots of hours, so start planning for some time off."

"Don't rush it," Erno said. "When you return, I lose Pep."

"Wait a minute," Sherry said with a pout. "Are you pitting your two offspring against one another?"

Erno tipped his head. "Promoting a little healthy competition isn't a bad ploy to get the most out of you both. A parent's secret weapon in the fight to raise industrious humans."

"Dad, you're incorrigible. I don't know how Ruth Gadabee puts up with you," Pep scolded.

"I'm going right over to her house to discuss the matter," Erno said with a wink. "My lovely girlfriend should win a medal for bravery when it comes to dealing with this family and all your interesting career and hobby choices. I never know when any of you are coming or going. Amber's the only one I can count on to be a constant."

"Thank you, Erno," Amber said. She blew him a kiss as he let himself out.

"Oh, great. Now Dad's favorite child isn't even a member of the Oliveri family," Pep said and laughed.

"What are you working on, Pep?" Sherry asked.

Pep slid his laptop computer across the sales counter to give Sherry a good look at the screen.

"My marketing plan. How to build name recognition for my truck and how to make my service appealing to the masses."

"First you need a name," Sherry said.

"Then, location, location, location, but not in the typical sense," Amber said. "Unlike a store, a food truck needs to find the location of its customers, not the other way around."

"You guys seem to have the answers," Pep said. "The name will be the thing people remember. I'm working on it. People can't come to the food truck if they don't know where I'm parked. I don't want to commit to a certain location until I've studied the sales analytics. I have to find my patrons first. Social media, direct advertising, an app—they all come into play."

"Whatever happened to the good old days of word of mouth? Someone in town likes something and tells someone, and on and on until, voilà, a best-seller is born," Sherry said. "Dad built a computerless business on the back of recommendations from satisfied customers."

"I agree, only my business is so time-sensitive I need the word out in a quick fashion, rather than when satisfied customers decide to spread the news by word of mouth at their convenience," Pep said. "By then, the toasts will be burnt, cold and/or soggy."

Amber tucked her strawberry-blonde hair behind her ears. "Pep's got me rethinking giving him some hours on his food truck when it's up and running full-time."

"Really?" Sherry said.

"Really?" Pep echoed. "That would be awesome."

"Does that mean we would lose you at the Ruggery?" Sherry asked.

"No, never. You'd have to pry my cold, dead hands off the cash register to get me to quit."

"Let's hope it doesn't come down to that," Pep said and laughed. "This is fantastic news."

"The news may not be too exciting. I'm only talking about a few hours on my days off. I had second thoughts after I saw how well the truck and its menu were received at the cook-off. Everyone had such positive feedback for what they ate, the service and the convenience. I really think there's a niche to be filled here in Augustin and Pep is on to something," Amber said.

"Wow. I like your sentiments," Pep said.

"We'll continue formalizing the hows and how-tos," Amber said.

"Best news I've had all day," Pep said. "You have made me one happy lunch server."

Pep returned his attention to his computer screen. "Besides the work I'm doing on the marketing plan, Charlotte is having email issues with her research email address. During down times I've been working on that, too."

"There are no down times at the Ruggery," Sherry said.

"Right. I meant to say I try to squeeze in parts of my other life while constantly attending to store matters."

"That's better," Sherry said and laughed. "Who knew you were a computer whiz among your many other talents?"

"It would be very useful if you could invent a way to have email sort itself according to the user's interests," Amber said. "Just a thought."

"I think you're on to something," Sherry added. "Less time wasted on scrolling through the in-box."

"That's what the *delete* key is for. Why are you two trying to give me more work? At this rate I'm going to have as many jobs as you, Sher," Pep said. "Before you two add to my to-do list, I'm getting back to the job at hand."

Sherry sensed an opening in the conversation to broach the pending subject. "Amber. Talk of emails has me thinking. Rickie was singing your praises for connecting the cook-off organizing committee with Washington Appliances after the Hemphill Appliances prize package was pulled."

"That's nice of her. Really all I did was make a recommendation. I saw an opportunity for an old acquaintance. If she wanted to run with my suggestion, the decision was hers," Amber said.

"I'm curious. Is there an email thread back and forth between you and Gray or did you text or go old-fashioned by using the phone?" Sherry asked.

"Yes. Email. All email. Is that important? I assume you're asking with reference to the murder investigation?"

"Probably. Investigators may want to subpoena the emails. Anything from Gray Washington, Washington Appliances, or Livvy Washington, for that matter."

"Nothing in the emails I wouldn't want anyone to see," Amber said. "I had a back-and-forth with Gray when I reached out to him with the suggestion he fill the void that losing Hemphill Appliances created."

"He jumped at the opportunity?" Sherry asked.

"Not at first. He was combative. He didn't trust my motives. He made me squirm a bit. He questioned me as to why I wouldn't let sleeping dogs lie. Why dredge up the past. Sounded paranoid I might be planning retaliation for something that happened years ago."

"That's what I was afraid of," Sherry said. "How did you respond?"

"I thanked him for considering stepping in as a sponsor. I told him I was glad Rickie O'Dell took up my suggestion of contacting him and I looked forward to seeing him if he accepted. Gray didn't seem very appreciative of my efforts. He ended up taking the opportunity, which I was happy about."

Pep straightened his posture. "There is, of course, another angle to look at this from," he said. He faced Sherry. "But that would only apply if we didn't know Amber as the wonderful kind person she is."

"You mean, if she were vindictive, she could have recommended Gray for the job to bring him within striking distance so she can seek revenge on an old nemesis?" Sherry said. The overdramatization in her voice was meant to indicate the lack of belief she had in the theory. After a brief pause, she added, "Nope, never."

"Another consideration is if Gray Washington's murder had anything to do with the animosity between you two, you may be next on the hit list. If not, then you still have to worry about getting off the suspect list."

"Why would you stay in communication with someone who held bad feelings about you for some length of time, and more importantly, why would you recommend his services to Rickie O'Dell if you thought he might bring a negative attitude with him?" Sherry asked.

Amber remained quiet as she met Sherry's inquisitive gaze. After a moment she said, "Second chances. The problem we had in the past could be resolved with a nice gesture on my part, I was hoping."

"I knew that was the reason. You're such a kind person," Sherry said. She glanced at Pep for reassurance.

"Do you have ideas as to why Gray had envelopes addressed to you in his hotel room?" Pep asked.

"Yes, I do have an idea," Amber said. "For now, I need to keep the details to myself while I work through them. You do believe I didn't kill Gray Washington, don't you? Why do I have to explain myself over and over."

"I believe you with all my heart," Sherry said. "But I'm not Detective Bease and his crew of investigators. Meanwhile, there are clues that appear to implicate you and we need to find who did kill Gray and put an end to any other speculation. And did you know Rickie received a letter a week ago suggesting there might be trouble at the cook-off?"

"I didn't. We need to get back to work." Amber turned her back to Sherry as she welcomed a group of customers entering the store. Her clipped tone was not lost on Sherry.

Chapter 12

Sherry spent Thursday morning at the doctor's office when her appointment was suddenly rescheduled from Friday. "When a doctor wants to take a day off, I say yes. Even if I have to change my appointment," Sherry explained to the receptionist. "I'm happy to accommodate the man who's unstitching my cooking hand."

"I'm so sorry you had to miss the cook-off," said the woman behind the glass partition. "My friend sat in the audience and had so much fun. I'm definitely going next year. I may even enter. I have a recipe I have perfected using glass noodles, shrimp, ginger and sugar snap peas. My mother-in-law likes it very much and she's impossible to please. Amazing how every culture has a wonderful use for noodles."

An hour later, made up of fifty-five minutes in the waiting room and five minutes getting snipped with surgical scissors, Sherry was on her way out of the doctor's office with verbal instructions to go slow with the recuperating hand for a few more days.

"See you at next year's cook-off, hopefully," the receptionist said as she handed Sherry her post-procedure care instructions. "Be careful with your knives until then." The woman was slow to release the paper from her grasp. She stood from her chair and leaned in toward the opening in the glass partition. "I had a theory about the poor man who died at the cook-off."

"It wasn't at the cook-off," Sherry was quick to point out. "He died before the cook-off."

"Yes. Right. Anyway, my theory is he was murdered by someone from the appliance company his company replaced. I'd be peeved, too, if I lost that deal at the last moment. Makes perfect sense. Plus, when I saw on the news Hemphill's appliances may spontaneously burst into flames and were under a recall, I had a strong suspicion Washington Appliances may be behind that bad publicity. Has anyone asked who made that claim about faulty electrical parts?"

"I don't know if it's possible to find out."

"Excuse me. I've been waiting thirty minutes. Will it be much longer?" a man whose arm was in a sling asked from behind Sherry.

"Thank you. See you next time. I mean, I hope I don't have to make a return trip," Sherry said. "Excuse me." Sherry edged away from the receptionist's window, nearly bumping the man's injured arm.

The rest of the day was spent collecting articles to edit for Augustin's newsletter, a job that was labor-intensive one day a week. Reminders had to be sent out and time delays reconsidered. Quick trips to pickup locations from those unwilling, or unable for some reason, to email their articles. After that Sherry spent time cataloging requests for additions and revisions to complete the editing. She would do the typing portion of the editing after her hand passed the flexibility test. She was certain she could type, at a reduced speed, without much discomfort but wasn't quite ready to commit to long-term use. Blocking the articles in their position within the newsletter template was as far as she was willing to go for the moment.

When the newsletter tasks were complete, she tackled the question nagging at her brain. Who made the complaint against Hemphill Appliances? She called the one person she thought would have the knowledge of how these processes work.

"Hi, Charlie. How is everything?" Sherry visualized her ex-husband in his law office seated behind his modern white acrylic desk. Every few minutes he, in his ergonomic chair, would roll from file cabinet to drawer, searching for facts and figures on whatever the law topic du jour might be. He was a rabid information junkie for the cases he worked on. Sherry couldn't help but admire him for that.

"All is well. Working on an environmental hazard case. A tough one. I want to make those sons of guns pay for polluting the beautiful stream I used to skip stones across as a kid. What can I do for you?"

"Good for you. Keep at it." Sherry paused before changing gears. "I know you're busy but I wanted to pick your brain. If a product has been recalled, a large household appliance say, because of a fire danger with the electricals, does the general public have access to the specifics of the recall. Meaning who initiated the complaint?"

Without hesitation Charlie came up with the answer. "The info is all out there, minus names and addresses. Check the consumer product safety commission website. There is a 'report an unsafe product' section. Any consumer can make a documented complaint."

"But no names?" Sherry asked.

"Not to be shared," Charlie said. "Using some detective skills, you might be able to learn something about the source of the complaint. More likely you won't."

"Okay."

"Check the website. If you know what the specific product under review is and the date the complaint was issued, you might learn a thing or two. Have I been of assistance?"

"Yes, you have. I took notes and I'll check the website you mentioned. Thanks, Charlie."

"My pleasure. Let's talk again soon," he said before he clicked off.

That evening Charlotte picked Sherry up for their sister-in-law date. They arrived at the Augustin Playhouse with plenty of time to mingle with other theatergoers in the main lobby before the doors opened and people could be seated. There were many familiar Augustinians who greeted Sherry as if she were family. Sherry and Charlotte chatted with Curt and Jean McDonald, who were beyond thrilled to be among the ticket holders for the night's performance of *Scrambled*.

"We stayed an extra day to take advantage of the play tickets the cook-off committee gave us. After the preview whet my appetite, I couldn't wait to see who kills who, and why," Jean said as she shook Charlotte's hand. "Curt, tell the ladies how much I've pestered you about coming tonight."

"I was interested in getting back to work but Jean insisted we stay one more night," Curt said. "She's the boss, so here we are."

"Speaking of murders, any progress with Gray Washington's real-life murder investigation?" Jean asked.

Over Jean's shoulder Sherry spotted Livvy and Bart wedging their way through the assembly of people. "Not that I'm aware of."

Before Jean had time to reply, Livvy swept past, uttering words Sherry couldn't decipher.

"Did you see that, Curt? She practically knocked me off my feet," Jean said.

"She didn't, did she," Curt simply said. "You're fine."

"That woman," Jean snorted. "We had one heightened conversation about the prize package being of diminished quality since the switch from Hemphill Custom Appliances I so sorely wanted to win, and she acts as if I badmouthed her firstborn."

"Could also be because you've complained to everyone with ears," Curt said with a casual tilt of his head, leaving Jean's mouth agape. "The doors are opening, let's take our seats. Enjoy the show." Curt grasped his wife's elbow and steered her toward the ticket-checking ushers alongside the newly opened theater doors.

Sherry and Charlotte exchanged quizzical glances.

"How upset do you think Jean was with Gray Washington?" Charlotte whispered as they approached the ushers. "Didn't you say her knife was missing? The same brand the poor man was stabbed with?"

"Oh, I don't think . . ."

"Welcome, ladies and gentlemen. The theater doors are now open, and if you'll take your seats the play will begin in approximately seven minutes," a voice announced from speakers overhead.

Sherry and Charlotte found their place in the forming line. When they reached the doors Sherry handed the usher two tickets. Torn ticket stubs in hand, the ladies took their seats in the eighth row from the stage.

"Great seats," Charlotte said. "We could almost be part of the performance if any of the actors need a stand-in."

"Let's hope not," Sherry said with a laugh. "I haven't memorized any lines."

As the lights dimmed, indicating the play was about to begin, a procession of actors in chef's coats appeared from the stage wings. The smartly dressed characters depicting chefs and detectives handed the aisle seat-holders a stack of recipe printouts to pass down their row. The papers were shared until everyone was holding a recipe for Bistro Chicken and Mushroom Crepes.

"Amazing," Charlotte whispered as she held up her recipe.

"I wrote a recipe very similar to this one. Can't wait to see what the differences are," Sherry said.

Before *Scrambled* began, a woman dressed in an elegant knee-length dress and sparkly heels parted the curtains and addressed the audience.

"Someone among you may hold the key to the murderer's identity. It's up to you to gather the clues, assess the motives and unravel the mystery that is *Scrambled*. Bon appetite," she said in a voice that mesmerized Sherry.

As the evening progressed, Sherry was witness to one chef's murder, one chef's jealous rage, and a stolen recipe recovered, a mystery she was determined to solve. By the end of the third of four acts Sherry had pinpointed the murder weapon, a meat tenderizing mallet. Charlotte wasn't in agreement. She insisted the mallet was a red herring and the weapon was the butt end of a food processor. With one more act to go Sherry and Charlotte whispered their best guess to each other as to who may have served the aggressively competitive chef his final meal.

Charlotte tapped her recipe printout lightly with her finger. "Don't forget about this. I think this is the biggest clue of all. I just have to figure out why."

Sherry squinted to get a better look at the recipe sheet on her lap. The theater's dim lighting made reading difficult. She ran her finger down the list of ingredients for the Bistro Chicken and Mushroom Crepes. Nothing struck her as pertinent to the play's content until she reached the preparation instructions. She leaned toward Charlotte's ear.

"One of the main reasons home cooks aren't satisfied with the results of recipes is because they don't read the prep instructions from start to finish before beginning execution." Sherry pointed to a spot on the recipe handout. "Sure enough, the final sentence in the prep instructions reads, 'If the crepe batter thickens add more milk, otherwise your delicate crepes will turn on you and become pancakes.' If the reader hasn't read all the way through the text, they'd miss this message."

Charlotte's gaze locked on the paper. "But what was the message exactly? Who turned on who after becoming something they weren't originally?"

"Exactly," Sherry said.

"Exactly what?" Charlotte asked as Act Four got underway. The question went unanswered.

The play ended with a rousing round of applause. The actors emerged from behind the curtain to receive the audience's appreciation of a mystery solved and a play well acted.

"I can't believe the sous chef murdered the chef with the skillet, but it all makes sense," Charlotte said. "Unrequited love, jealousy, greed, desperation. Her motive was blackmail gone wrong and her botched attempt at having two lovers who hate one another for their individual successes."

"We both were wrong about the murderer's identity. Phew, I'm exhausted from all the intrigue," Sherry said as she made her way across the lobby. Brushing past groups rehashing the play's plot, Sherry was amused at the bickering she overheard.

"Sherry. Maybe you can settle our argument." A woman waving the recipe handout approached.

Immediately, Livvy gripped Sherry's forearm. Before Sherry could beg off, she found herself in the middle of a disagreement.

"Bart thinks the recipe wasn't a red herring. Says the biggest clue was in the last line of the printout. Something about adding milk if the batter becomes too thick to save the crepes from being something they weren't meant to be."

Sherry checked behind her to locate Charlotte, who became detached from her side when she was whisked away by Livvy. Charlotte was chatting with a couple Sherry recognized as classmates of Pep's from Augustin High. Content her sister-in-law was occupied, Sherry entered into the debate.

"I need to give the plot more thought. I missed a clue along the way. Probably daydreaming. Did you have the right suspect at the end?" Sherry asked Livvy.

"No," Livvy said. "I was positive I did. I was wrong."

"Did you?" Sherry asked Bart.

"Yes, and I bet you did, too," Bart said.

"No, I didn't. It was tough deciphering the clues. I agree with you, I also was struck by the last line of the recipe. If the batter becomes too thick it makes pancakes. At that point the title of the recipe, Crepes, no longer applies and the recipe is no longer valid. If that mishap occurred at one of my cook-offs I would be out of the running. Names of recipes are very important and a highly considered component."

Bart blew out a breath. "The sous chef wrote the recipe."

"You think she did?" Sherry asked.

"Think about it," Bart said. "Both chefs were her lovers. The recipe was her way of choosing between the two men. One would live and the other would die, depending on the outcome of the recipe and following her preparation instructions. I think the last line is a foreshadowing of how the recipe might come out, as well as their relationships."

"You're right," Livvy said. "The young lady was really in charge of the kitchen. Not the chefs. Especially if she wrote the recipe they were expected to execute flawlessly."

"Bart's a good detective," Sherry said.

Livvy tapped Bart's arm with her palm. "Yes, he is."

"While everyone was focused on the recipe handed out to the audience, we should have gone a step further back and considered its author. Hmmm." Sherry mulled over her words.

"I don't know how crimes get solved without such creative thinking," Livvy said. "On the other hand, I don't know how criminals get away with murder with all you smart sleuths out there on their trail."

"Bart, any news as to Walter Hemphill's medical state?" Sherry asked.

"I followed up with the Nutmeg Motor Inn's front desk. The inn's manager couldn't tell me fast enough the incident was not their fault. Seems Hemphill brought a space heater with him. He told the ambulance crew he doesn't like the inconsistent heat hotels are known for. Cheap hotels, I'm inclined to add. The manager referred me to the hospital," Bart said. "I made a call, but the hospital is tight-lipped about giving patient info out."

"A space heater? Giving off noxious gas?" Sherry said. "That doesn't sound right."

"Right or wrong, that's the story I got from the inn. They shut the door on any further discussion, saying they were confident it was an isolated incident brought on by the patron himself." Bart held Sherry's gaze, giving her the impression he wasn't interested in second-guessing the information he was providing.

"Could be an accident," Livvy suggested. "The timing is suspicious. Hemphill being in the center of an investigation. Could someone be after him? I'm so confused."

"Hey, Sherry. I'm ready to go," Charlotte said. She didn't give Livvy and Bart more than a quick goodbye before she took a step toward the door.

"Have a good evening," Sherry said. "I have to catch my date. She has a little one at home she wants to get back to." Sherry trotted up behind Charlotte, and when she joined her side, she once again had reason to pause. "There's Amber. Let's say a quick hello."

Amber and Tig were involved in a conversation when Sherry caught Amber's eye. Did Amber's animated expression droop into a frown or was Sherry's imagination playing tricks on her? Sherry put the brakes on her approach.

"Hi," Amber said. "How did you two enjoy the play?"

"We loved it," Charlotte said from behind Sherry. "Nice to see you again, Tig."

Tig turned his attention to Sherry. "I imagine this play is most interesting to you. Amber has told me about all your cooking successes. Fascinating. Who knew being a competitive cook could yield such great rewards? That's the reason I came to the cook-off. When I heard Amber was in one, I begged my way into the audience."

"I wish I'd done better," Amber said. "You'll have to come to my next one, if I enter another."

"You will," Sherry said. "I have no doubts."

"Sounds great," Tig said. He split his glances between Sherry and Charlotte.

"Tell me, Tig. Between you and me, how was it working with Amber in the therapy practice," Sherry asked. She avoided Amber's glare as she waited for the reply.

"Amber is a gem. So professional. She was the heart of the group. Sad when we broke up the practice," Tig said. The corners of his mouth dropped as his gaze softened.

"She's one of a kind," Sherry added.

"Can we please change the subject? Sounds as if you're giving my eulogy."

Sherry kept her sights on Tig. "Speaking of eulogies, you knew the man who passed away the day before the cook-off, Gray Washington? From your therapy practice?" Sherry wondered if there was anything Tig might add to the mystery of Gray's correspondence with Amber.

"Yes. Although, he was Amber's patient, not mine. Pleasant fellow the few times we spoke in passing, until he wasn't. If Amber hasn't supplied you with details I don't want to be the one to. We both believe in patient confidentiality, even years after treatment."

Amber puffed out her cheeks. "Sherry, I told you I wasn't comfortable talking about my ex-patients." Her tone was sharp.

"I asked if Tig knew the man, that's all," Sherry responded.

"You don't give up, do you," Amber said. She curled her fingers inward and let her shoulders slump. Her purse slipped down her shoulder and dropped to the wooden floor. A light curse word tumbled from Amber's lips.

"She's looking out for your best interest," Charlotte said as she took a step toward Amber. "Sherry, we should get home. Mimi might wake up and Pep will need reinforcement."

"See you at the store tomorrow," Sherry said. She searched Amber's face for any sign she wasn't as aggravated as she sounded. She didn't see any. "I'm spotting Pep for a few hours in the morning while he tends to some truck issues. Good night, Tig."

Amber rotated away, mumbling what Sherry chose to believe was a wish for a good night. Judging by her friend's sour expression, she reconsidered she may have been wrong.

On the drive back to Sherry's house the conversation bounced from the play to Amber to the murder of Gray Washington.

"You think Amber knows who killed Gray Washington, or at least is sitting on important information?" Charlotte asked after a prolonged silence.

"I don't think so. She'd share her suspicions. What is she so worked up about? Do you think I came at her too hard?"

"Sometimes people need a bit of cage rattling to get their thinking straight. She may not understand what trouble she's in."

"She had a falling out with Gray in the past. She tried mending fences by offering his services to a national cook-off. That's fine, except why was he in the process of reaching out to Amber by mail for some reason? And before he could, was murdered? And Rickie said she received a warning letter from someone about a bad occurrence that could happen during the cook-off. A letter. Like the unwritten letters in Gray's hotel room. Who under the age of seventy-five even writes letters these days?"

"Does Amber have a solid alibi for the time of the murder?" Charlotte asked.

Sherry sighed. "I didn't get her entire story, but she was seen at the convention hall that evening in the company of the Washingtons. The time of death hasn't been pinpointed, last I spoke with the detective."

"Her hackles are up," Charlotte said.

"Absolutely, and I'm the one who gave them lift. Something's missing in Amber's story. Something's missing in the Washingtons' story. I'm not seeing what may be right in front of my eyes. Like in the play tonight. And I missed the clue in the play. One of my best friends, who I see nearly every day, has a secret and she doesn't see me as a worthy confidante."

"May not be a secret. More likely she isn't ready to let you in on whatever nugget of information she's sitting on. There's a huge difference," Charlotte said. "Timing."

Sherry peered out her passenger-side window. Passing the lodge entrance on their left and the moonlit pathway leading to the bluffs, Sherry was reminded of her childhood excursions to the dilapidated old house that once stood on the property and to the rocky beach below.

"I'm feeling a bit down about Amber. I want to help her but not at the expense of our friendship."

"Okay, let's do it. Let's help her," Charlotte said. She slapped the steering wheel with the palm of her hand. "Maybe there's a recipe with a message you should be considering? Like in *Scrambled*? A crepe isn't a crepe if it's a pancake sort of clue."

"My thinking was going in another direction. The sous chef may have killed Gray."

"The sous chef? Now I'm the one who's missed a clue."

Chapter 13

The following morning brought wind, rain, and colder than average temperatures. Sherry knew that would spell trouble for Don spending much time out on his boat, giving her the opportunity to catch him on dry land. She had subjects she wanted to broach with him and he wouldn't give her his full attention if there were looming boat projects distracting him.

Making her coffee, she was pleased to discover her hand was marginally less stiff and sore. She could actually manipulate the coffee scoop with her hand well and bear the weight of her mug. Was it healed enough to work on an evolving recipe she hoped to finalize by an impending cook-off contest deadline? The coffee mug slipping out of her hand answered that question. And the little accident hurt the palm of her hand when she overflexed the joints to divert the mug from hitting the countertop and smashing.

Sherry groaned, cleaned up the mess and refilled her cup. Recipe creation was out, so she moved up her call to Don.

"Ahoy, Captain." Sherry saluted as she greeted Don as if he could see her. "That joke never gets old. What are you up to today?"

"Hi, honey. I've haven't been a captain for very long, so I'll give you a little more mileage on that joke before I claim overuse."

"Where are you? I can hardly hear you," Sherry said over the revving and rumbling reverberating through her phone's speaker.

"Take one guess."

"Marina?"

"You're close. I've driven the boat down to the service center. I'm getting the radar upgraded so I can manage days like today." Don's voice was exploding with enthusiasm. He was in his element.

"That's essential," Sherry said. How could she deny him his new love? Maybe her questions could wait. "Safety first."

"Getting the boat in position to be checked below the waterline wasn't easy," Don said. "Not like lifting a bike onto a bike rack and motoring down to the store for repairs. This involves forklifts, hoists, and whatever else it takes to check the underside of the boat. Did you know they put sensors on the lower hull like a car would have to avoid collisions with unseen objects?"

"Makes you wonder about the olden days when explorers set out for parts unknown with no weather forecasting tools besides their intuition. How did any of them survive?"

"A lot of them ran aground. Thank goodness some of them made their trips successfully. Sometimes luck was on their side. We've come a long way," Don said, his enthusiasm never waning.

"On the other hand, intuition can get you pretty far," Sherry said with a curl of the lip.

"Why do I have the inkling we're not talking about my boat anymore?"

"We can discuss the situation at lunch," Sherry said. "What time and where?"

"Sounds serious if there's a situation. Let me see," Don said before he let out a hum of consideration. "I only have an hour at noon. That's the best I can do today. I'm getting the boat ready to run folks back to Long Island. Everything needs to be ship-shape."

Disappointed, Sherry checked her emotions before she made the mistake of sharing the thoughts flooding her brain. The dead air went on longer than she had intended while she swallowed hurt feelings that were swelling up. If she was his priority, he would carve out time for more than an abbreviated lunch date with her. She had to remember, the cook-off had dominated most of her time and he was entitled to his time, too. Maybe a short lunch was enough for him. He was starting up a business. They both knew time together would most likely be in short supply for the foreseeable future.

"I'd be happy for as much time as you can give me," Sherry said when she was confident she wouldn't apply unappreciated pressure through her tone. *Don't be that needy girlfriend who makes everything about herself,* she silently recited. "Short lunches are fine with me."

"Short lunches, plural? I only said today was a short lunch and not by choice. Don't you want to spend time with me?" Don whined.

Sherry burst out laughing.

"What's so funny? I'm serious."

"I was afraid I was the needy one. Glad we need each other. See you at the Whale's Tale at noon," Sherry said before bidding Don farewell until midday. As she did, a text came in from Ray Bease. He requested a meeting at the lodge at Sherry's earliest convenience.

At Sherry's feet, Chutney yawned and refreshed his sleeping position. "The detective is on the move. But is it in the right direction? Away from Amber? Like the creator of the recipe in *Scrambled*, I think finding out who wrote the complaint against Hemphill will be invaluable." Sherry searched for the written list she'd made headed up with Amber's initials. She reviewed each word. The second half of the list was composed of questions Sherry needed answers to. To that list she added:

Who wrote the complaint against Hemphill Appliances?

"My right hand works. Sort of." She scrutinized her penmanship. "Mimi has better handwriting than me right now."

Sherry found her laptop under two magazines at her kitchen workspace. She hadn't typed more than a keystroke or two for days. One-handed typing was so inefficient. She tested her right hand on the keys and was pleasantly surprised at the result. She began a search for the government agency Charlie recommended for appliance recalls. A few halting keystrokes later, Sherry was staring at a recall for Hemphill Gold Standard ovens.

"Eureka. I've struck gold," she said, enjoying her pun. She read the recall notice concerning the potential electrical wiring hazard on the Hemphill top-of-the-line oven. The notice described a reported incident of burning and smoking associated with the oven's outlet wiring. No injuries were reported.

"Only one report? I would have thought you'd need more complaints than that." She could find no trace of where the complaint originated. "Dead end."

Sherry closed up her laptop. She made a phone call and set up a meeting.

"There are a few hours until lunch with Don. What do you say we go take a ride over to the lodge and see what the detective is up to?" Chutney picked up on the word *go* and bounced to his feet.

An hour later, Sherry clicked Chutney up to the leash and helped him out of the car. The spring air had a nip of chill to it and Sherry regretted her decision to forgo her heavier coat in favor of a light quilted barn coat. She picked up the pace of her walk to the lodge's lobby to generate body heat. Chutney, indignant he wasn't allowed to sniff the unfamiliar landscaping, strained against the leash.

"Sherry, give the dog some slack. His legs are so short." The voice came from behind Sherry.

Sherry did an about-face, certain she recognized the familiar voice. The khakis, the sensible shoes, the hat updated from the last time she laid eyes on Ray, and a surprisingly stylish leather coat greeted her sights.

"Ray, you've never looked so fashionable," Sherry said. Her first thought was the man has met someone he fancies and his new look reflects the influence she's having on him. She was happy for her friend.

"With age comes good taste," Ray said. He shrugged. "Or something like that. Thank you."

Sherry followed Ray through the entryway and into the lobby.

"I've set up a chat with Livvy Washington and Bart Foster," Ray said.

"Haven't you spoken to them?" Sherry asked.

"Not with you present," Ray said. "Are you willing?"

"I did want to ask them a few questions myself. What is it you have in mind?"

"To lessen the interrogation aspect. Make the conversation more of an interaction rather than a grilling, which it's not. Just a preemptive strike bringing you on board to soften the mood for the grieving wife," Ray explained.

"I have to say I haven't gotten much of a grieving widow vibe from Livvy." Sherry clipped her next thought when she glimpsed Livvy and Bart rounding the corner across the lobby.

"These folks are leaving by Saturday and I can't hold them here any longer than that without any formal charges. Thank you for your cooperation."

Livvy made a beeline for Ray, and on her way did a subtle double take when her sights found Sherry.

"Good morning," Ray said. He shook Bart's hand when he approached, steps behind Livvy. "Sherry's going to sit in on our conversation, if that's alright."

Livvy shrugged. "Fine with me. Nice to see you again, Sherry. What a sweet dog." Livvy reached down and patted Chutney's head. "I hope you'll be riding with us when we take your friend Don's boat back to Long Island."

"I would like to, schedule permitting," Sherry said.

"Let's take a seat over in the library." Ray directed the group to the wood-paneled room lined with bookshelves. A chess set sat on a coffee table. Everyone claimed a chair and pulled up to the board game. Chutney parked himself at Sherry's feet.

"How's your hand?" Livvy asked.

"Better, thank you. The stitches came out and I'm almost as good as new. Be careful of knives is the lesson I've learned." As soon as the words left her mouth Sherry wanted to crawl under the table. "I'm sorry. I wasn't thinking." Sherry winced until she was certain her words hadn't offended Livvy beyond repair.

"Please. It wasn't your fault my husband was murdered," Livvy said.

"I assume that's what we're here to talk about?" Bart asked, shifting his gaze from Sherry to Ray.

"That's right," Ray said. His matter-of-factness paved the way for Sherry to gain a fresh start on the meeting. "I've asked Sherry to join us because her friend Amber is on my radar. You two may have something to say about that."

As much as Sherry wanted to shout out Amber was innocent, she stifled her response. She shifted her sights to Livvy. Maybe a flinch or twitch produced by Livvy would reinforce Sherry's suspicion she may know more about her husband's death than she'd shared. She didn't move a muscle.

"Amber Sherwin has more than a passing reason to want Livvy's husband gone," Bart said. "I'm a private investigator, as you both know, but the reason the Washingtons hired me was not as I stated. More accurately, Gray didn't hire me, Livvy did. She was investigating Gray. She had every reason to believe Gray was blackmailing Amber and she wanted to know why."

"What?" Sherry blurted out. "Livvy? You were investigating your own husband? Gray was blackmailing Amber? What else was Amber keeping secret?"

Ray cleared his throat and sent Sherry a stern glare. She must keep her emotions in check was the message he was sending, or this meeting would end prematurely.

"Blackmail is a strong word," Ray said.

"If the shoe fits," Livvy said. "We have to call it what it is. What do you think those envelopes in his hotel room were for?"

"Amber said she hadn't received any letters from Gray. Had he not begun what you suggest is a blackmailing plan?" Ray asked. "And if he hadn't, how do you know what his plans were? Were you in on them? We can arrange a plea deal if need be, as long as you cooperate."

"No, no. Nothing like that," Livvy said, beating Bart's swift reply by a word. His head bobbed up and down, reinforcing her denial.

"Let me explain," Bart said.

Livvy and Bart exchanged glances. Sherry shifted in her seat as the anticipation of the coming details made the back of her neck prickle with discomfort.

"That's okay, Bart. I can explain," Livvy said. "Years ago, I wanted out of our marriage. We were living in Boston at the time and, without going into specifics in terms of my marriage, I'd had enough of him. We could work together but that was all. Business, no pleasure. He begged to go to a marriage counselor, but I refused to join him. He went to Amber's practice without me."

"She was very good. He made the right choice," Sherry said, for which she received another glare from Ray.

"I'm sure she's helped many. Unfortunately, Gray wasn't one of the lucky ones," Bart added. "After spending hours in her office over the period of many months, Gray threatened to file a formal grievance against the Back Bay Therapy Group. His claim was ineffective, overpriced treatment and malpractice. A real shame."

"He spent so much money trying to fix something unfixable and I wouldn't budge, so he wanted his money back. We were in a financial crisis at the time. The luxury appliance market was in a slump with all the big box stores opening. Too much choice for the consumer. Anyway, Gray felt it was within his rights to get reimbursed," Livvy said. "I felt awful about it, but that's the truth. I'm sorry Amber had to be involved. Gray was like a dog with a bone. He had to get those thousands back."

"Are you, I mean, were you and Gray together, as a couple, at the time of his death?" Ray asked.

"Sort of. And sort of not. It's complicated. But the inner workings of our marriage has no bearing on his murder, I assure you," Livvy asserted.

Sherry witnessed a slight tip of Ray's head, which she interpreted as a gesture of doubt. Again, Sherry scrutinized the woman and her mannerisms. Cool as a cucumber.

"Can we return to the blackmailing allegations?" Ray said. He picked up a chess piece and placed it on an empty square on the board. "Besides the letter paper and addressed envelopes in Gray's hotel room, what proof do you have Amber was being, or about to be, blackmailed?"

Bart picked up a different chess piece and set it in a blocking position to Ray's move.

"I have evidence Gray sent Amber an email rehashing a situation that occurred at her practice years ago," Bart said. "Livvy discovered the email. The text of the email did not discuss the matter in specifics, which is a good fear tactic for the blackmailer. Puts the victim in a defensive posture because she has a fear of what's to come if there are secrets to be told. More leverage for the blackmailer."

"You went into Gray's email?" Sherry asked.

"That's not the point of the story, but yes, I did," Livvy said. "Sometimes a wife does things for her husband's own good. I don't have any remorse. Besides, the email account was originally a general Washington family email created the very first year email was available to the general public. No one had the foresight to understand email would be the mega method of communication it is today, so many families shared one address. After I created my own, I did check the old one every so often, even though it was technically Gray's at that point."

"Was this email from Gray to Amber recent?" Ray asked. "As in the last few months?"

"Yes, very recent. Around the time Washington Appliances got the call from Rickie O'Dell to inquire about stepping into the cook-off sponsorship position," Livvy said.

"Amber said she had an email thread with Gray about the sponsorship opening at the cook-off," Sherry said. "Amber was the person who recommended your company to Rickie. I believe she did it to offer an olive branch. An old wound she'd like healed. She's a wonderful person." She reached across the board and moved one of the smaller pieces, having no recollection how the game of chess worked. "Why would Gray consider blackmailing her after her kind recommendation?"

"I'm not sure you know all the details of Amber's last year in Boston," Bart said. "I've spent a lot of time looking into those months before she left town as part of my investigation."

"I know Amber's marriage therapy practice disbanded. Feeling untethered, Amber moved down to Augustin after competing in a cook-off here, deciding relocation was a fresh start after her divorce. Her marriage fell apart, propelled, in part, by the fact her ex-husband took up with another woman."

"She told you that?" Bart said. He reached for the chess set's queen piece, inspected the wooden carving and replaced her where he found her. "Beautiful set. Handmade, I suspect."

"Yes, she told me that," Sherry said.

"There's more to Amber Sherwin you may not be so familiar with. Her life prior to living in Augustin had complications. Digging around in her not-too-distant past has unearthed surprising facts," Bart said.

"Such as?" Sherry prompted. She had her guard up to deflect Bart's response and her tone reflected as much. She sat up as straight as she could. A rigid posture would send the message she had a firm belief in her friend's upstanding character.

Livvy glanced at Bart, who nodded, presumably giving her the go-ahead to respond. "Gray sent Amber a correspondence suggesting he may require compensation to withhold some information that could be detrimental to her. Maybe ruin her chances at her successful new life in Augustin."

Before Sherry could form two words Livvy continued. Only the word *what* escaped her lips.

"What was the information? Is that what you were going to ask, Sherry?" Livvy said.

"Yes. I know Gray sought counseling from Amber. I also know Amber takes her clients' confidentiality very seriously. Even to this day she won't talk about their sessions. Another reason I have the utmost confidence in Amber's innocence. Her integrity," Sherry explained.

Bart slid the king chess piece between spaces. He lifted his head and locked his gaze with Livvy's. After a moment he spoke.

"What I uncovered is damning for Amber. Gray was very dissatisfied with the professional help, or lack of, he received from Amber," Bart began.

"Not a crime. Not everyone is cut out to benefit from therapy," Sherry stated in no uncertain terms.

Bart continued. "Yes, of course that's true. And it's unusual to have someone go the extra mile and file a grievance against a therapist as Gray did. That's a lot of effort in time and money and can affect livelihoods eventually. As it did in this case. The cost of fighting the allegations may have cost Amber her career."

"By the time the grievance was a step away from being filed, Gray backed off," Livvy said. "Backing off didn't matter, the damage was done."

"He had a change of heart?" Sherry asked.

"Hard to say. I honestly don't know why he changed his mind about proceeding with the grievance. Over time things settled down between Gray and the practice," Livvy said.

"Okay, so time goes by and Amber reached out to Gray and presents him with a business opportunity. All he has to do is accept. Amber isn't part of the deal, only the point contact. After that she's out of the loop when Rickie steps in. As a thank-you, Gray blackmails her? And what are the terms of the blackmail? It's now obvious the envelopes in his hotel room were for the demands to be sent in," Sherry said.

"Makes sense," Ray said.

"Maybe she awakened a sleeping bear when she thought she was performing an act of kindness. He'd suppressed his anger for years and when the opportunity arose he couldn't resist getting back at Amber in a twisted scheme," Sherry said. She scanned the chess board. Pieces were scattered off their starting positions. They made no sense in the squares they rested on. "If the scenario were a chess match, what would be the next logical move? Amber's move."

"She could pay up, convince him to give up his plan, or let whatever information he was dangling over her head become public knowledge, busting the plan."

"I'd hope he'd withdraw his attack," Ray said as he moved the king piece away from the board and set it aside. "And seems as if he did. He never mailed the letters."

"Or his time ran out before he could," Livvy said.

"Whatever occurred, Amber didn't kill Gray for attempting to blackmail her, or any other reason. Who did?" Sherry asked.

Livvy shook her head. She turned her attention to Bart. "Bart? Your time is almost up. I can't pay you anymore if you've hit a brick wall. Time for Detective Bease and Sherry to take the reins. I may not have loved Gray anymore, but I liked him, and I want to see whoever killed him brought to justice."

"I have one more piece of evidence I've uncovered," he said.

Everyone's sights bore down on Bart.

"What's that?" Ray asked with a note of skepticism in his tone.

Bart shifted in his seat. He uncrossed his legs and leaned forward. Before he could reach for a chess piece Livvy knocked his hand away from the board.

"Enough. Leave the game alone. What is the piece of evidence you have, Bart?" Her voice gave Sherry the chills.

"Give me a little longer to double-check my sources," he said, imploring Livvy with widened eyes.

The intense look Ray sent Sherry's way stole her attention from Bart. She was certain she knew what Ray was thinking. *Bart wants to remain on the payroll and he's hoping Ray and Sherry get his job done for him.*

"A day or two longer and then I'm pulling the plug, Bart. I can't afford you any longer. Find the murderer," Livvy said as she stood. "Are we done here?

Chapter 14

Sherry arrived at the Whale's Tale ten minutes early. The early-bird lunchers were well into their juicy hamburgers, artisan salads and locally caught fish fillets.

"See anything you'd like to order?"

Without turning, Sherry replied to the commanding voice, "Everything looks and smells wonderful." She spun on her flats and received an invigorating kiss from Don. He appeared to have put extra effort into dressing up for the date. His nautical-themed sweater was a reminder of his current occupation. The tiny anchors appliquéd across the cable stitch screamed his commitment to the boating life. His freshly shaved face was scented with an earthy musk Sherry wanted a second whiff of.

"You smell like man-heaven," she said. "I haven't seen you without scruff in a long time. How did you even have time to shave?"

"Why, thank you, pretty lady. For you, I make time," Don said. "I wanted to make an impression in case the days get as busy again as the last few and I don't see you for a spell. I don't want you to forget me."

"No way," Sherry said. "Not if you're going to smell this good."

Sherry and Don were given a table out on the patio overlooking the salt marsh. A space heater positioned in the middle of the covered patio warmed the chilly spring air. There was room for only four tables on the small patio, and with the limited fit an intimate conversation was an impossibility. Only one other couple was seated outside when Sherry and Don sat down. A double take confirmed she knew both members of the party.

"Amber? Is that you? I didn't know you'd be here." Sherry popped out of her seat and greeted Amber and Tig tableside. "Want to join us? We're having a quick lunch before Don goes back to servicing his boat." She found Don with her gaze and he waved from the table. Amber and Tig returned the wave. Sherry turned her attention to Tig, seated across from Amber. "Hi, Tig. So nice to see you again. I'm sorry to hear you're leaving town soon."

"Hi, Sherry. Nice to see you, too." Tig deferred to Amber with a glance.

"Hi," Amber said.

Was that an icy tone? No, Sherry had to have misheard Amber over the hum of the restaurant's activity.

"Would you two like to join us?" Sherry asked.

Amber's sights dropped to the table. "No, thanks."

"I understand," Sherry said. She shifted her gaze to Tig when Amber failed to lift hers. "Did Amber mention she's going to join my brother in his food truck venture? They'll make a great team."

Amber cleared her throat. "I haven't committed. I'm leaning toward saying no. As a matter of fact, I'm thinking of relocating to another town altogether."

"Oh, she's just kidding," Sherry said with a stilted chuckle. She imagined Tig would be more comfortable under the table than seated in between the women at that moment. Sherry couldn't decipher the tone of the conversation, but *pleasant* wasn't one of the choices. "I'd better get back to Don. See you soon, Amber, and safe travels, Tig." The words had a hollow ring to them.

"You look like you just gave blood. What happened?" Don asked when Sherry sat down. "Take a sip of water."

"I could use a shot of brandy."

"Wow. What's going on?"

"Amber said she's contemplating moving away from Augustin. I thought she was joking. She wasn't. What have I done? We have to get out of here. I can't stay. I'm about to have a full-on panic attack." Sherry snatched her purse off the empty seat to her right and headed for the door. She felt Amber's eyes on her as she scurried by her table.

"Can we get a sandwich at the deli, please?" Sherry said with total lack of enthusiasm.

"Goodbye, pistachio-crusted local cod on a bed of kale Caesar salad." Don looked longingly back at the entrance to the Whale's Tale. "I'll meet you there unless you want to ride together."

Sherry didn't wait to give an answer. She let herself into Don's pickup truck. "I'm too upset to drive."

On the short drive to the deli, Sherry mulled over the scene at the restaurant until she suddenly called out, "Stop the car! There's Rickie. I have to talk to her. Pull over." Don steered the truck illegally into a fire lane in front of the Augustin Cinema. "Order me a turkey bacon avocado wrap and I'll be right over."

She hopped out of the vehicle and trotted up to Rickie, who was putting coins in a parking meter. "Rickie, hold on," Sherry called out when she saw the woman make a beeline for the hardware store.

When Sherry reached Rickie she made short work of getting to the point. "Do you know who reported the Hemphill appliance electrical defects to the consumer protection office? Who got the ball rolling on recalling the products?"

The confusion projected on Rickie's face while she took a moment to orient herself—being questioned by a woman who had run up to her on the street with no warning or greeting—was almost enough to bring a smile to Sherry's face. Were it not for the seriousness of the matter.

"Oh, Sherry," she said. "You caught me by surprise."

"Rickie, I need to know. Do you have the answer?"

"I don't know the answer to that question. I do know I was made aware of the situation by the media, not a direct contact. Thank goodness I found out as early as I didi or the cook-off would have suffered terrible embarrassment. I would rather have learned the truth from Walter Hemphill himself, but I didn't. He has some nerve to put me through the ringer trying to replace him at the eleventh hour and not advising me of the situation himself as soon as he was aware of it. When I called him to say I no longer could honor his contract, you would have thought I was the one who began the recall process. He was livid, his anger aimed squarely at me!"

"You really don't know? I checked the consumer recall website and saw the recall. No luck on who made the complaint, though."

"Best guess is the author was an unsatisfied consumer. Those custom appliances are considered the gold standard and have a price tag that reflects that sentiment. These people want their money's worth, and when they don't get it there's hell to pay, especially if there's a question of safety. That's likely the reason for the swift action on the recall."

"You know swift action was taken from the time of the complaint to the recall?" Sherry glommed on to a possible hint at inside information.

"Another best guess, as the cook-off had the contract with Hemphill Appliances up until about two and a half weeks before the cook-off. The news services reported the complaint was made and the recall accelerated for public safety concerns within a few days," Rickie explained.

"Someone made a very strong claim against the product's safety," Sherry said as she pondered whether that person wasn't someone she might know. "Maybe someone with a lot of clout."

"You need to ask Walter himself, but be advised he's still very disturbed by the situation surrounding his participation in the cook-off and the most recent incident with possible toxic gas in his room. He claims he wanted what he deserved, which I found quite a chilling proclamation."

"Thank you. I think I'll pay him a visit, if I can find him," Sherry said. "He's one hundred percent healthy?"

"Absolutely. It was just a scare. He fainted and was checked out at the hospital. Doctors cleared him for any activity."

"Okay, good."

"Why is knowing who filed a formal complaint important? Do you think that may be the same person who murdered Gray?"

"Quite possibly."

"I'm glad you're interested in getting to the bottom of Gray's murder. I just hope it doesn't lead you to someone associated with the cook-off. I'd hate to think I was in such close proximity to a killer."

"Now the problem is tracking down Walter Hemphill," Sherry said.

"I know exactly where he'll be for the next hour. I ran into him when I was leaving the lodge a few minutes ago. He's staying there now. We moved him from the inn, as a courtesy. He invited me to have lunch with him at the Whale's Tale restaurant. Quite a surprise after what we've been through. I didn't see any harm in accepting his invite. I told him after one quick errand I'd meet him there. Please join us. Actually, he said you recommended the restaurant to many people at the cook-off and now the place is hopping."

"I accept your invitation. I'm with my friend Don. He's at the deli. We can give you a lift to the restaurant and be back here in an hour," Sherry said.

"Why not? My errand at the hardware store can wait. I'll go put some more money in the meter," Rickie said. "Thanks."

"Let me get this straight," Don said after Sherry tapped him on the shoulder and lured him out of the lunch line before he placed their orders. "We're going back to the Whale's Tale after having just left there to drive to town to buy sandwiches? And we're now a party of four when I told you I only have an hour?"

"That's right. Rickie's outside waiting for us and Walter Hemphill is waiting for her at the Whale's Tale by now. Can you squeeze out a few more minutes and make your lunch hour start when we get back to the Whale's Tale?" Sherry pleaded.

"Do I have a choice? What about Amber? She undoubtedly hasn't finished her lunch. She's the reason we had to leave my longing for pistachio-crusted local cod unfulfilled," Don said. He held the door open for Sherry.

"Thank you for understanding. I'm on a mission. I let my emotions get the better of me. We've got a job to do. Come on, let's hurry." She increased her pace and hoped Don would do the same.

On the short drive back to the Whale's Tale, Rickie went over the plans for Don to return passengers to Long Island to pick up their cars. "And you'll ride with the group on the boat, won't you, Sherry?"

"If Don has room, yes."

"There's always a seat on the *Current-Sea* for you, my dear," Don said.

"Aw," Rickie cooed. "Young love. How nice."

Sherry's face warmed as Don side-eyed her.

The conversation stayed light until they reached the restaurant. At that point, Rickie leaned forward from the rear seat. "Do me a favor. Please don't rile Walter up with talk of his recall. I'm trying to avoid him bringing legal charges for breach of contract, which wouldn't go anywhere, but I'd have to hire a lawyer to thwart his charges. More honey than vinegar, please."

On her way across the dining room, Sherry passed Amber and Tig handing cash back and forth between themselves. They didn't seem to see any of Sherry's party pass as they were sorting through their bill. Sherry was more than a bit relieved not to have to explain her comings and goings to her friend. The trio found Walter seated at the same table Sherry had abruptly evacuated moments before.

Walter's expression was quizzical when his lunch date showed up with two tagalongs. "This is a pleasant surprise," he said. "The more the merrier."

Sherry returned the smiley greeting.

"Good start," Sherry whispered to Don when they took their seats. "He's in a jovial mood. Rickie has nothing to worry about."

"I hope you're right," Don said.

The lunch moved along at a hastened clip. Sherry didn't want to keep Don from his work, while at the same time she was motivated to keep Walter in good spirits. When the sandwich, soup and salad dishes were cleared and the check was on its way, Sherry recognized her opportunity had come. The conversation had wandered to the cook-off and what goes into organizing such a monumental event. After Rickie gave her insight on the process, she yielded the topic to Sherry's contestant point of view.

Sherry, in turn, passed the conversation topic ball to Walter.

"Walter, I was wondering if you have any idea how your wonderful appliances ended up on a nationwide recall list? By that I mean, have you been able to trace back the source of the original complaint, if that's at all possible?" From across the table, she heard Rickie exhale loudly.

Walter began cracking his knuckles, a habit that made Sherry's skin crawl.

"I do know where the person's from," Walter said as another pop was released from his noisy knuckles. "I was driven to find out as much as I could because I wasn't aware I had enemies who would try to rip my livelihood out from beneath me. I wasn't aware I had enemies at all."

"The complaint filer doesn't have to be an enemy. Could have been one faulty appliance. Just bad luck," Sherry said.

"You can't deny I have reasons to believe someone may be out to get me. Someone tried to kill me with poison gas at the Nutmeg Motor Inn."

"Has that incident been a confirmed attempt on your life?"

"No, but I'm staying at the lodge now so at least I can get a good night's sleep without fear of suffocating."

"Could have been stopped-up ventilation," Sherry suggested.

Walter shook his head. "All evidence points to ill intent. How could a heavy cloud of carbon monoxide only be in one single room in a building? The window was cracked open a touch. Just enough to let someone pump in the gas. There is a parking lot right outside the window. Even a child could easily run a hose from a tailpipe through the window."

"You've got a point," Sherry said.

"I've been asked to hang around Augustin while the matter is investigated. Thank you for paying for the upgrade, Rickie. I realize I made a pain of myself to hang on to the perks my contract laid out, even if my products weren't promoted as I'd hoped. The organizers went above and beyond to make me feel welcome, even if it did take a strong nudge on my part. I won't be taking any legal action to challenge the dismissal of my contract, but I do want to know who is out to get me."

Rickie forced a smile and directed a look of distress Sherry's way.

"Who filed the product complaint?" Sherry pressed cautiously.

"A man in Boston," Walter said.

"Do you have his name?" Sherry asked.

Sherry couldn't hide her disappointment when she saw Walter shake his head no. Back to square one.

"How do you know the person was from Boston?" Don asked.

"When the consumer product safety agency contacted Hemphill Appliances, we asked if we could be advised of the origin of the complaint. We were told the name of the complainant couldn't be revealed pending further investigation, if ever, unless consent was given," Walter said. "I didn't let that stop me from further research. I was able to match an unhappy customer with the same complaint on the most popular social media website that reviews businesses. A site I monitor regularly. No name attached to the review. Signed as *Buyer Beware in Boston*."

"You think the same unhappy reviewer also is the person who tried to do you harm at the Nutmeg Motor Inn?" Rickie asked. "I could see how that's a possibility."

Walter shook his head. "Anything's possible. Big effort to come down to Augustin to find me. The irony of it all is, I do know I was high on Gray's murder investigation suspect list."

"And my list," Sherry whispered to Don.

"Until I was almost added to the victim list."

"You can see how you would be considered a suspect with your animosity toward the Washingtons."

"I admit, I came to the cook-off to vent my frustration for what happened to my company. Pride is a strong motivator for me. I hold firm Hemphill's was wrongly accused of manufacturing dangerous products without any evidence whatsoever excepting one person's critical and unsubstantiated opinion. After I suffered the vengeful act against me in my hotel room, I came to realize how lovely the people of Augustin are after they saved my life. I have made a complete turnaround in my attitude and will forever be thankful rather than bitter. Life's too short."

"I agree," Sherry said.

Walter turned his attention to Sherry. "But, the matter's still out there, as is the person who wanted me dead. You want a name, I want a name. Someone out there has a powerful vendetta."

Sherry suppressed her disappointment at coming away from lunch without a name. The name of the person who initiated the product recall that triggered the need to switch appliance vendors. The act that may have gotten the victim to the desired location, the cook-off.

Sherry retrieved her car from the parking lot and dropped Rickie back in town. Don followed in his truck. The two met up to say goodbye at the municipal parking lot.

"What now?" Sherry asked. "I think I've lost a friend, I'm at a dead end in my search for clues to Gray's murder, and Amber is still on the suspect list. Walter Hemphill is off the suspect list. Is that considered progress?"

"You still have me," Don said. He garnished his comment with a kiss.

"Thank goodness," Sherry said with a lengthy return kiss.

Sherry drove her car to the Ruggery, guided by nerves and trepidation. Amber's proclamation left a rumbling agitation in Sherry's stomach that only a face-to-face conversation would soothe. Or make worse. And it was about to happen. After a deep exhale Sherry entered the store.

"Good afternoon, fine people," Sherry said, paving the way for a jubilant greeting.

"Erno's not in this afternoon. Pep will be back soon. He's picking up a late lunch," Amber said with as much warmth as an ice cube.

"I'm here to help. Just tell me what needs to be done," Sherry said.

"Erno wrote a list. Next to the register," Amber said without raising her head.

"If you have any additions, let me know." After a pause, Sherry added, "Did you have a nice lunch?"

"Do we have to keep dancing around like this? What I said today at lunch, I meant. I can't work with folks who don't trust me and I can't live in a town where I'm considered a murderer." Her words became breathless.

"You can't mean that," Sherry said. "Of course we trust you without question. Listen to what you're saying."

"I'm going to give Erno my two weeks notice next time I see him." Amber's voice quivered. A tear ran down her cheek before she blinked away another. She wiped her face with the back of her hand. "I could use some help filling out today's customer profiles, please." She pointed to the Rolodex, a pile of index cards, and a stack of orders. She crossed the floor to the yarn cubbies without waiting for Sherry to reply.

After Pep brought his lunch back to the Ruggery, Sherry took the opportunity to test Amber's mood again.

"Amber, would you please give me your opinion on what shade of brown works best for a squirrel's fur?" Sherry asked.

Amber raised her head from the canvas she was outlining. "Can it wait?"

"Mrs. Remington is coming in by four and I'm only halfway done," Sherry implored.

Without a further word Amber made her way to Sherry's side. Sherry was certain her friend saw through the ploy to bring them closer.

"I'm so sorry I've upset you," Sherry began. The two shades of brown yarn in her hand shook as her emotions flowed. "But you owe me more of an explanation as to why you're thinking of leaving your job and Augustin altogether."

Amber pointed to the lighter brown yarn bundle. "Gray wanted money, hush money," Amber said in a near whisper. "My ex-husband did something terrible and I still feel the need to protect someone I once loved. I offered the idea of sponsoring the cook-off as a last resort and, in response, Gray did a flip-flop and changed his mind about blackmailing me. Period."

Chapter 15

"Gray was asking you to pay him off for something Jeff did?" Sherry asked.

Pep strolled up to the sales counter. "What's with all the solemn faces? I need to make some plans." He scanned his audience and his smile disappeared.

Sherry gave Pep a look that chilled his joviality.

"Oh, this is a serious conversation. Forgive me," he said.

"Amber is announcing she may be leaving," Sherry said.

"You can go. I'm here till closing," Pep said. "Sherry, if you're here there's no problem."

"No. I mean go, as in Amber might leave town because she thinks we don't trust her anymore. Our efforts to get her off the suspect list, as misguided as they seem, have convinced her we don't love her as a member of our family and a most valued friend." Sherry's voice trembled as she let loose her emotions once again.

"No. No. No. Amber, listen to me. Sherry's heart of gold may have steered her brain in the wrong direction, but you're a believer in second chances. That I know," Pep said.

"You admitted you gave Gray a second chance. Why not us?" Sherry begged.

"We all love you very much." Pep wasn't pleading. He was so calm, in fact, Sherry wondered if his tactic might backfire. What if Amber didn't feel the passion behind the plea?

"Amber was telling me Gray was set to begin a blackmailing campaign, the goal of which was to keep a secret about her ex-husband," Sherry said. She turned to Amber. "Forgive me, but why do you even care about Jeff at this point? How bad could it have been? If he can't help himself, is the matter in your hands? That doesn't sound fair. He's ancient history."

Amber took a deep breath. "When I hired Jeff to do the bookkeeping for the Back Bay Therapy Group, I only thought I was doing the practice a favor. Him, too. He was out of work but was good with numbers and had solid accounting skills. Our bookkeeper was on maternity leave, so it was a win-win, I thought."

"Another kind gesture on your part," Sherry said.

"Turns out, he was a fox in the henhouse. Dipping into the cash reserves without anyone looking over his shoulder. In no time flat, we didn't even have enough money for payroll. Didn't take much detective work to trace where the leak in the cash flow was coming from. If word got out, we'd begin losing patients and referrals. Word gets around quickly in the health-care industry."

"I imagine you had to turn him in or the practice would implode."

"It wasn't that cut-and-dried," Amber said. "I was addressing other issues at the same time. Darn social media was giving Back Bay a hard time. One review site was especially and relentlessly harsh, giving us terrible ratings. Many people read those reviews and are influenced by them. It's a helpful method of referral if the reviews are positive."

"How did Gray get involved in all that? Do you think he was behind the negative reviews being published?" Pep asked.

"That would be a logical conclusion," Amber said. "Gray knowing Jeff had his fingers in the practice's pot is something that puzzles me. The matter was handled with discretion and kept very well contained."

"Do you recall whether any of the reviews were signed by someone who goes by *Buyer Beware in Boston*?" Sherry asked.

"Yes. That, I wouldn't forget. How did you know?"

"See? I'm trying to help you," Sherry repeated.

"As a patient, wasn't Gray interested solely in getting his money back for his therapy sessions?" Pep asked.

"Good question," Amber said. "At the time, over three years ago at this point, we had managed to avoid Gray pursuing a formal grievance against us. I won't go into details, I feel as if I've broken my oath of patient confidentiality already by sharing all this. Suffice it to say, he went away satisfied. Then he suddenly reached out. I didn't know what to think."

"So, he reached out to you first? Not the other way around? He brought up Jeff's shady activities?" Sherry asked.

"All these years later, yes. I don't even know how Gray got hold of the details he knew about what Jeff had done. It wasn't public knowledge. On the other hand, nothing seems to be a private matter these days."

"I'm guessing Jeff got away with just a slap on the wrist?" Sherry asked.

"Not even a slap," Amber said. "But it didn't end all bad. He agreed to a quickie, no-contest divorce and he was out of my life. That's all he wanted, besides the money he stole. I couldn't ruin his life with formal charges."

"Even though he nearly ruined yours?" Sherry said.

Amber's expression soured.

"Sorry, I shouldn't judge. I'm not you and I can't walk in your shoes."

"Desperate times call for desperate measures," Pep said. "As for Gray, he may have considered Amber his financial salvation. But you're saying what Jeff did wasn't common knowledge?"

"That's right. Jeff was able to carry on with his life as if nothing had ever occurred, since I didn't press charges. I wanted out of the practice at that point. I needed a fresh start. Tig understood and didn't try to stop me. Leaving was best for me and the practice. Since then, I've maintained out of sight, out of mind where Jeff's concerned."

"Saving Jeff's hide may not be worth all this excess trouble he's put you through," Sherry said.

"Do *you* hate your ex-husband enough to throw away any shred of kindness you have the ability to show him?" Amber asked Sherry.

Sherry's eyebrows lifted.

"I'm not that person. I suppose that's my downfall, but I'd rather go down with my compassion intact. If Gray wanted to bring up the past with the idea of exploiting my association with Jeff for his financial gain, I figured, let him try. I was on Jeff's side no matter what happened between us."

"I know. You're such a good person. That's why you need to let us help you," Sherry pleaded. "Please."

"I can't stop you," Amber said. "I'd rather not continue this conversation. I haven't made up my mind what the immediate future holds. Seems like the time to move on may have presented itself." Amber trekked across the showroom floor. When she reached the other side she called out, "The lighter gray-brown is squirrel fur color, definitely."

Pep leaned into Sherry. "Does Detective Bease know all those nuggets of info? They only add to a case against Amber. She had more than enough reasons to want Gray gone if he was harassing her about a family scandal. This isn't good. Not at all."

Sherry shook her head. She wasn't sure of anything at the moment.

"Why didn't you come right out and ask Amber whether she was pushed too far by Gray after being forced to deal with Jeff's indiscretions," Pep said.

"And have her up and leave this very minute? No way. You heard her. She will walk away from something if the situation warrants. You know what? If she did kill Gray Washington, maybe he deserved it." Sherry raised her fist to pound the sales counter. She stopped short, remembering her tender, mending flesh.

"Call Ray," Pep said.

"Okay. Soon," Sherry said.

"You're stubborn."

"You're right."

Pep paced back and forth. "Gray was about to begin a blackmail scheme with Amber as victim. She thwarted his effort with a brilliant plan of her own. Kill him with kindness and generosity. Unfortunately, he ended up dead." Pep tapped his temple with his index finger. "What's the chance Amber's ex put Gray up to attempting blackmail? Kind of a backhanded reverse blackmail, with Gray being the middleman?"

"You know who might know? Livvy's private investigator, Bart Foster." Sherry picked up her phone. "He said he was sitting on some information. Maybe it's time he shared."

"What are you doing now?" Pep asked.

"I'm texting Livvy and asking her if she'd like a tour of one of Augustin's treasures, the Ruggery. Where she goes, Bart always follows." Sherry retrieved her phone and typed in a text inviting Livvy to a private showing of a hooked rug collection specifically designed for food lovers."

"I thought she had already stopped in."

"Only to recruit me to find Gray's killer. She never gave the store its due deserve, as Augustin's landmark hooked rug business."

"When is this impromptu showing?" Pep asked.

"I suggested in one hour. That will give her time to catch a ride but not enough time to change her mind about coming," Sherry said. She lifted the phone to her face. "That didn't take long. She's coming, and surprise, surprise, she asked if Bart could tag along. Let's get going and stockpile any rugs that have a food theme about them."

"Are you going to warn Amber?" Pep asked.

"I think it's better if they mosey in organically, unannounced, don't you think? She can chat with them if she wants to, or she can avoid them."

"Sher, you're playing with fire," Pep warned before heading to the stock room. "Hope you know what you're doing."

Within the hour Livvy and Bart arrived at the Ruggery. Livvy appeared excited to see what the shop had to offer. She gushed over the colors and design of each rug Sherry showed off. Bart hovered in the background, absorbing the interaction between the two. Sherry explained the history of hooked rugs in the New England area and how her family entered into the trade by chance when Erno's father acquired the store from a deceased artisan. Rather than sell the remaining stock and rebrand the store, Ernesto Sr. taught himself everything there was to learn about the craft, thereby saving a town treasure from extinction. Every opportunity Sherry had to tell the story was another addition to her pride reserve.

Sherry was also counting on the fact that the store's origin story never failed to ignite the desire for keepsake purchases by intrigued customers. Many times after the story of the store was told, a small purchase like a key ring sampler or an investment piece like a huge area rug would end up leaving with the satisfied customer. As Sherry had hoped, Livvy was no exception. She purchased an oval fireplace rug with a springtime leafy greens theme. During the showing of the rugs Sherry spotted Amber peeking out from the storeroom.

"Bart, are you interested in a rug?" Sherry asked. "I'll show you a different theme if you'd like."

Bart had a deer in the headlights glare on his face when Sherry addressed him. He must have been somewhere else in his head because he blinked the fog from his unfocused gaze before answering Sherry. "Sure."

"Pep, you take Livvy and her rug to the sales counter and I'll spend a few minutes with Bart. Wait for us before you ring up the orders."

Sherry led Bart to the farthest corner of the store, where she was sure no one could hear them converse. Bart's discomfort about being separated from Livvy was evident from the way he was surveying the entire store.

Sherry cleared her throat and mustered up a strong whisper. "I wanted to ask you a question in private. Do you know who may have begun the recall for Walter Hemphill's appliances? He's from Boston and I'm wagering the same person had a connection to Amber's therapy practice. Possibly Gray? Or Amber's ex-husband, Jeff? Either could be *Buyer Beware in Boston*."

"I could see how you might think there's a connection," Bart said. His attention drifted to a rug on display. "Gray is certainly a possibility. If he began the recall process for his own gain, he didn't achieve his goal. Why would Jeff Sherwin be involved in taking down Hemphill Appliances? We don't even know if he was acquainted with the store."

"*Buyer Beware* could be anyone." Sherry sighed.

Bart nodded and kept his sights on a particular rug.

"You like that one?" Sherry asked as she followed his line of sight to a beach scene rug.

"Yes, I do," Bart said. "I'm about to move and this would look sensational inside the front door of my new townhouse."

"I'm offering a special discount if you can give me a name of who initiated the recall," Sherry said without missing a beat.

"I don't have a name, that's the problem. I was prepared to wrap up the case after confronting Hemphill and getting him to confess to Gray's murder, but when he was taken to the hospital, he fell off the list. Someone was after him, not the other way around. I was back at square one." Bart paused. "How about a discount for trying?"

"I'll see what I can do. The rug is last year's design, maybe I could apply the past season discount," Sherry said.

"Doesn't Amber Sherwin work here?" Bart whispered. "Can I speak to her?"

Sherry peered over her shoulder. She glimpsed Amber's shadow through the doorway across the room. "She is, but she's on inventory duty in the back room this afternoon while I'm up front."

"Have you made a selection?" Livvy asked as she appeared at Bart's side. Sherry held up a rug. "That's lovely."

"Livvy, can I ask you something?" Sherry said. In her peripheral vision she caught sight of Bart's frown.

"Of course," Livvy answered. "I know you're on a mission to find my husband's killer in order to save your friend. I assumed that's what was behind the invitation for this private showing."

Sherry's breath caught in her chest. Was she that transparent? Most likely. But the plan worked, Livvy and Bart were at the store. Why second-guess herself?

"My hopes were to have everyone associated with the cook-off visit my family's store," Sherry said. She watched Livvy's face soften. "And, since you're here, I'd like to clear something up."

"Then why are we the only ones here?" Livvy's vision panned around. "Go ahead."

"Do you and Gray have an ongoing relationship with Jeff Sherwin since you all still reside in Boston?" Sherry's mouth dropped open when Amber entered the room before Livvy could respond.

"Did I hear the good name of Sherwin?" Amber said as she strode toward Sherry.

"You have excellent hearing," Sherry said. "Boston came up in conversation and you came up as a Bostonian."

"That's right and proud of it," Amber said.

"Livvy and Bart will be returning there Saturday, taking the long route by heading south to Long Island to retrieve her car first." Sherry picked up Bart's rug.

"Looks like you could use some help," Amber said. "Would you like me to ring that rug up?"

Livvy made a small step in Amber's direction. "I want to apologize for Gray's behavior over the years. I never in a million years thought I would ever run into you at a cook-off, then come to find out you were instrumental in getting our products the sponsorship. We owe you a great thank-you for the exposure."

"But Gray was murdered . . ." Amber began.

"We *will* find out who killed him. That's a separate issue." Livvy was emotionless in her insistence.

"There are some who think it was me," Amber said with a quick glance at Sherry.

"Gray caused you all manner of trouble. He tried to hide it from me, but what Bart has uncovered has horrified me. I would have killed him if I were you," Livvy said.

"I don't hold grudges," Amber said and again glanced in Sherry's direction. "At least that's a goal of mine and something I used to preach to my patients. Too much misdirected energy. I wanted to help Gray, not punish him."

"The question is, who did want to punish him?" Livvy said.

Amber shook her head slowly. "Let me help you over at the register."

"Yes, please," Sherry said. "Oh, and I've worked in a special discount for them both."

After checking out, Livvy and Bart exited the store, satisfied with their purchases. Sherry was left with no more information than she had before the duo stopped in. Closing time couldn't come fast enough. The tension in the air between her and Amber had settled into an uneasy quiet that prevented Sherry from her usual banter with her friend about cooking, tennis, gardening and the topics being covered in the next Augustin newsletter. Amber seemed to be doing her best imitation of someone who wanted to not be seen or heard. She stayed in the back room most of the remaining store hours, leaving Sherry and Pep to greet and assist the customers. Then Pep left early to attend to some truck business with the help of Don.

When five o'clock arrived, Amber snatched her coat off the hook. With one hand on the front door and the other on Bean's leash, she bid Sherry an unenthusiastic goodbye.

"Doing anything fun tonight?" Sherry asked in a desperate attempt to liven the tone at the last moment.

"Tig convinced me to take a walk on the beach, that's the reason I'm rushing out the door. Doesn't stay light much past six and I need to drop Bean at home. Tig's leaving on Don's boat. He's very excited about the crossing to Long Island."

"Does he have a car there? He didn't take the boat on the first leg," Sherry said.

"Yes. He was out in the Hamptons before the cook-off. He rode the train here, not aware of Don's new service."

"And would you like to come on the crossing? You, also, missed the first leg and Don would love to show off his new love."

Amber stared at her friend for a moment. "Maybe."

Relieved Amber was less guarded, Sherry called it a victory and ended the brief but positive chat.

After pulling the door open Amber paused. Turning her head slightly in Sherry's direction she asked, "Are you doing anything fun tonight?"

Sherry stifled the urge to launch into a full-on explanation of the night's activities. Preserving the peace was the number-one priority, and the less talk the better seemed to be the right formula. "I'm meeting Don at Pep's house. They're working on his spreadsheets for the truck. That's why Pep left the store early. Not a terribly exciting evening, but necessary."

A wave sealed the goodbye.

Twenty minutes later Sherry and Chutney arrived at Pep's house. The first thing she did was scoop Mimi up into her arms. "Did you guys accomplish the task at hand?"

"Ten more minutes. It's taken us about an hour so far, and I can see the light at the end of the tunnel," Don said. "Pep's knowledge is invaluable. Numbers are my thing, so we're a great team."

Pep peeked out from behind the laptop screen. "One of us should fold their business and join the other in their venture."

"Not me," Don said. "I can't cook under pressure. And I've never cooked to please customers. I think I'd have to pay them to eat my food. I better stick with captaining a boat."

"Not me either," Pep said. "I wouldn't be much help being a crew member on a boat. I'm really a landlubber at heart. And I don't mind cooking under pressure as long as it's not for a cook-off judge."

"I don't believe a word either of you two are saying. Safe to say, probably for the best you two don't team up," Charlotte said. "They say relationships between family members who work together often suffer irreparable damage."

"Don's not a family member, unless you and Sherry have an announcement you'd like to make," Pep said.

"Pep, leave them alone," Charlotte scolded.

"How did this conversation go so far off the rails," Sherry said. "Don's never coming over here again if we harass him."

"I'm having fun being the fly on the wall," Don said. "Maybe I'll find out how serious Sherry is about me from this inquisition."

"Charlotte, isn't there something you'd like to show Mimi and me until these two are done with spreadsheet building?" Sherry asked. "Your new garden? Your she-shed?"

"You've scared her away," Pep said to Don.

"As a matter of fact, I do have something to show you," Charlotte said. "Follow me."

Charlotte led Sherry out the side door, down the short driveway to the one-car garage. Mimi was snuggled in Sherry's arm. Chutney shadowed alongside.

"I have an idea about using the back of the garage for a project area and I want your opinion as to what shape table Pep can build me. Right now, the space is being used for the bags of garbage Pep's had to haul from his truck location, but I don't think that will continue because I can't imagine the smell won't attract unwanted critters in here. We need a solution to that problem."

Not one to often admire garages, Sherry couldn't help but appreciate the miniature version of Pep's main house. Colonial in appearance and robust in strength. Nothing showy, but the impression of a solid structure that had withstood a century of New England weather extremes.

"This is a wonderful space. A window for light, these shelves. All you need is a table, you're right," Sherry said as she surveyed the space in the back of the small garage.

"Let me move these bags so you can get the full picture." Charlotte slid one large black garbage bag across the space. The area opened up nicely. A second bag was more difficult to wrestle with. After one failed attempt at sliding it, Charlotte lifted the unwieldy sack.

"Watch out!" Sherry warned when a large shiny object pierced through the black plastic. "The blade!"

The knife landed so close to Charlotte's sandaled foot she had to hop from foot to foot to avoid the subsequent bounces as it vaulted off the cement garage floor with a clang. When the knife came to rest, Charlotte's face was blanched with shock.

"That was close," Charlotte said. "Glad you were holding Mimi. Also, glad Chutney wasn't close by."

Sherry stepped toward the knife, which came to rest at a menacing angle, blade tip aimed in the women's direction. The wooden handle boasted the familiar initials *S.O.*

"Those are my initials. Don carved them into the wooden handle of the knife. He knew I'd be bringing it to my future cooking competitions and some identifying mark would be useful in case I misplaced it. He was right. I need a paper towel to pick that up, in case of fingerprints, besides my own and Amber's."

"I'll grab one from the kitchen. Back in a sec," Charlotte said. She carefully placed the torn bag in the corner and ran from the garage.

Sherry resisted flipping the knife over to check for smudges, smears or splatters. None of which she welcomed finding. The side facing upward was clean, too clean. If the murderer used the knife, he or she did a stellar job of cleaning the surface afterward.

"Here you go," Charlotte said between heaving breaths. She handed Sherry a thick stack of paper towels after retrieving Mimi from Sherry's embrace. "I didn't even stop to explain the find to Pep or Don. Should we call Detective Bease?"

Sherry held her stance while she considered Charlotte's question. "How long has the garbage bag been in the garage?"

"Let me think. Could have been since the first day Pep parked his food truck at the Sound Shore Lodge, or possibly from the next day's lunch over there. He had to remove his garbage both times."

"So, a day or more," Sherry surmised. "In that case, Ray can wait a little longer. I'd like Amber to know of our find before he does. He doesn't necessarily need to know he wasn't the first I contacted, does he?"

"Whatever you say," Charlotte said. "You're the sleuth here, I'm only in training."

Sherry knelt down and flipped the knife over using a paper towel as protection from contaminating the handle any further. The other side of the blade was spotless, as if it were run through the dishwasher. Maybe the knife wasn't used as the murder weapon. If Amber thought the knife was recovered she might be more inclined to fill in some of the ambiguities in her story.

"Amber lost her knife, and I use the term *lost* loosely because I feel it was taken. Anyway, she discovered the knife was missing the day of the orientation. The same day Gray's body was discovered."

"You're positive these bags only contain waste from the lodge lunches?"

"One hundred percent sure. We wanted to keep the truck's trash separate and recorded, as part of Pep's data analytics," Charlotte explained. "He wants to make his truck as eco-friendly as possible, so reducing waste over time is one of his goals."

"Gives me the shivers to think what could have gone wrong when the knife poked through the plastic if you hadn't reacted so swiftly," Sherry said as she wrapped the knife carefully in a paper towel coat. "Home cooks call that the knife dance when a knife falls off the kitchen counter. Fancy footwork is essential to avoiding an injury."

"Where should we store the knife until you're ready to talk to the detective?" Charlotte asked.

"Can we use the highest shelf?" Sherry pointed to the top shelf on the back wall to the side of the window. "We have to tell Pep so he doesn't have a repeat of our near miss."

"Good plan."

"Sherry, time for a romantic walk on the beach before dinner," Don announced as he entered the garage. "Okay, what are you two schemers up to. I've never seen two guiltier faces in my life." He kissed Mimi. "Make that three."

Sherry walked Don through their discovery. "I can't believe you had a walk on the beach before dinner in mind. You must have ESP. That's exactly where we're headed."

Chapter 16

It was nearing twilight by the time Sherry and Don parked at the lodge.
"We have about thirty minutes of daylight," Sherry estimated. "The sunset should be gorgeous."

"This wasn't the beach I had in mind. A bit rocky here, don't you agree? And you chose a treacherous way for us to get down to the beach in dim light," Don said as they stepped onto the steep path leading to the strip of rocky beach.

"I know. It's the beach Amber's on, so I didn't have much say in the matter."

"Wait. You painted the picture of a romantic walk on the beach at sunset with your boyfriend. How does Amber fit into that scenario?"

"Tig and Amber will be here, if we've timed this correctly."

"That doesn't really answer my question."

"As for this path, if I could hike down the bluff as an adolescent, why can't I trek through the brambles and sea roses now?"

"I won't doubt your ability for fear of retribution," Don said. "To be safe and romantic, hold my hand." He reached out and guided Sherry through the overgrown bushes only deer may have navigated recently. "Why didn't we park down at the beach?"

"I was hoping for the element of surprise," Sherry said.

"Amber certainly will be surprised if we Jack and Jill down this hill, in a tumbling mess." Don caught the toe of his sneaker on a wandering prickle bush branch as he made his joke. His resulting lurch forward yanked Sherry's hand out of his. "See?"

"There she is," Sherry said in a hushed tone. "Where's Tig? I wanted him in on this, too. I think he can help us with suggestions as to who wrote the review of Back Bay and Hemphill Appliances. He must know his patient clientele well."

Sherry followed Don through the clearing to the open rocky beachfront. Amber was yards away gazing out over the water. The sun was nearly down and Amber's dark silhouette made for an artistic contrast to the oranges and purples of the approaching dusk. She turned as they neared.

"So pretty," Sherry said. "One of the loveliest sunsets I've seen in a while."

"You're right. Were you looking for me?" Amber asked.

"I'd be lying if I said I wasn't hoping to run into you here," Sherry said. "Where's Tig? I counted on him being here."

"You missed him. We met here for a walk and a talk about me moving back to Boston. We're thinking of restarting a practice together. Revisiting my roots as a therapist. I like Tig. Not romantically, but as a person. I think the fit is a good one," Amber said.

"Wow, I wasn't expecting that. But that decision only makes me want to act faster, for your sake," Sherry said.

"Can't you let the investigation take its natural course? Sometimes you have no control over these things," Amber said. "If I'm at the top of the list, so be it."

"This doesn't sound like you." Sherry implored Don to reinforce her side of the argument with an eyebrow lift.

"Sherry's made a discovery at Pep's house. You need to listen," Don said before throwing the look back in Sherry's direction.

"We found my knife." Sherry waited for Amber's reaction. She didn't get enthusiastic reaction she was hoping for.

"I'm so relieved. Whereabouts?" Amber said.

"In a garbage bag Pep brought back from the lodge grounds. The management over there made him take care of his trash, so he stores the bags in his garage until he consults with his sanitation pickup service."

"I feel better," Amber said. "I was going to replace the knife. I hadn't had a chance to shop yet. If there's anything wrong with the condition I take full responsibility and will still replace it. I'm so glad that mystery's solved."

"Still doesn't resolve whether the knife was the murder weapon or not. Gray's wound matches the knife's blade length and width exactly, Ray told me," Sherry said. "My gut feeling is my knife was not the murder weapon. It was so clean."

"You still think I did it?" Amber said.

"I don't think you did it and I never have. I want proof beyond a shadow of a doubt for the benefit of skeptics." Sherry tried to keep an even tone, but insistence snuck into her delivery.

Amber picked up a stone and tossed it in the ocean.

"I'm trying to help you, Amber," Sherry said.

Amber pitched a larger stone into the break of a small wave. "I don't want Tig involved in this. He and I have come a long way since the conflict

Gray caused for our practice. Jeff was a terrible source of discontent between us and all of that seems to have smoothed itself out over time. I may even get a friendship struck up with Jeff."

"That guy better head in. It's getting dark," Don said. He pointed to the rumbling jet ski on the water.

Sherry shaded her eyes from the setting sun with her hand. "He looks familiar," Sherry said. "I think it's the man I had a brief chat with at the marina before Don's first trip. His windbreaker had that bright flash of neon yellow." She looked again. "No, maybe not."

"The driver came over to the beach when he saw Tig and me here. The beach is so rocky he didn't dare try to pull the jet ski on shore, which disappointed Tig, who was hoping for a demo."

"This is not a good beach for landings," Don said.

"If that's all you need from me, I'd like to head home," Amber said. "I'm happy you found your knife."

"Me, too," Sherry said.

Sherry watched Amber dust the sand off her hands and stroll toward the parking lot. She suddenly left Don's side and ran to the water's edge. She bent down and retrieved a soft oval object with an animal pictured on one side. It was a keychain with a single key attached through a small hole. "Litterbugs are the worst." She examined the keychain closer. "Maybe this is what Bart was referring to," she said softly.

"Saving the planet one piece of garbage at a time. That's why I love you. Where are we having dinner?" Don asked.

"I love you, too. Why don't we eat at the lodge's smaller restaurant since we're here. They have less variety, but I've heard their seafood is to die for."

"We have to survive the trek up this bluff first," Don said as he clasped Sherry's healthy hand. "Try to keep up."

Fifteen minutes later, the sun had set and Sherry and Don were seated in the small dining room decorated in beachy colors. Sherry admired the attention to detail on the walls. Ocean scenery paintings, sea life figurines on driftwood shelves and one detail she found near and dear to her heart. An Oliveri rug lay at the foot of a fish tank sunk into a side wall. The diners were welcomed with a water's edge landscape rendering, an exclusive design commissioned by the owners. The familiar rug prompted Sherry to name-drop her family's business and the hostess immediately called for the chef to come greet her and Don.

"Welcome to Fire and Ice," the man, dressed in a food-splattered chef's coat, said. His beard was neatly trimmed. His chef's hat flopped over to one side of his head. "I am Chef Alexi. I was told you are a member of the Oliveri family." The chef's Italian accent caressed each word he spoke. "What an Augustin treasure. Look at your beautiful handiwork." He swept his hand in the direction of the hooked rug. "Your family made me something special that brings me joy every day. Tonight, I will make you two something special. You are Mr. and Mrs. Oliveri?"

Before Sherry could nip the false information in the bud, Don nodded his head and said, "Maybe one day, I hope."

Sherry steadied her surging heartbeat. "Thank you so much, Chef Alexi. We're honored."

The hostess handed Sherry and Don a wine list after Chef Alexi returned to the kitchen with the promise of a wonderful meal to come.

"Well, that was unexpected," Don said. "The Oliveri influence reaches far and wide."

After reading the wine selection they were told their orders were already underway and to expect offerings only special guests received. Sherry and Don ordered a glass of wine and a beer. Sherry waited for the drinks to arrive in hopes the jovial spirit of the restaurant would segue the conversation back to Don's comment to the chef.

"What a treat," Don said.

"Good evening, you two."

Sherry peered behind her and was met with Livvy's round face. Her brown eyes glowed with warmth. Her hair was tucked under a gorgeous multicolored headwrap. Gold hoop earring adorned her ears. In response to the woman's striking appearance, Sherry ran her fingers through her own hair to spruce up her look. She hadn't checked her image in the mirror since leaving the house that morning. She immediately found a knot created by the beach wind. A moment later she gave up the fight with the tangle.

"Good evening, Livvy. Are you arriving or on your way out?" Sherry asked.

"All done. Had a wonderful scallop dinner on my last night. Don, looks like you have a full boat for the ride to Long Island. I've organized the remaining people to meet at the Augustin Marina at four tomorrow afternoon, as you said."

"That's right," Don said. "Looking forward to the trip. Keep an eye on the weather and you'll know what to wear."

"Good idea. Any progress on the search for Gray's murderer? That Detective Bease hasn't contacted me in the last twenty-four hours. Hope the clues haven't run dry."

Sherry studied the woman's pretty face. Age lines lent her an intelligent, caring aura. "Clues aren't always as recognizable as one would hope." She made a snap decision to dive right in. "Did Gray write the negative review of Hemphill Appliances that may have led to a recall?"

Livvy put up her hand. "Stop right there. Gray didn't write the Hemphill review. I read it. He showed it to me, as a matter of fact. You know why?"

"Because he was happy someone wrote a scathing review of a competitor?" Don guessed.

"Surprisingly, the opposite. Gray and I are very fond of Hemphill appliances. Our kitchen is exclusively Hemphill custom-designed. Washington Appliances might sell the second best but, believe me, I only wanted the very best for our house."

Sherry's mouth dropped open. She reached for her glass of wine and took a swig.

"I know, I know. It may be hard to swallow. But I'm confident he was a Hemphill fan," Livvy said as Sherry tapped Don on the back. "On the other hand, I can't say Gray didn't write the review of Back Bay years ago. He had plenty to say about the practice and what his hours spent in the therapist's office didn't do to resolve our marital issues."

"Buyer Beware in Boston," Sherry said. "Both reviews were penned with the same moniker."

Livvy cocked her head to the side. "Makes perfect sense his would be signed that way. He often said 'buyer beware,' as if he coined the phrase. We could be at the pharmacy and he'd say 'buyer beware' when I suggest we buy off-brand pain reliever. Or 'buyer beware' if we're at a restaurant and the fish on the menu wasn't local. He said it as late as the night before he was murdered. We were at the contestant dinner and Rickie O'Dell brought up the quality of the prize packages. Never mind, that's a bad example. Gray didn't say 'buyer beware' that night, Rickie did. She was relaying the story of Hemphill's product recall. You see? Anyone could use that term."

"You might be following a dead-end trail, Sherry," Don said. "Even if Gray had written both Hemphill and Amber's negative reviews and angered one, the other, or both, Hemphill wasn't Gray's murderer and we certainly know Amber wasn't either. Why do the reviews matter?"

"I think Gray wrote the review about Back Bay." Sherry was adamant.

"I think so, too," Livvy said. "There's power in a written review and that was his first step to announcing to the world he was unhappy with the therapy he heavily invested in."

"If he didn't write the Hemphill review someone copied his style and wrote the second, possibly to implicate him. There were too many style similarities," Sherry said. "But who? And why?"

"I wish I knew," Livvy said.

"What I don't fully understand is what prompted Gray to reach out to Amber after a long period of uneasiness between the two. She's down here now and he was up in Boston. She hasn't traveled back there since she moved to Augustin," Sherry said.

"My belief was Amber thought of us when the cook-off needed a sponsor fill-in. I was wrong."

"Wrong?"

"Turns out it wasn't her idea. Gray said she had someone push her in our direction. That's what Amber told him. He didn't share the name."

"Jeff," Sherry whispered.

"Does Bart think Jeff Sherwin killed Gray?" Don asked.

"It's crossed his mind. Jeff had reason for revenge if Gray had attacked his wife's livelihood. Or was withholding hurtful information."

The waitress arrived with plates and parked herself next to Livvy.

"Time to eat," Livvy said. She yielded her spot to the waitress. "I'll see you tomorrow at the marina, Don. Will I see you there, Sherry?"

"I'm definitely planning on coming along on the boat trip," Sherry said. She was too distracted by racing thoughts to give a convincing reply. She watched Livvy stroll away. "The name that keeps popping into my head is Jeff Sherwin."

"Are you also thinking Amber's ex-husband killed Gray?" Don asked as he scanned his surroundings. "I better keep my voice down."

Sherry shuddered as she analyzed her Caesar salad. The croutons were homemade and flecked with seasoning. The anchovy fillets were shimmering with olive oil and the Parmesan shavings were pungent with the aroma of tangy aged cheese. Nothing worse than a half-hearted Caesar salad. The salad Sherry was admiring was anything but. Even the romaine lettuce appeared to have recently been harvested out of someone's well-tended spring garden—vibrant green and sturdy with robust veins and ribs.

"Sherry? Are you there?"

"Sorry. Just lost in what my fork is about to transport to my mouth. Looks perfect."

"Amazing how you can switch gears and topics so seamlessly. Especially when there's food involved."

Sherry nodded in agreement.

"Let me ask again. Do *you* think Jeff Sherwin could have killed Gray Washington?" Don speared a pink shrimp out of the cocktail sauce.

After swallowing her first bite, Sherry was ready to give Don's question it's due consideration. "He had his reasons. Gray was the catalyst for the demise of Amber's practice, maybe even their marriage, although Amber gives some of that credit to a seductive secretary in Jeff's prior job. Jeff doesn't have a spotless character record. He embezzled from Amber's practice when she hired him to do some bookkeeping. The situation was dealt with and kept quiet but maybe word got out? That occurred years ago now. People do hold grudges."

"Why isn't Amber telling the police her ex-husband may be stalking her here in Augustin?"

Sherry used her hand to illustrate the shift from point to point. "But maybe she doesn't know he's here."

"He's here? What do you know, young lady?" Don said between bites.

"Nothing for sure. Once again, I need to hear it from the source. And I haven't. Right now, Amber's not volunteering much, and when I bring up any information I've stumbled upon, the reception I get isn't welcoming. We haven't even spoken about Jeff being involved, beyond Amber telling me about his embezzling. The prospect is nerve-racking. What's even more nerve-racking is Amber might be next on the hit list."

Chapter 17

Don left Sherry's house before breakfast Saturday morning. The prior evening's plan wasn't to spend the night together, but once they returned to Sherry's house to catch an episode of their favorite crime drama, Don fell asleep on the couch. He woke with a stiff neck and yesterday's outfit needing an iron. Sherry's offer of steel-cut oatmeal with banana and walnuts was refused due to time constraints. She sent him off with a more portable blueberry muffin.

"I have a few hours before I ride the *Current-Sea*. There's one more bullet point on my Gray Washington list to check out. Are you listening, little man?" She bent down and ruffled Chutney's fur. He sniffed her hand and licked a stray muffin crumb off her finger. "I'll be back soon."

Sherry arrived at the inn as the last of the breakfast diners were leaving the dining room. As she hoped, she caught Tig on his way back to his room.

"Tig? Can I have a quick word with you?" Sherry called after Tig as he was reaching for the elevator button. He retracted his hand and turned.

"Hi, Sherry. Bringing some coffee back to my room." He held up a thermos. "Of course. What do you need?" He made no move away from the elevators.

As Sherry closed in on Tig she realized she hadn't practiced her opening line. She needed to find the words that would pry vital answers from a man she barely knew. Knowing they would both be seeing Amber in a few hours, she had to be sensitive to her approach. A rehash of the conversation would surely make its way to Amber next time the two spoke.

"I'm interested in helping clear any doubt investigators have about Amber's involvement in Gray Washington's murder."

"I know. Amber has expressed her concerns you've overstepped the friendship boundaries between you and her in your efforts. Do you think you should leave well enough alone and let the experts do their jobs?"

That was the most she had ever heard Tig say since she met him. She was taken aback by his candor.

"Our friendship means the world to me," Sherry said in her defense. "I was hoping to have this conversation with her yesterday when you two were at the beach after dinner, but I missed you by the time I found Amber."

"I wasn't at the beach yesterday. I thought about a walk on the beach but never got around to it." The elevator door opened and a couple with giggling children spilled out. Tig put his hand on a button to keep the door from shutting.

"Just before sunset? You weren't at the beach with Amber? She said you were."

"Nope." He looked back at the elevator as the doors struggled to close. "Anything else?"

"Before you go, I have a question about Jeff Sherwin. Is he in Augustin now? Would I have seen him at the marina a few days ago?"

Tig removed his hand from the elevator and the doors merged shut. "Now? Maybe. At the marina? I'm not sure. He does love jet skis."

"Was he here the night Gray was murdered?"

"Yes."

"Was he at the beach yesterday?"

"I believe he was jet skiing just before sunset," Tig said.

A woman rushed past Tig to push the elevator button.

"Did I answer your questions?" The elevator dinged and the doors slid open. Tig followed the woman inside.

"Yes, thank you."

"See you later. At the boat. I think Amber's joining us." Tig waved goodbye as the doors slid shut.

Sherry returned home to walk Chutney and organize her thoughts. Jeff Sherwin was, and may still be, in town. Amber never mentioned a word. Did she know? Of course, she had to know. Even if Jeff didn't contact Amber, Tig certainly would have mentioned her former husband and his best friend was in Augustin during her cook-off. They could all be friends, couldn't they? Unless Jeff was harboring resentment. Unless he was a murderer. By the time Sherry and Chutney passed her neighbor Eileen's house, Sherry's pace had increased from a leisurely stroll to a determined strut.

Back inside her house, she gathered her cool weather gear as she had seen the clouds increase and the wind pick up. Not the weather she would choose for a boat ride across the Long Island Sound, but she was resigned to the mission. She left the house with an hour to spare. Enough time to make a stop before meeting Don at the marina.

The brick building a block down from the marina's entrance welcomed its clientele with an array of paraphernalia on display. A water sport enthusiast's dream. A paddleboard, a jet ski, a tiny sailboat, a kite surfboard and water skis were all lined up to give potential renters and purchasers many choices of equipment. H-2-OH! wasn't a store Sherry frequented, and she felt more than a bit out of place shuffling past the merchandise in search of the manager or any salesperson.

A young man dressed in board shorts and a flower-print T-shirt hustled over to Sherry when she neared the rack of wetsuits. His bleached white hair stood vertical in an impossibility of physics. Sherry pulled her light down coat tighter around her. His lack of warm clothes projected a chill onto her.

"May I help you, ma'am?"

"Hi. I'm planning on renting a paddle board later in the season and I was wondering if you had a price list? Also, I'd like the jet ski prices for another outing, please."

"Awesome. Follow me." He led Sherry to the sales counter.

"You'd think it was July the way you're dressed." She laughed and waited for the young man's bountiful chuckle to end before continuing. "You remind me of my brother. He used to wear shorts all winter."

"I'm a hard-core summer celebrator year-round," he said. He handed Sherry a lengthy price sheet. "This should have everything you're looking for and more."

"Do you get many equipment rental requests this time of year?"

"This was a busy week. Unusual for early spring. There's some epic cooking event going on that brought in lots of out-of-towners. Bonus for me when that happens. Weather's been awesome. Snow at night, fifties in the day. Blows my mind."

"My friend recommended your store to me after renting here. I wonder if you'd remember him. Handsome, athletic guy, name is Jeff Sherwin. You waited on him a few days ago? He had such a positive referral for you."

"You've just described every dude that comes in here. Let me think. Did he rent a wetsuit?"

"I have no idea. His top layer was a windbreaker. Still, he's a hardy guy. Must have been chilly."

"Yep. I know exactly who you're talking about. Said he wanted to surprise his friend. Said she was riding on a boat and he would catch up to her. I didn't know how he'd do that unless he was familiar with the Long Island Sound, but he seemed determined. Rented for an hour and returned the jet ski right on time. Said he never found his friend, which was a bummer. The sound is a lot bigger than people can wrap their heads around." He shook his head and amazingly not one luminous piece of hair shifted out of place.

"Jeff Sherwin? You're sure of the name?" Sherry asked.

"One hundred percent. If a rental agreement is signed, I always require identification. My father's name is Jeff, so the name stuck in my brain."

"How about a man named Walter Hemphill? Did he rent a jet ski? Maybe at the end of the day?"

The young man twirled the leather bracelet on his wrist between his fingers. "Oh, man. I messed up. It's been a rough week with no shut-eye. I drive a car service after hours and the cook-off meant so many more calls for rides I didn't know what hit me. The minute I left work here I was on duty. I went all night until the calls stopped."

"No wonder you can't think straight," Sherry said.

"Let me see. The Hemphill dude rented a few days ago and the Sherwin dude rented yesterday afternoon. I was confused because they came into the store at the same time the first time. Only Mr. Hemphill made a purchase. Mr. Sherwin returned days later, which I was glad about because he really wanted to rent and seemed to blow a fuse when Mr. Hemphill was helped before him. He hit the road without his ID. I had to hoof it after him to return it."

"I know Walter Hemphill," Sherry said. "A nice man. I know he had fun on the water." Her exaggeration of knowing Walter more than slightly seemed to soothe the salesman's agitation.

"Say, are you a cop? Are these guys in hot water?"

"No, no, nothing like that. Just a friend," Sherry said with no further explanation.

"Good. Hey, I didn't even ask. Why not rent a board today? A little cool on the water. I'd recommend a wetsuit."

Sherry checked the huge wall clock. "I would, only I have an appointment in half an hour. I'll definitely file these price lists for my next adventure."

"Awesome. See you when I see you."

The drive to the marina gave Sherry a few minutes to consider the pieces of the puzzle and how they did or didn't fit together. Jeff Sherwin was in town. Good chance Walter Hemphill was the jet skier who veered into the path of the *Current-Sea*. Why would he do a thing like that? Does Amber even know her vindictive ex-husband may have been a stone's throw from her at any given time over the last few days? Sherry's temple began to pulse. She reached in her pants pocket and found the keychain she'd collected off the beach.

"Hey, good-lookin'. You going to sit in your car all day or can you give me a hand with the boat ropes."

Sherry replaced the keychain in her pocket. Through the open window she received a welcome kiss.

"Hey there, yourself." Sherry gathered her purse off the passenger seat and closed the window. After stepping out of the car, she accepted Don's chivalrous hand as she crossed a large puddle.

"You have something on your mind besides me and the boat. Care to share?"

Sherry unfurrowed her brow and relaxed her shoulders. "You read me like a book. I think Jeff Sherwin was here at the marina the day we made the crossing to Long Island. He went to H-2-OH! to rent a jet ski to harass Amber because she was supposed to be on the *Current-Sea*. He didn't get a chance to, though, because Walter Hemphill rented before him, so he left in a huff. I think Amber is in real danger."

"But someone did harass us. If it wasn't Jeff, who was it? And why?"

"It was Walter Hemphill and I'm not sure why. I imagine he was angry with the cook-off organizers and venting. He's over the whole situation now, so he's riding the boat today rather than toying with us."

"That's a lot," Don said. "I don't want to put a damper on your sleuthing progress, but right now I need to concentrate on the commute to Long Island. The passengers are arriving in twenty minutes and I have a few more details to attend to. Mind if I assign you a job?"

"You're right. I'm sorry. That's why I'm here."

"Plenty of time to sort out all those details. Amber will be with us for the next few hours so she's safe. Right now, would you please double-check there is a life vest for at least fourteen passengers. We don't have that number of passengers, but more is better than less. And please lay them out so they are easily accessible once the bin is open. They get jostled around, and in case of emergency I want the procedure to be easy." Don adjusted the *Current-Sea* logoed cap resting on his head.

"Understood," Sherry said.

"I'll pay you later," Don said simply, before waving Sherry down the dock toward the boat. The sea air cooled the warm rush Sherry felt sweep across her face.

Sherry had completed her safety check of the life vests and was next assigned to greeting and logging in the passengers. Walter Hemphill was the first passenger to arrive, fifteen minutes prior to the scheduled time. Walter had picked up a bronzed glow since Sherry last saw him. He projected an attractive confident air as he struck up a conversation while waiting for Don to give the all-clear to board.

"Sherry, again, let me apologize to you and Rickie for my temper. You know I wasn't happy when I came to Augustin days ago. Someone had a beef with my product and the criticism hit me hard. I was hoping to find whoever it was if I came to the cook-off. Now none of that matters. Gray is dead. I had a health scare. I'm fine. My business will recover. Gray won't."

"I'd like to find who killed Gray," Sherry said. "Do you have any ideas?"

"Sherry? Livvy Washington and Bart Foster are behind you," Don called from the boat.

Sherry flipped her sights to the duo making their way down the dock. "Welcome, welcome," Sherry said.

Livvy flowed down the dock in linen pants and striped sneakers. Bart followed a step behind wrapped in a warm overcoat. "You coming, Bart? Which seats do we want?"

Sherry considered Livvy's cotton sweater was no match for the ocean winds. "Are you going to be warm enough, Livvy? I can lend you my coat."

"I have a windbreaker you could borrow," Walter said as he approached. "Works great. Kept me warm on my jet ski ride the other day."

"Hi, Walter. Thank you for the offer, both of you. I'll see if I need another layer when we get underway. I have a lot of insulation on these bones. I'm hardly ever cold." Livvy laughed while pinching her forearm.

"The last of the passengers are arriving," Don said as he shuffled across the dock. "Sherry, would you show this group to their seats? I'll greet Amber, Tig and the McDonalds."

"I wanted to say something to you, Livvy," Walter said as Sherry held the group up at the gangplank. "I thought you and Gray were behind my company's recall. I believe you when you say you weren't. I'm so sorry about Gray. I've enjoyed our rivalry throughout the years. Boston's kitchens are better places because of the healthy competition."

"I understand," Livvy said. "And I hope you accept my apology for thinking you killed my husband."

Sherry's breath caught in her throat and she gagged. When she regained her composure, she led the group aboard the boat. "Outside seating?"

"Yes, please," Livvy said.

"All aboard," Don shouted. Amber, Tig, Jean and Curt filed across the gangplank to wait for further instructions.

"Welcome," Sherry said. "For those who have not been on the *Current-Sea*, the rows are three across. There isn't a bad seat in the house. The view is wonderful, and today's weather is really perfect for spring. Cloudy, breezy. I would recommend an extra layer if you need to fish one out of your bags before we secure them under your seats." Sherry observed some reaching for their suitcases' zippers. "Be careful. Watch your step. Tig, you might want to do that at your seat."

Sure enough, Walter caught his toe on the suitcase lid, scattering the contents as a result, as he attempted to bypass a squatting Tig. He swallowed half a curse word and hopped to his seat, keeping his sore foot off the ground until he was seated.

With jackets on, passengers stowed their luggage under the roomy seats. Jean and Curt sat in a row across from Amber, Tig and Sherry. Rickie and Bart claimed the front row of seats and had a close view of Don's impressive instrument console. Walter sat solo in the row across from Rickie and Bart. While Amber and Tig nestled into their seats, Sherry returned to the captain's chair and whispered in Don's ear.

"After your safety talk, I have something to say to the group before we set sail."

Don clutched the steering wheel. "Sherry, what are you up to?"

"Why, nothing. You make it sound as if I'm up to no good. Just a few words, that's all." She planted a kiss on Don's cheek and strode the short walk toward the stern to sit next to Amber.

Don faced the passengers and welcomed them aboard the second inaugural voyage of Captain Don's Commuter Cruiser. He pointed out the bin containing the life vests, described their usage and gave a run-through of emergency procedures in the case of fire, power loss or collision. Sherry crossed her fingers and said a little prayer none of the stated emergency procedures would need to be executed during the voyage. When Don was done explaining emergency survival techniques, he made eye contact with Sherry.

"Sherry, do you have something you'd like to say?"

"Yes, thank you. One minute." Sherry rose from her seat and shimmied down the deck toward the captain's chair. As she passed the front row of seats, Walter tapped her on the forearm.

"Sherry, can I tell you something?"

Sherry leaned down to his eye level. "Yes, Walter, what is it?"

He lowered his voice to an airy whisper. "I banged my toe on a mermaid."

"I'm sorry, I don't think I heard you correctly. Don's radio is blaring."

She shifted her attention to Don, who punched the radio receive button and the connection crackled to life. "*Current-Sea*, over," Don said.

"*Current-Sea*, this is Marina Dockmaster. There is a man here who would like to join the commute. I have added him to the passenger list since you haven't departed. He's on his way down. Please, hold up a minute."

"Copy," Don said. "Looks like we have one more passenger. Sherry, I'm sorry. Go ahead with what you have to say."

Sherry turned to face Walter.

"Thermos, not mermaid. When I banged into it, something metal rattled around inside." He pinched his face up tight. His eyes begged her to understand. She wasn't sure she did. "He's been carrying the same thermos every day I've seen him. We shared a shuttle bus back to the inn. He put the thermos on the floor of the bus and it fell over with a hefty clang. Unless he had metal ice cubes inside, I can't imagine what he stores in there. Maybe drug paraphernalia?"

Sherry's mouth hung open. She returned her attention to Don. "I don't have anything to add," Sherry said to Don. She made her way back to her seat.

A moment later, Amber grabbed Sherry's thigh and gasped. "What is he doing here?"

"Well, well, well. Look what the cat dragged in," Tig said. He stood and stepped over Amber and Sherry to get to the edge of the boat. "You accepted my invitation after all."

The man Sherry had chatted with at the marina days ago extended his hand toward Tig as he climbed aboard. "Hi, buddy."

"Is that?" Sherry began.

Amber answered before Sherry could finish the question. "Yes, that's Jeff."

"Hi, Amber," Jeff said from a row away.

Don stepped forward and introduced himself to Jeff, who, in turn, gave his name.

"Sherwin? Are you a relation to Amber Sherwin?"

When Don's gaze crossed Sherry's, the expression on her face was enough to stop him in his tracks. "Oh my gosh, you were married to each other. I'm an idiot."

Jeff nodded.

"Well, you could knock me over with a feather," Don said. He pointed to an empty seat in Walter's row. "We're about to get underway. Why don't you have a seat next to Walter. Tuck your case under the seat, please."

Sherry watched Jeff sidle across the row of seats to sit next to Walter, pulling his rolling suitcase behind him.

"Jeff made a surprise appearance at the cook-off, thanks to an invitation from Tig." Amber's words were clipped. "I was going to tell you, but I honestly was so conflicted about him being here I couldn't process talking about him. It's hard to explain."

"I don't really understand but I have to respect your feelings," Sherry said. Her chest was tight with an emerging emotion she fought hard to control.

"If everything is secured, especially your hats, we'll be getting underway, folks," Don announced from the bridge. "We have a nearly full load, which I'm thrilled about. Hope everyone is comfortable. If anyone would like to visit me up here on the bridge, Sherry will walk you up. I just ask we only have two people at a time. Space is limited. Thank you. Bon voyage."

"We'd love to," Jean called out. "Right, Curt?"

"Okay. I'll let you know when the time is right," Don said. He pushed buttons, turned knobs and the motors rumbled to life. The water churned around the boat as the vessel backed away from the dock.

Sherry leaned into Amber's ear. "How are you feeling right now?"

"I don't like this," Amber said. "What does Jeff want? Why didn't Tig tell me he was coming on the trip?"

The boat jerked as Don's hand threw the throttle forward to begin the navigation out of the marina.

Chapter 18

The *Current-Sea* picked up speed as the last of the harbor's "drive slow" markers disappeared out of sight.

"Ladies, I would like a tour of the captain's bridge. Would that be alright, Sherry?" Tig said as he leaned across Amber.

"Of course," Sherry said. The wind took hold of her words. She hoped they were delivered.

Tig stood and motioned to Jeff. "Want a look?"

Jeff nodded.

Sherry touched Amber's shoulder as she passed her. "Be right back."

Sherry joined Tig and Jeff at the bridge. The sun's rays flashed off the shiny metal cylinder in Tig's hand and blinded Sherry for a second. She blinked to regain her vision.

"It's okay to have some iced tea, isn't it?" Tig asked.

"It's tricky getting the liquid in your mouth while bouncing over the open ocean," Sherry said and laughed. "Oh, and I'm not so sure Don allows food or beverage near the captain's area."

"Welcome, gentlemen," Don said. Sherry sidled up to him with Tig and Jeff following close behind. "This is where the magic happens."

Don went through a litany of purposes for each control, gauge and meter on the console. He explained the new radar system read the depth of the water below and kept an electronic eye out for potential obstacles off the bow. Tig was particularly fascinated with the radar's capabilities. He had a number of questions about safety protocol, as if he may one day buy a boat. Sherry was proud of the answers Don provided. He wasn't stumped by any questions until Tig threw in a curveball.

"You need to take me to the Westerly Point State Park. Amber and I are taking a trip. How long until we can get there?"

Sherry's brow pinched together. Had she heard Tig correctly? The wind rushing past her ears was making for some sketchy interpretation of the conversation. She set her sights on Don to get confirmation she had heard Tig ask to be taken to an unscheduled destination.

Don kept his eye on the horizon ahead. "We are on a preset itinerary. That's impossible." His tone left no room for negotiation.

Sherry peered over her shoulder at Amber. She had her sights pinned to Sherry as if she could read the change in mood and was waiting for further instruction. Did Amber know Tig would make such a request?

"Just do it," Tig said.

"Tig. What are you talking about?" Jeff said. "We can't head north to Rhode Island. We're going south to Long Island."

"I have a knife in this thermos. Does that persuade you?"

Don's head swiveled from his instrument panel to the passengers in their seats and back again. Sherry's heart began to pound. She turned her attention to Jeff. If he decided it was time to join Tig in hijacking the boat, Don would be outnumbered. They were already outnumbered in weapons—zero to one.

"Okay, Tig," Don said. He took one hand off the boat's steering wheel and showed Tig his palm. "Take it easy. We have already registered our itinerary with the Coast Guard. If we don't follow the planned route they will come looking for us in no time. That's their job."

Tig sidestepped Sherry. He unscrewed the lid from his thermos and tipped the mouth in Don's direction. He pulled out the knife. "See this? I'm using it on Sherry if you don't aim this boat north." He replaced the knife and the lid.

"Is that my knife?" Jean called out. "If there's a red nail polish dot on the handle, that's my knife."

"Yes, it is," Tig said. "Thanks for leaving it on the picnic table when you visited Pep's food truck. Made things quite easy for me. I had Amber's knife, but it had some initials on it, so I threw it away. Too identifiable. She wasn't the one I wanted pinned for the murder. Why do you cooks insist on monogramming all your kitchenware?"

"Don't you even think about it," Jeff shouted through clinched teeth. He grappled with Tig's arm. Tig juggled the thermos before swinging it into Jeff's head, knocking him into Sherry before he tumbled down to the ground.

Screams and cries rolled forward from the other passengers. Don swung the boat hard left and everyone was scattered across the seats. "Hold on," he shouted. The boat slowed down so abruptly those not securely planted in their seats were thrown askew.

Sherry had a firm grip on the captain's console, but she wasn't happy about her close proximity to Tig. Before she could take a step back, she heard Amber shout, "Sherry! Look out!"

Sherry ducked to avoid Tig's grip seeking her neck.

"Get down," Don commanded. He lowered his voice. "Hold this and don't let go." Don handed her a coiled lanyard, one end clipped to the console. She went down on all fours and reverse-crawled from the jostling bodies. She backed into Jeff, who was moaning as he tried to regain his footing.

"I came here to stop him. I won't let him hurt Amber, or anyone else," Jeff said. He made a guttural groan as he lifted himself to his feet with the help of the captain's chair.

"Stay down," Don yelled.

Before Jeff could react, he was struck again, this time by the butt end of Tig's thermos. Jeff crumbled to the deck floor.

"Doesn't pay to be a hero. Amber, get up here. Everyone else, stay where you are."

Tig shoved Don from the captain's chair and the two wrestled for control of the boat's steering. Again, Tig pulled the knife from the thermos. This time he tossed the thermos overboard. "Amber, I'm waiting. Get up here. Don, change of plans. Take us to that beach landing over there round the bend. Do what I say and no one else will get hurt." He motioned for Don to take back the steering.

"We can't land there. Too rocky. My boat will be destroyed."

"Not my problem. Slow the boat down and don't try anything. People, get back in your seats. Don't pick up anything or I'll use this knife on our captain."

"What do you want from me?" Amber implored as she approached Tig. When she reached Sherry, crouched on the deck next to Jeff's limp body, she stopped.

Sherry rose from her knees with Amber's assistance.

"I want what you owe me," Tig said as he brandished the knife over Don's head. "You and Jeff ruined my life. I have nothing. When you left the practice, patients never returned. I was responsible for half of what Jeff stole because I was your partner and his best friend. I had no way of explaining to potential employers my situation without sacrificing Jeff's reputation. I kept that secret, Amber. You went on to a new life while I was left with nothing." Tig pounded his fist on the radar screen.

Don flinched as if he were the one being pummeled.

"He hid the knife in the thermos," Walter called from his seat. "That's what I tripped on."

Tig pointed at Walter. "And you! You're lucky to be alive. Since you were always in the way of my plans, you were going to take the rap for

Gray's death. You made the perfect decoy for the investigators. You had a beef with the cook-off organizers, but it was nothing in comparison to my situation. When you went over to the convention hall that night, I almost killed you instead of Gray to get you out of my hair. But I was reminded of the play, *Scrambled*. That saved your hide."

"How so?" Sherry asked.

"How so?" Walter echoed.

"Remember the last line of the play's handout said the recipe wouldn't result in a crepe if instructions weren't followed correctly? That advice resonated with me. If I didn't stick to my plan to dispose of Gray, I wouldn't be able to blackmail Amber, as Gray would tell her everything. The ingredients for a big payday would turn into a bust. Like a crepe without enough milk. Pancakes just don't have the culinary flair crepes do. Same way revenge done wrong can only be called remission."

"You took things too far." Sherry shook her head.

"I could have gone a step farther. Walter wasn't worth killing, then and there. That would spoil my plan. Things were getting complicated. I imagine the sous chef in the play felt the same way."

"Those were your wet footprints in the hallway at the convention building?" Sherry asked Walter.

"Among others. I had to see the prize package for myself. If the side door hadn't been unlocked, I'd have been out of luck," Walter said. "I let myself in the building, thinking I was alone. Boy, was I wrong. Last thing I saw before taking off was Tig heading toward Gray, who was up onstage. I had to get out of there. Tig had seen me. Something was going on I didn't want to be a part of. I shadowed the others back to the lodge in the dark."

"When I heard Gray solicit Amber to get him into the convention hall that night," Tig said, "I bid my farewells to Amber and promptly circled back to the hall via the edge of the bluffs. Nearly fell down the embankment twice trying to stay hidden. Dropped my thermos once. Took forever to find it in the thick undergrowth." He held up his scratched hand.

A wave rocked the boat and Tig nearly lost his footing. Sherry saw Don bend his knees slightly to absorb the boat's instability. If the captain went down, all hope would be lost.

"Since you didn't kill me that night, then why try to asphyxiate me in my hotel room?" Walter asked.

"Who said I did?"

Bart cleared his throat. "I said you did. Unlucky for you, Walter pulled down his window shades at night and lifted them each day. Walter described the car parked outside his hotel room window the day of his mishap. Big rent-a-car sticker on the windshield."

"Hotel parking. Not assigned spots," Tig said with a shrug. "Big deal. Could be anyone."

"I took a chance and followed the trail. You left this behind." Bart held up a plastic tube segment he retrieved from his coat pocket. "Trimmed from the hose you attached to your tailpipe and ran in through Walter's cracked window. I found the remnant on the car's tailpipe when I tracked it down at the rental dealer. Matched a piece found on the windowsill. I have a picture, given the rental dealer's blessing to document the finding."

"So, I'm not the handiest guy. Whatever. I figured if it looked like Walter committed suicide by self-inflicted asphyxiation, he'd be considered the likely guilty party and he'd be out of my hair. Genius, right?" Tig nodded in agreement with himself. "I rented a car for the day so I could feed the hose from the exhaust pipe through those cheap windows at the inn that are so easy to jack open."

"You just forgot to put the *Do Not Disturb* sign on my door. The daily maid service saved me," Walter said.

"You shouldn't have gone that night. You saw too much," Tig said. His voice was trembling with anger. "Once inside the convention hall, I had a long wait until everyone but Gray left. I didn't know Walter had slipped in the side door. I saw him when I followed Gray behind the stage curtains, but on second glance he was gone. I would have to take care of him later."

"Why did you have to kill Gray?" Livvy asked Tig.

"Jeff and I had a few beers one night and we reminisced about the good old days of Back Bay. He was kind enough to spill the beans about Gray's unhappy time under Amber's care. The fact Gray almost sued the practice was my ticket to a new partner in my plan to force Amber to pay for financial difficulties that have only mounted since she left Boston. Of course, Amber would pay anything to keep Jeff's past indiscretions under wraps. Gray wanted compensation years ago, why wouldn't he still want it? I pursued him to join me in my plan to get what Amber owed me, with the addition of what she owed Gray. The rest fell into place. Until the eleventh hour before the cook-off got underway and he had second thoughts. He wanted out. Too late. I had everyone here together. It was perfect, until it wasn't. By then, Gray knew too much."

"Gray sent me one letter," Amber said. Her voice was weak. Sherry saw the face of a woman who had the rug ripped out from under her and didn't know which end was up. "It said if something happens at the cook-off, please forgive him. I really didn't know what to make of it. He never asked for any sort of payment."

"I got a similar letter," Rickie called out. "He was trying to warn us."

"Gray didn't deserve to die," Bart shouted.

"Blame it on Amber. She made the mistake of reaching out to Gray and offering him a business opportunity he couldn't refuse. Always the nice one, right, Amber? You weren't so nice to me."

"You killed Gray because he wouldn't go along with your blackmailing scheme?" Sherry asked. She knew the answer.

Jeff moaned. "I'm to blame. Over the last weeks, I began to realize Tig was way too interested in Amber's cook-off. Constantly pumping me for information. I was afraid he'd gone to the dark side and I was right."

Sherry turned in Amber's direction. "When Amber said she was meeting Tig at the beach, it was Jeff she was meeting. She didn't want me to know because of my suspicions of Jeff. On the beach I found a foam keychain with an image of a Jack Russell on it. I'm very familiar with Amber's initialed keychain, so it wasn't hers. I suspected it might be Jeff's. Amber told me the two owned a Jack Russell together prior to Bean."

"Keys must have been tossed out of my pocket on the jet ski and floated to the beach. I was trying to keep Amber safe. She might have suspected me of wrongdoing but I had to risk it." Jeff struggled to get the words out. "Days before, when I ran into Walter at the jet ski store, I abandoned the idea of heading off Amber's boat. He was telling the salesman all about the cook-off and I didn't want to take any chances of being identified as a cook's ex-husband. Turns out I left my driver's license with the guy anyway, I was in such a rush to leave. Days later, when Amber and Tig invited me to the beach, I had to go. I felt something horrible was about to happen."

"That's the piece of information I was holding on to," Bart said.

"That Jeff was in Augustin?" Sherry asked.

"That's right. I made a visit to H-2-OH! In a search of jet ski renters and Jeff, your name came up. I didn't want to rush to judgment but I sure did think you were the murderer up until this boat ride."

"I almost told you, Sher. I know you suspected Jeff was in town. He jet skied to the beach but couldn't get over the rocks to land," Amber said. "He was coming to rescue me. He had been trying to convince me Tig was up to something, but he hadn't figured out what. Frankly, I didn't believe Jeff. Tig was so sincere in wanting me to move back to Boston and restart a practice with him."

"It was only a matter of time before he convinced you. Jeff always had the power of persuasion over you." Tig shook his head. "I was planning on killing him that afternoon on the beach. Couldn't after Jeff failed to come ashore. I was watching from the top of the bluff. Why am I telling you this? Enough! Everyone, sit down and shut up," Tig commanded. "Listen up. Amber and I will be departing. Don't bother trying to use your phones to contact anyone, there's no service out here."

"I don't like that he's telling us all this," Amber whispered to Sherry. "That only means one thing for our future. There won't be one. We have to keep Tig engaged."

"Be patient," Sherry said. "Trust me." She saw her friend's expression relax.

"We need to speed things up so Jeff can get medical attention."

"I agree."

The boat was motoring at a slow cruising speed, bashing across the crest of the waves created by the increasing winds. The boat paralleled the shore for a few minutes before Don made an announcement. "Folks, seems we have a disgruntled passenger on board who is forcing us to make an unscheduled stop. We have another passenger who needs medical attention and that's first priority. So, we will be landing at the beach to our left."

"You ready to take the plunge?" Tig said. His jaw was pulsing with anger. He grabbed Amber's arm and twisted it until she shrieked.

"Don!" Sherry called out. She examined Don's face. Would he sacrifice Amber for the safety of the others? Why was he letting Tig's demands dictate? His eyes were on the radar screen. Sherry checked the readout and could see a flashing red warning signal. She shifted slightly to get a better look and saw they were heading into dangerously shallow waters.

"There's something wrong with the steering," Don said. He made eye contact with Sherry and contorted his head in the direction of the red lanyard she was holding. "Pull it," he mouthed.

Sherry yanked the coiled lanyard attached to the ignition's emergency cutoff switch and the motor died. She made the instantaneous decision to toss the lanyard overboard.

"What's the matter with this thing? Why aren't the engines on?" Tig grumbled.

Relentless waves pushed the boat toward the shore. The ear-piercing screech of the boat's hull scraping the top of rocks just below the surface gave Sherry goose bumps. After a jarring smash of metal meeting rock, the boat came to a rest, tipped precariously to one side. Sherry took inventory of the others on the boat. Dead silence was followed by cautious commentary.

"Don't move," Rickie said. "We don't know which way this thing's going to tip."

Tig stepped away from Don with Amber hooked inside his bent elbow.

"Don't you dare hurt another person," Don said. He lunged at Tig but glanced off the steering wheel and was knocked backward.

Tig gripped the knife so tight his knuckles were white. "Come on, Amber. That's our cue to exit this sinking ship. We're gonna get wet. As long as I have you no one will risk your life by being a hero. I came to see a cook-off and I'm leaving with the cook." Tig waved the knife across Amber's core. "One, two, three."

Tig yanked Amber onto the edge of the boat, safeguarded with a metal railing. He forced her to climb the railing in front of him and with a shove threw her overboard. He leapt in after her.

"Don, do something. Amber, swim!" Sherry rushed to the edge of the boat.

"Damn rocks. I think I broke my foot." Tig dropped the knife and was floundering with his hands up above the water's surface.

"I'm going in after them," Sherry called out.

"No!" Don said.

Sherry recoiled. "Then you go!"

"I can't leave the boat, Sherry. All these lives. Amber's doing her best and it's working. His plan is a dud."

Rickie let out a scream. She joined Sherry and leaned over the side of the boat. "Look, who's that? Pep! Help! We need help!"

"And the police!" Curt yelled out.

Sherry watched from the side of the boat as Amber swam away from Tig.

Bart shouldered his way through the gathering to reach Sherry's side. "I had Detective Bease meet us at the lodge's beach. I texted him before we left the dock when I saw Jeff board at the last minute. The case against Jeff just didn't add up. If he was guilty, I doubted he would suddenly show his face after eluding my search for days. Had to be someone else."

"I knew you could solve the mystery," Livvy said.

Sherry unzipped her coat and tossed it on a seat. "I'm going in." She hoisted her legs over the railing and gingerly lowered herself down the side of the boat. Even hanging by outstretched arms, she had a full body length to drop before hitting the water. Rocks were looming to greet her if she didn't ball up her legs. A flash of regret for a rash decision crossed her mind.

Sherry didn't hear Don's voice warning her, so she let go. The shock of the frigid salt water pulsed through her body. She stroked as she had never stroked before until she made the short swim to the beach. She struggled to stand and slipped twice when her soaked shoes trod on the slimy submerged rocks.

"Out for a polar bear swim?" Ray said as he met Sherry on the beach. He was holding Tig's upper arm, hands cuffed behind his back. "Officer, do you have a blanket for this lady?"

"Amber, are you okay? Ray, is Amber okay?" Sherry's teeth chattered as she tried to make sense of the scene.

"Yes, I'm a drowned rat, but I'm okay," Amber said. She was shivering under her blanket, her feet dancing to stay warm. "I hope Jeff will be all right." She pointed to a boat with flashing lights, pulling up to the *Current-Sea*. "The Coast Guard." She barely uttered the words before Sherry smothered her with a hug.

"They'll get him to the hospital. He'll have the finest care. Coastal Health and Wellness Hospital is the best," Pep said as he approached. "Mimi was born there. And so were Sherry and I."

"Pep, how'd you know what was going on?" Sherry asked.

"Ray texted me."

Ray rubbed his forehead. "Something you should have mentioned? About a knife in your brother's garage or garbage bag?"

Sherry shot Pep a glance.

"I had to tell him," Pep said. "Someone on the boat was most likely the murderer and the knife may have been the weapon. Since I'd seen Tig eat lunch with Amber with Sherry's knife carrier poised between them on the picnic table, I took a chance he was the culprit."

"Why'd you put the knife in the garbage, Tig?" Sherry asked, ignoring Ray's reprimand.

Tig raised his head. The moment of defeat was drawing his mouth down to a scowl. "When Amber left her knife kit with me during lunch while she cleaned up, it made for easy pickings. Later, upon further inspection, I saw Sherry's initials and I tossed the knife in the garbage. Who takes their garbage home with them?"

"Thank goodness I did," Pep said.

"I need a lawyer." Tig lowered his head.

"Yes, you do. We'll be heading to the station house now where you can make a call," Ray said.

"What happened to you?" Sherry asked Ray.

Ray handed Tig off to two police officers and Tig limped away.

Ray swiped at the bramble and twig bits on his jacket and pants. "Pep called us to meet him at the lodge's beach. I didn't know there was a very poorly marked parking lot right over there. Instead, we hiked down a poorly maintained path from the top of that bluff."

"He fell more than once," Pep added. "He'll be picking brambles out of his clothes for days."

"Welcome to our childhood, Ray," Sherry said.

Chapter 19

"Thanks for having us to dinner, Sherry and Don. Cheers to you," Pep said as he raised his beer mug. A chorus of "cheers" followed. "After the week we've been through, a gourmet meal is beyond welcome."

Everyone agreed. When plates were full the conversation flowed in all directions until Sherry decided the time had come to revisit the murder.

"Amber, there's a question I've been wanting to ask you. How did Tig know you were in a cook-off?" Sherry scooped up the last of the goat cheese spread. "Help yourself to seconds everyone." She swept her hand toward the table's offerings, from the lemon sole fillets to the Caesar salad.

"You can thank social media," Amber said as she reached for the almond rice. "I was so excited to be in the cook-off's final round I posted on all my platforms. Tig emailed me he'd like to come watch me compete. After that Jeff contacted me and said he'd enjoy attending. I should have been suspicious I had that many fans."

"You knew Jeff was coming?" Sherry asked. "And you never mentioned the fact?" She squeezed her forehead tight in advance of Amber's reply. Sherry had let slide her interest in the subject since the confrontation with Tig on Don's boat, but held tight to the intention of discovering the answer at some point.

"I did," Amber said. The short reply hung in the air like a thundercloud waiting to burst open. A moment later Amber added, "Can you forgive me?"

"You don't even have to ask. Where was Jeff staying?" Sherry asked.

"Not with me, in case enquiring minds thought otherwise. I believe he stayed over in Hillboro."

Sherry shook her head. "Tig was so desperate for payback he overlooked how many people he ended up involving. One situation he underestimated. The minute he came between Amber and me, it was game on." She placed a forkful in her mouth.

"Would you consider Tig the sous chef in the mystery?" Charlotte asked.

Sherry's mouth turned up into a satisfied grin. "Like the sous chef in *Scrambled*, Tig wrote the recipe he counted on Amber following. He was hoping Amber would execute his instructions perfectly to get his desired result. If she didn't . . ."

"And I didn't," Amber added.

"I'm afraid he was going to . . ." Sherry swallowed her next word.

"I know. You don't have to say it," Amber said. "Thank goodness for you all, and Jeff and Walter, who all stuck their noses in to try and nudge me forward."

"How is Jeff doing?" Charlotte asked. She passed the garlic toast to Amber.

"He'll be fine. A mild concussion and some bruises. I owe him big-time," Amber said.

"No, you don't," Sherry and Pep said simultaneously. They laughed at their unified chorus.

"Okay, maybe not," Amber said. "But he risked his life to save mine, so I'm calling things even Steven between the two of us."

"That was Jeff I saw at the marina prior to the cook-off. Funny, my first thought was that stranger and Amber would make a gorgeous couple."

Amber smiled a coy grin. "Maybe once upon a time."

"Is that all you have to tell us about you and Jeff?" Sherry asked between bites.

"He and I had some unfinished business. I still care about the guy. I admit I was testing his loyalty. I wasn't going to risk my life for someone who wouldn't do the same for me. Well, actually I probably would. We shared a kiss before the ambulance took him to the hospital but we both quickly returned to our senses after the moment passed. One and done."

"You won't catch me and Charlie testing our loyalty that way," Sherry said.

"That makes me feel a whole lot better," Don said. "Can we change subjects, please?"

"And your boat, Don? Is it in good shape after running aground on the rocks?" Charlotte asked.

Sherry knew Charlotte was aware of the dents and dings the *Current-Sea* sustained while dealing with Tig. If the outcome had been any worse it may not have been advisable to ask for an update.

"The boat will be shipshape in no time. No damage other than cosmetic," Don said with the pride of a man with a new toy. "Pep, would you pass the roasted asparagus, please?"

Don helped himself to the garlicy green spears. "Sherry, I've wanted to apologize for raising my voice on the boat when I thought you were risking your life to save Amber. You do know how to test someone's love."

"How can you not forgive the man?" Pep asked.

"I forgive you," Sherry said. "You'll note I took the plunge anyway."

"Sherry's stubborn side will endear itself to you over time, if you're willing to stick around," Pep said.

On the count of two beats everyone in the room shouted, "Pep!" He was duly reprimanded.

"Maybe you taking the plunge off the boat was foreshadowed in your dream about taking the plunge into marriage," Amber said.

"Did you discuss your dream with everyone?" Don asked.

"Pass the salt, please," Sherry said with the full understanding her request wouldn't provide enough of a diversion from Don's question. She felt his touch on her knee.

"Let's get to the elephant in the room," Pep said.

"You mean there's a bigger elephant than the cook-off murder?" Charlotte asked.

"Like who took all the toasted walnut, goat cheese and fig spread?" Pep said. He held up the empty glass serving bowl.

"Guilty," Sherry said. "It's my favorite. Should be your next toast topper special."

"Already on the menu," Pep said with a thumbs-up.

"Elephants come in many different sizes," Sherry said. "I'll go first with the largest." She scanned the dining room table to ensure all eyes were on her. "Amber, have you decided whether you'll be staying in Augustin, whether you'll be working at the Ruggery, and whether you'll be Pep's sous chef on your off hours?" A moment later, Sherry didn't realize she was holding her breath until Amber took too long to reply and she lost her wind.

Amber toyed with the flakey fish on her plate. She took her time sampling a savory bite. No one else moved. After she swallowed, Amber smiled. "Move away from Augustin and miss delicious dinners like this?"

The room erupted with polite applause.

"Such good news. And have you settled on work plans?" Sherry said when the clapping died down.

Pep straightened his posture. "I hope you pick me."

"I'm so sorry, Pep. I'm going to stick with the Ruggery. If I work as a sous chef with you on the truck, I will disqualify myself from all future amateur cook-offs and I don't think I'm done with those yet."

Sherry couldn't contain her pride in her friend's enjoyment of her favorite hobby. She raised her wineglass in a salute to Amber's choices.

"I kind of saw that decision coming," Pep said. "I've been interviewing for the position since the second lunch at the cook-off."

"You sneak," Amber said. "What if I change my mind?"

"Too late. I hired the third person I interviewed. A young chef slash entrepreneur-in-training with energy to burn. He's perfect," Pep said as he puffed out his chest.

"Okay, well, that's all settled. Now for a smaller elephant in the room," Sherry said. "Pep, what's the truck's name?" She stood and carried her empty plate to the kitchen. "Hold that thought until I return. I'm bringing out the dessert."

"Ready for the big reveal?" Pep called out.

Sherry emerged from the kitchen. "Hold on." She set a chocolate mousse roll cake down on the table. She took her seat next to Don. "Okay. Thanks for waiting."

"I've decided on Toasts of the Town." Pep's sheepish smile punctuated his announcement with a sweetness Sherry knew meant he was completely satisfied with his choice but wasn't sure others would be.

Silence. Sherry watched her brother's eyebrows lift, encouraging her to speed up her reaction. Sherry flashed a broad smile. "Love it."

Recipes From Sherry's Kitchen

Sausage and Asparagus Roll-ups

This recipe is a variation on Sherry's Spring Thyme Asparagus Roll-ups.

Serves 8–10

24 fresh asparagus, ends trimmed off
6 ounces Boursin cheese
1 tablespoon Dijon mustard/mayonnaise blend
1 tablespoon fig preserves
12 bread slices, crust trimmed
1 cup sausage, browned and crumbled
¼ cup butter, melted
paprika

Preheat oven to 400 degrees.

Steam asparagus until crisp-tender, let cool.

Stir together cheese, Dijon-mayonnaise blend, and preserves.

Roll each bread slice with a rolling pin to flatten. Spread one side of each bread slice with 2 tablespoons cream cheese mixture and top with 1 tablespoon sausage. Place 2 asparagus spears in the middle of each prepared bread slice and roll up. Place each roll, seam side down, on a baking sheet and brush lightly with butter. Sprinkle with paprika and bake for 12 minutes, until golden. So good!

Recipes

Red Pepper Glazed Rustic Mushroom Toast with Crispy Prosciutto

Served at Pep's Toasts of the Town food truck.

Serves 4–6

2½ cups crimini mushrooms, thinly sliced
4 ounces prosciutto, cut in very thin strips
4 ounces soft goat cheese
½ cup red pepper jelly
4 slices sourdough country bread, ⅛-inch-thick sliced
salt to taste
pepper
fresh thyme sprigs

Heat a large skillet over medium heat. Add mushrooms and prosciutto and sauté for 6 minutes, stirring occasionally, until mushrooms are softened and prosciutto edges are browned. Remove mushrooms and prosciutto to a bowl.

In a small saucepan, heat red pepper jelly over low heat until melted. Remove from heat.

While jelly is melting, place bread slices, two at a time, in the large skillet and brown lightly on one side. Flip and spoon goat cheese across toasts. Top with one-quarter of the prepared mushrooms and a sprinkle of crispy prosciutto. Cook until bottom of toast is light brown. Remove from heat and drizzle with red pepper glaze. Repeat steps for the remaining bread slices.

Serve garnished with fresh thyme.

Bistro Mushroom and Chicken Crepes

Serves 4–6

2 tablespoons unsalted butter plus 2 tablespoons, divided use, plus 1½ tablespoons or more if needed for making crepes
1½ pounds boneless skinless chicken thighs, cut in thin strips
sea salt
2 teaspoons sea salt plus 1½ teaspoons, divided use
2 tablespoons fresh lemon juice plus 1 tablespoon, divided use
2 tablespoon Worcestershire sauce
16 ounces crimini mushrooms, sliced thin
1 tablespoon apricot preserves
1 tablespoons fresh tarragon, chopped or ¾ teaspoon dried
¾ cup all-purpose flour
1¼ cups whole milk
1 whole large egg
5 ounces crumbled goat cheese

Heat 2 tablespoons butter in a heavy skillet over medium-high heat.

Sprinkle chicken with 2 teaspoons sea salt. Add the chicken and 2 tablespoons lemon juice to the butter and cook until chicken is cooked through. Remove chicken to a plate.

Maintaining heat, add 2 tablespoons butter, Worcestershire sauce, ½ teaspoon sea salt and mushrooms to the skillet and cook for 8 minutes, stirring often. Reserve ½ cup of mushrooms in the skillet and combine remaining mushrooms with the chicken on the plate.

Add the apricot preserves to the skillet with 1 tablespoon lemon juice and tarragon. Stir until preserves are melted and coat the mushrooms. Remove from heat.

In a large bowl combine flour and 1/2 teaspoon salt. Whisk in milk, egg and 1 tablespoon butter until well combined. Let batter rest for 5–10 minutes.

Prepare crepes by melting ½ tablespoon butter in a 9-inch heavy skillet over medium heat. Stir crepe batter; pour 3 tablespoons into center of skillet. Lift and tilt pan to coat bottom evenly. Cook until top appears dry.

Dot 2 tablespoons goat cheese down middle one-third of crepe and top with a layer of chicken and mushroom blend and fold in each side to cover filling. Remove each crepe to a serving plate as it's prepared. Add butter to skillet for each crepe preparation, as needed.

Prepare 4–6 crepes and top each with apricot-tarragon glazed mushrooms.

Serve warm. Enjoy!

About the Author

Devon Delaney is lifelong resident of the Northeast and currently resides in coastal Connecticut. She is a wife, mother of three, grandmother of two, accomplished cooking contestant and a recent empty nester. She taught computer education and Lego Robotics for over ten years prior to pursuing writing.

Devon has been handsomely rewarded for her recipe innovation over the last twenty-plus years. Among the many prizes she has won are a full kitchen of major appliances, five-figure top cash prizes, and four trips to Disney World. She won the grand prize in a national writing contest for her foodie poem "Ode to Pork Passion." Combining her beloved hobby of cooking contests with her enthusiasm for writing was inevitable.

When she's is not preparing for her next cook-off, Devon may be found pursuing her other hobbies, including playing competitive USTA league tennis, gardening, needlepointing, painting, jarring her produce and hooking rugs. Her standard poodle, Rocket, is her pride and joy and keeps her on the path of sanity.

You can learn more about Devon at www.devonpdelaney.com.

Made in United States
Orlando, FL
25 July 2024

49541223R00124